SOVIET AND RUSSIAN PRESS COVERAGE OF THE UNITED STATES

St Antony's Series
Series Standing Order ISBN 0–333–71109–2
(*outside North America only*)

You can receive future titles in this series as they are published by placing a standing order.
Please contact your bookseller or, in case of difficulty, write to us at the address below with
your name and address, the title of the series and the ISBN quoted above.

Customer Services Department, Macmillan Distribution Ltd
Houndmills, Basingstoke, Hampshire RG21 6XS, England

Soviet and Russian Press Coverage of the United States

Press, Politics and Identity in Transition

Jonathan A. Becker
Dean of Students
and
Dean of Studies
Bard College

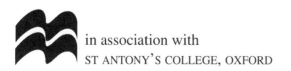

in association with
ST ANTONY'S COLLEGE, OXFORD

First published in Great Britain 1999 by
MACMILLAN PRESS LTD
Houndmills, Basingstoke, Hampshire RG21 6XS and London
Companies and representatives throughout the world

A catalogue record for this book is available from the British Library.

ISBN 0–333–64314–3

First published in the United States of America 1999 by
ST. MARTIN'S PRESS, INC.,
Scholarly and Reference Division,
175 Fifth Avenue, New York, N.Y. 10010

ISBN 0–312–21907–5

Library of Congress Cataloging-in-Publication Data
Becker, Jonathan A., 1964–
Soviet and Russian press coverage of the United States : press,
politics, and identity in transition / Jonathan A. Becker.
p.   cm. — (St. Antony's series)
Based on the author's thesis (Ph. D.)—University of Oxford.
Includes bibliographical references and index.
ISBN 0–312–21907–5 (cloth)
1. United States—Relations—Soviet Union.   2. Soviet Union–
–Relations—United States.   3. United States—Relations—Russia.
4. Russia—Relations—United States.   5. United States—Foreign
relations—1981–1989.   6. United States—Foreign relations—1989–
7. United States—Press coverage—Soviet Union.   8. United States–
–Press coverage—Russia.   I. Title.   II. Series.
E183.8.S65B434   1999
327.47073—dc21   98–47674
                                                             CIP

This book is printed on paper suitable for recycling and made from fully managed and sustained forest sources.

10   9   8   7   6   5   4   3   2   1
08   07   06   05   04   03   02   01   00   99

Printed and bound in Great Britain by
Antony Rowe Ltd, Chippenham, Wiltshire

To my parents,
Alvin and Arlene

Contents

Acknowledgements

This book started as a doctoral dissertation at the University of Oxford, St Antony's College. At that time, the Soviet Union still existed and the Cold War was just beginning to abate. In my wildest dreams, I never imagined that by the time the book was completed, the Union would collapse and I would have spent five years teaching and working in the former 'Eastern bloc'.

I am indebted to the many people who have helped make this book possible. I should start by thanking Alex Pravda, my dissertation supervisor, who has been tremendously supportive over the years, even after I had long departed Oxford. Richard Kindersley, Archie Brown, Mary McAuley and Neil Malcolm offered helpful comments on many of the chapters, as did Dave Keen, Philip Murphy and Kate Flynn. Alexandra de Brito was particularly helpful in pushing me to broaden my horizons and explore new and invaluable literature. Christine Zapotocky and my wife, Jessica, provided fresh perspectives on the many restructured chapters. Alfred Stepan deserves special thanks for his encouragement and for never failing to remind me that I had a book to complete. I owe a debt of gratitude to Jackie Willcox of St Antony's College who demonstrated tremendous patience in responding to my numerous requests and my ever expanding presence in the Russian library. I am also thankful to the many Russian journalists who generously granted interviews. I only wish that they could now work in better conditions. I am indebted to several students at the University of Kiev Mohyla Academy and the Central European University who provided critical research assistance. I would also like to thank Philip Longworth for first drawing my interest to Russia. Although I have moved forward a few centuries, many of the themes remain the same.

I gratefully acknowledge research support from the Anglo-Jewish Association, St Antony's College, the Social Science Research Council and the Central European University.

Finally, I would like to thank Penny Dole of Macmillan who has been supportive and shown the patience of an angel.

J.A.B.

Introduction

> The press is the prime instrument through which the party speaks daily, hourly with the working class in its own indispensable language. No other means such as this for weaving spiritual ties between party and class, no other tool so flexible, is to be found in nature.
>
> Joseph Stalin[1]

The Soviet press was assigned a unique role by its communist rulers. The Party leadership did not fear the power of the press and simply suppress it, as did many old European and recent Latin American, African and Asian rulers. It also did not envision the press serving as a free marketplace of ideas, nor as a fourth estate, roles it supposedly fulfils in modern Western democracies. The press in the Soviet Union was assigned a more transformative role; it was to do nothing less than foster the creation of new people who would both forge and form a new society. In short, it was an instrument which would help the Communist Party build communism.[2]

To the disappointment of those who had such high hopes for it, the press, and the entire system of ideological education, was not successful in transforming society as the Party prescribed. People's beliefs changed, but public opinion failed to converge with official doctrine. The 'New Soviet Man' internalized some official values, but he did not conform to the Party's blueprint.[3]

The press even had difficulty with the more mundane task of mobilizing the population in support of the leadership's short-term goals. Press campaigns, when not backed by coercion, frequently failed to fulfil their tasks. Despite numerous attempts, the press rarely persuaded the masses to work harder or to stop consuming excessive amounts of alcohol, nor could it restrain rampant bureaucratism. The press's effectiveness in promoting Party goals diminished with time, particularly as society grew more educated and the chasm between the promises of socialism and Soviet reality widened.[4]

In spite of the failure of the Soviet press to attain its idealized form as an instrument of social engineering, it did play an important role in the Soviet polity. Two areas are of particular interest. First, the press made an important contribution to the creation

1

and reinforcement of a negative identity, that is, a perception of what one is not.[5] In the Soviet case, this meant that it had some success in conditioning society to be critical of capitalism and bourgeois values, particularly those reflected by the West and its leading power the United States of America. Soviet citizens might not have known what it meant to be socialist, but at least they were hostile towards socialism's capitalist enemies.[6]

Second, the press contributed to the imposition of a limited discourse on society. In the Soviet Union, it did not matter so much if people believed the press, or even comprehended it; more important was that they understood that as far as public expression was concerned they were required to adopt the official discourse reflected in the press.[7] The limited discourse helped to perpetuate the status quo because people could not express alternative views in public. Instead, they were forced to communicate through the constraining lexicon of double-meanings or 'Newspeak.' As Goldfarb said about the much less severe East European experience:

> The special language of officialdom distorted communication and obfuscated clear and critical thought. People were forced to use an official rhetoric to get on with their lives, and for decades the independently minded had to try and use the prescribed ideological discourse to say or do something original, critical, or creative.[8]

The press thus helped to perpetuate the hegemony of the party/state over civil society.

This book examines the transformation of the Soviet and Russian press during a period of over ten years. The goal is to demonstrate how a press dominated by totalitarian discourse and committed to ideological struggle undergoes liberalization. It is argued that, in part due to the absence of a language to support the reform strategy, Soviet leaders and the Soviet press increasingly used images of the Soviet Union's chief ideological opponent, the United States, as a means of supporting arguments for domestic reform. The trend was so powerful that near the end of the Gorbachev period, Soviet press content was nearly inverted with, if anything, the United States being portrayed in an overly positive manner. It is also argued that the initial changes in both foreign and domestic coverage of the United States were part of a deliberate policy of *glasnost'*, a policy which sought to use the press instrumentally as a means to support reform. However, like other countries which attempted a limited form of press liberalization, changes went beyond those initially envisioned by the leadership. The result was that a press which was once dominated by Party-imposed consensus became increasingly dominated by what can be called legitimate controversy. Indeed, given the lack of underlying societal consensus towards the end of the period, the mainstream Soviet press often showed far greater diversity than its Western counterparts.

The primary focus of the book is from March 1985, when Mikhail Gorbachev was named General Secretary of the Communist Party, through July 1990, when the new Soviet press law was adopted. The study explores three primary issues: press liberalization, Soviet press images of the United States and how those images reflected Soviet identity, and mass communications during the breakdown of Party-imposed totalitarian discourse. It also revisits the post-Communist Russian press notionally operating under more of a 'free press' model.

Press liberalization in the Soviet Union is approached from two perspectives: change from above and change from below. The former involves a government-controlled liberalization of the press (*glasnost'*). The latter concerns pressure, primarily from journalists, which forced the liberalization process to expand wider than its initiators had originally foreseen. Examples of press liberalization in other countries have been taken into account in order to highlight important patterns of change in the Soviet press.

The study of changing Soviet images of the United States forms the empirical heart of the book. The United States was selected as the subject of the empirical study for several reasons. The most distinctive characteristic of the Soviet press prior to the Gorbachev period was its commitment to 'ideological competition' with the West, particularly the 'mother-country of imperialism,' the United States of America. Indeed, the Soviet press frequently devoted more detailed attention to American political, economic and social issues than to comparable developments in the Soviet Union.[9] The United States constituted the most important 'other' in Soviet self-definition.

The importance of press coverage of the United States means that it poses a good test of the Soviet policy of *glasnost'*. The study was originally conceived in a period when *glasnost'* had produced significant changes in Soviet press coverage of domestic issues, but only mild changes in international press coverage. It was seen as a means of updating past works on the Soviet press,[10] including some written early in the *glasnost'* period,[11] and as a way of testing the policy of *glasnost'* in order to determine whether the policy was related to Western notions of press freedom.

Press coverage of the United States has also been selected because it is an important topic in its own right: the capitalist enemy played such a central role in Soviet thinking and discourse that changing images of the US reflect the process of breakdown of the officially imposed ideology and a re-evaluation of Soviet identity. This study updates the work of several authors who could not take into account the scope of change in the Gorbachev period and beyond.[12] It also takes a different approach from most works on Soviet and Russian images of the US by focusing primarily on the popular press instead of on leaders or institute specialists. Although all three are related, the changes in the popular press are this study's focus because the popular press reflects broad changes in official discourse rather than inter-elite communication.[13] The ultimate test of the depth of changing images and ideology is not the narrow forum of specialists, but in the broader arena of mass communication.

In analyzing changing Soviet and Russian press coverage of the United States, a number of publications have been consulted. In the period from March 1985 through July 1990, every issue of five publications has been consulted: *Pravda, Izvestiya, Argumenty i Fakty, Moscow News,* and *Literaturnaya Rossiya.* The newspaper *Sovetskaya Rossiya* and the weekly journal *Krokodil* have also been examined selectively.

These publications represent a cross-section of the Soviet popular press. *Pravda* and *Izvestiya* were the official publications of the Party and state and thus traditionally considered the most important newspapers in the Soviet Union, serving as guides to other publications for the interpretation of political and socio-economic phenomena.[14] *Argumenty i Fakty* became the most popular publication in the Soviet Union in the Gorbachev period, with a weekly circulation surpassing 30 million, the largest in the world. Its commitment to providing significant amounts of raw information contrasted with the other publications which primarily focused on interpretation. *Moscow News* was one of the flagships of democratic reform in the Soviet Union.[15] As an official organ of Novosti news agency and the Society of Friendship, it was not as 'official' as *Pravda* or *Izvestiya*, and was thus less constrained during the liberalization process. *Literaturnaya Rossiya* had a reputation as a conservative publication and, as an organ of the Russian Union of Writers, was also 'less official' than *Pravda* or *Izvestiya*. Because its sphere of coverage of international events was somewhat limited, *Sovetskaya Rossiya*, another newspaper with a conservative reputation, was selectively examined. As the official publication of the Central Committee of the CPSU and the Supreme Soviet and Council of Ministers of the Russian Republic, its standing fell between that of *Pravda* and *Izvestiya* and the other publications. *Krokodil* was the most important publication in the Soviet Union devoted exclusively to political satire. It was studied to understand changing images of the United States in Soviet political cartoons.

By drawing on a variety of 'official' and 'unofficial' publications, and those with reputations for pro- and anti-reform stances, it is hoped that this study will reveal patterns indicative of changes throughout the Soviet print media.

In order to contextualize changes in content and to understand their significance, two approaches are taken. First, there is an exploration of changes in the organization and operations of the Soviet and post-Soviet press. This includes changes in the press's relations with the Party and the government and in journalists' attitudes, especially concerning news values. Second, there is an examination of changing leadership policies both towards the press and the United States. These changes are then examined chronologically with reference to changes in press content. It is only through studying these three areas, content, organization and government policy, that it is possible to understand why press coverage of the United States changed and consequently the nature of the liberalization process of the Soviet media.

The book is divided into two parts and consists of eight chapters. The first part of the book, Chapters 1–3, examines the Soviet press. Chapter 1 explores the theoretical literature on press systems. An attempt is made to bring the study of press systems closer to political science than communications or media studies by combining it with research on regime transitions.

Chapter 2 examines the pre-Gorbachev Soviet press. It is argued that the Soviet press in the pre-Gorbachev period can be described as post-totalitarian. This system is distinguished by a press which largely retains the linguistic structure of a totalitarian press, even as belief in the ideology waned and its mobilizing capacity weakened. It then explores the failure of previous regimes to change press content, attributing it to Gorbachev's predecessors' concentration on the ideological battle with the West, particularly the United States. They preferred a largely ineffective press over one which might give ammunition to the capitalist world.

Chapter 3 highlights the Soviet press in the Gorbachev period. It juxtaposes change from above with change from below. Relying extensively on interviews with Soviet journalists and speeches of Soviet leaders, it demonstrates how the liberalization process went beyond the bounds originally intended by the leadership, but also how some of the most important constraints on the press, both internal and external, continued throughout much of the Gorbachev period, especially in the field of international press coverage.

Part II of the book, which consists of Chapters 4–8, shifts the focus from an analysis of media systems and the structure of the Soviet press to a study of Soviet and Russian press coverage of the United States and the importance of identity in contributing to that press coverage. Chapter 4 points to the importance of the United States in the psychology of the Soviet Union, demonstrating that the Soviet identity was as much a product of what the Soviet Union was not (bourgeois and capitalist) as what it was.

Chapter 5 begins the examination of press content. It focuses on qualitative and quantitative changes in the depiction of the United States in Soviet political cartoons. In doing so, it places significant quantitative changes within the context of changing Soviet policies and developments in US/Soviet relations.

Chapter 6 explores the changing portrayal of US foreign and military policies. Although change in this sphere was not as dramatic as in other areas, due to the unique nature of press coverage of international relations, a softening of images occurred, with dramatic alternations in the discourse which traditionally governed descriptions of US foreign policy. Many of the key changes also followed the same chronological pattern as those in political cartoons and in domestic press coverage, suggesting that they were controlled from above. Towards the end of the Gorbachev period, particularly in 1989 and 1990, significant differences also began to emerge between reporters and between different publications, indicating a growth in diversity in the Soviet press.

Chapter 7 constitutes the most detailed part of the book, exploring changing press images of domestic America. It divides press coverage of domestic America into three spheres: politics, socio-economics and culture. Two main trends emerge. First, the portrayal of domestic America was humanized, meaning that the enemy images typical of the ideological struggle diminished. Second, there emerged what can be termed affirmative-didactic press coverage, that is, press content which used US experience as a model for Soviet reform. The latter signified not only the abandonment of the ideological struggle with the United States, but a near inversion of Soviet priorities.

Chapter 8 is essentially a postscript. Revisiting the Russian press five years after the end of the Soviet Union, it explores how market influences inherent in a 'free press' system affect print media, and how Soviet popular attitudes towards the US have changed since the breakdown of Newspeak.

Part I: Politics and the Press

1 Press Systems

Nowadays nomenklaturist propaganda does not even take the trouble to try to make people believe what it says. Its aim is a different one, namely to make Soviet citizens understand that they must use a definite phraseology.

Michael Voslensky[1]

The press reflects the political environment in which it is situated.[2] In pluralist, competitive regimes, the press can serve as an active force, a fourth estate, which is accessible to the public, provides a wide array of information, and enjoys relative autonomy from the government. However, in highly centralized, non-competitive regimes, access and information are limited. In some cases, governments settle for a conservative approach, controlling and censoring the press in order to maintain order and stability. In other cases, they give the press a more transformative role, using it to promote policies, inculcate ideology, and even to help create a new definition of humanity. At the peak of Communism, the Soviet press was an extreme example of the latter.

This chapter seeks to identify some of the defining features of totalitarian and post-totalitarian press systems. The vast literature on mass media systems has been augmented by that on regime typologies and liberalizations/transitions in order to contextualize the material and situate the study more firmly in the field of politics.[3] The goal of the chapter is to offer background which can help explain the changes which took place in the Gorbachev period.

TOTALITARIAN AND POST-TOTALITARIAN PRESS SYSTEMS

At the beginning of the Gorbachev period, the Soviet press can best be described as a post-totalitarian press system. In order to understand the specific components which constitute such a system, it is best to begin with a description of a totalitarian media system, in part because the distinction between the two has not been effectively elucidated in the media systems literature.[4] Drawing

11

from Linz's work on regime typologies, one can say that the essential attributes of a totalitarian press system include the following:

The press is consciously identified with and subordinated to a monistic centre of political power which maintains positive and negative control over it. The political centre views the press as an instrument for promoting its authority, policies and ideology.

The ideology promoted by the press is modern in that it is supposed to be scientifically determined, represent some ultimate meaning, a sense of historical purpose and an interpretation of social reality. It is expressed in a particular discourse or political language called Newspeak.

All legal publications are required to present information which serves to educate the readership and/or mobilise it towards the fulfilment of the regime's goals.[5]

The key elements which distinguish the totalitarian press system from the other press systems are access, control and ideology.

Access to the press in the totalitarian model is not simply sanctioned by the party/state, as it may be in other authoritarian systems.[6] Rather, the party/state exercises both positive and negative control over the content of the entire (legal) press.[7] It controls all elements of the publishing process, including everything from paper distribution to the appointment of media personnel. Journalists serve as little more than extensions of the party apparatus, contributing to the general ideological education of the populace.[8] All publications are viewed instrumentally and are expected to continuously perform the function of educating and teaching the population about how to think and act. The press also must attempt to mobilize the population to help achieve the regime's goals. Interestingly, the totalitarian press model emerged in part because of the modern belief in the indoctrinating and transformative power of mass communications.[9]

Totalitarian press systems are further defined by the constraints imposed by the distinctive form of ideology which governs them.[10] Totalitarian ideologies are unique in that they offer scientifically determined truths which explain history and the nature of human order while promoting an archetype of humanity, the Aryan or the New Soviet Man.[11] This produces univocacy: 'for every politically significant word, one meaning; for every historical event, one interpretation; for every social problem, one solution . . .'.[12]

The comprehensive nature of totalitarian ideology has a tremendous impact on communications. It justifies party dominance of the press in the name of a pre-ordained scientifically determined 'truth'.[13] More importantly, it creates a distinct totalitarian discourse which Orwell termed 'Newspeak'. As Goldfarb puts it, 'While the simple idea of class struggle or racial harmony is the ideational core of the official truth, Newspeak is its linguistic structure.'[14] The shell of Newspeak protects the core ideology, and thus the party's justification for its rule. Words become so loaded with prescribed values that it is difficult for them to express ideas beyond accepted, official beliefs. Words to articulate criticism or to describe alternatives may simply not exist; at a minimum they cannot be used within the form of ritualized public expression.[15] Those who attempt to criticize or challenge the ideology from within its own language structure end up conforming to the inner logic of the ideology, thus perpetuating it.[16]

That having been said, I would question Goldfarb's assertion that 'the chief problem of living in the world of Newspeak' is that 'the individual no longer knows what exists beyond the official language and no longer exists apart from the official lie'.[17] While some might internalize the mode of thinking associated with Newspeak, the existence of relatively free communication within non-public environments (most notably the ubiquitous 'kitchen' conversations) in the post-Stalin period, and particularly in Central Europe, the subject of Goldfarb's study, raises questions about the degree and scope of internalization. For this study it is important to note that in the sphere of public communication, speech was ritualized and words lost critical meaning. Ritualization of public speech was so ubiquitous that alternative ideas often could not be expressed without challenging the basic tenets of the regime, something which authorities would not permit. As we will see in later chapters, this condition was critical because when the authorities decided to implement reform, and when public communication was opened and the bounds of 'Newspeak' removed, the flood of communication had unanticipated consequences which undermined the ideology and the regime's legitimacy.

The role which Newspeak plays in distinguishing totalitarian from other press systems lies in its scope and impenetrability. In free press systems, associated with liberal democracies, totalitarian ideologies may be expressed by political and social groups, but in the pluralist context they do not dominate public expression. They must compete in a marketplace of ideas.[18] In authoritarian press systems, totalitarian expressions are normally censored because the regimes are typically anti-totalitarian and conservative. The dominating ideology is focused on national rebirth and/or economic development; it is not deemed to be scientifically determined and thus, even if there is a form of dominating discourse it is not as embracing.[19] Its impact is further limited by the persistence of competing forms of public expression from autonomous or semi-autonomous institutions, creating a condition where meaning is not uniquely defined by totalitarian ideologues.[20] It is only totalitarian press systems where the ideology and the language produced by the ideology dominate all public expression, including the press. As long as public expression conforms to Newspeak, there is little possibility of challenging the ruling party or party control of the press.

   In spite of this domination in the totalitarian press model, the press is not monolithic. The press, just as the monistic centre of political power which oversees it, does not manifest absolute unity and uniformity. There may be some level of what can be called *manufactured diversity*, small differences in press coverage encouraged by the state in order to appeal to audiences of different regions, education levels and occupations. There may also be some degree of evolution of the ideology and thus the discourse. What is important is that central power retains strict positive and negative control over the press and that for the press, as for other groupings in totalitarian regimes, 'whatever pluralism . . . exists derives its legitimacy from (the) centre, is largely mediated by it, and is mostly a political creation rather than an outgrowth of the dynamics of pre-existing society'.[21]

POST-TOTALITARIAN PRESS SYSTEMS

As stated earlier, the Soviet press in the 1980s can best be described as a post-totalitarian press system. A post-totalitarian press system is the product of the ageing and partial degeneration of a totalitarian regime. As the party's promise of utopia remains unfulfilled and in some cases after a violent leader dies, there is a routinization and rationalization of power within the ruling party in an attempt to 'assure continuity, safety, and a certain degree of predictability' after a highly volatile and violent totalitarian period.[22] Concomitantly, two important phenomena occur which have significant implications for the press. First, there is a reduced emphasis on mobilization. Mobilization cannot be sustained indefinitely, and, more importantly, a continual high state of mobilization is undesirable for a regime which seeks safety and predictability.[23] Second, there emerges a decline in ideological fervour in the leadership and the masses, particularly the best educated, and with it a less rigid approach to ideological orthodoxy.[24]

The de-emphasis on mobilization and the reduced standards of ideological orthodoxy permit an increase in diversity in press content. What emerges can be called *sanctioned diversity*, which entails a selective scaling back of control and the appearance of non-uniform press content which, although not explicitly endorsed by the leadership, is tolerated by it. The party/state retains the power and the potential to exercise both positive and negative control of the press, but the press is still permitted a relatively greater degree of autonomy than in totalitarian press systems, even to the degree of expressing what Spechler calls 'permitted dissent'.[25]

However, the relaxation of controls is both narrow and selective. Sanctioned diversity and permitted dissent are most likely to be found in publications with limited, elite audiences, such as cultural and literary journals,[26] or in specialty academic journals.[27] Standards are also eased for subject matter which is not of central importance to the regime. Foreign press coverage, for example, is likely to be tightly restricted.[28]

In spite of a certain level of weakening in the scope of control, the post-totalitarian press system remains imprinted with the mark of totalitarianism. Access to the press remains highly restricted, and the press on the whole remains identified with and subordinated to the centre of political power. More importantly, the restrictive ideological language of Newspeak is still imposed on the press. The linguistic structure of the ideology continues, even as the ideology loses its vibrancy. In other words, although the ideational core of the totalitarian ideology deteriorates, the outer shell, in the form of Newspeak, remains largely intact.

This shell plays a crucial and defining role in post-totalitarian regimes because it reinforces the authority of the centre of political power. It does this in two ways. First, it binds together the ruling elite in a common language, uniting it even as differences of opinion within that elite sharpen.[29] Second, it helps to exclude the public expression of alternative ideas. To paraphrase Voslensky, the role of the propaganda is not to convince, but to demonstrate to citizens that they have to use a specific language structure in public

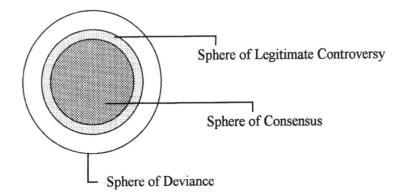

Sphere of Legitimate Controversy

Sphere of Consensus

Sphere of Deviance

Figure 1.1   Post-Totalitarian Press System

communication.[30] As discussed earlier, this language structure inhibits the expression of ideas beyond the ideology, to say nothing of ideas opposed to the regime. It does not matter whether journalists believe what they write nor if readers believe what they read. What is important is that they all conform to the official language in public expression.[31]

The post-totalitarian press system can be understood if we imagine press content as being divided into three concentric circles with the area within the innermost circle representing what can be called the sphere of consensus, the area between the first and second circles the sphere of legitimate controversy and the area between the second and third circles the sphere of deviance.[32] The innermost sphere reflects consensual issues. The middle area represents non-consensual issues which are regarded as normal and permissible topics of discussion. The outer area represents information or opinions which are understood to be inadmissible or inappropriate.

Post-totalitarian press systems, like totalitarian systems, have a strict delineation between consensus and deviance. However, needs of different sectors of society and the weakening of ideological orthodoxy allow for the emergence of a limited sphere of legitimate controversy which contains sanctioned diversity, particularly in literary and specialty journals. Most issues which fall within this sphere are of little importance to the regime. Arguments are also likely to continue to be made through the medium of Newspeak and thus are appreciated by only limited sections of the political and intellectual elite. In spite of the changes associated with a shift to post-totalitarianism, there is an overwhelmingly strong predisposition in the press to present material which broadly represents the government-imposed consensus.

CONCLUSION

For the study of the Soviet press upon which we are about to embark, it is crucial to underline that even if belief in the ideology begins to fade, and the regime slides into a form of post-totalitarianism, the press can continue to function largely as it had in the totalitarian phase. The press may contain a small degree of diversity sanctioned by the ruling party, but it still performs its primary function, promoting a language which both binds the leadership and protects the ideology that justifies the regime's claim to rule.

2 Soviet Communications Policy

The system of ideological education should act like a well-tempered orchestra, where every instrument has its voice and plays its part, and harmony is achieved by skillful conducting.

Konstantin Chernenko[1]

The Communist Party has been and will be the only master of the minds and thoughts, the spokesman, leader, organizer of the people in their struggle for communism.

Pravda, 7 July 1956[2]

This chapter examines how the Soviet press functioned in the pre-Gorbachev period and explores its effectiveness in implementing the tasks prescribed to it by the Communist Party. The primary focus will be Soviet communications policy, or the means through which the Soviet party/state exerted control over the press and its contents. Particular attention is devoted to international journalism, the focus of the empirical study.

It is argued that the pre-Gorbachev Soviet press represented a post-totalitarian press system. A combination of organizational biases and pre- and post-publication controls meant that the Soviet press was both controlled by and identified with the Communist Party, its policies and its ideology. However, Soviet communications policy was fundamentally deficient, failing to transform the population according to the Party blueprint and proving incapable of mobilizing the population to achieve even short-term ends. While the pre-Gorbachev Soviet leadership recognized the shortcomings of Soviet communications policy, it failed to offer a cure, especially in the area of foreign press coverage. Two factors explain the latter. First, the leadership's commitment to the ideological struggle with the United States precluded change from above, or what will be called controlled change. Second, coverage of the West remained relatively static because the Communist Party continued to hold firm control over the press. This persistent control ruled out changes instigated from below, by the independent actions of reporters and editors.

POST-TOTALITARIAN PRESS

The Soviet press in the pre-Gorbachev period most closely approximated the post-totalitarian press model outlined in Chapter 1. The Leninist dictum that the press serve a utilitarian role as a 'collective propagandist, agitator and organizer' of the masses guided the Soviet press into the Gorbachev period.[3] The press was to serve as a key tool in the Party's experiment in social engineering, helping to build *Homo Sovieticus*, the New Soviet Man.[4] As Stalin said, the press was the 'prime instrument' through which the Party communicates with the masses on a daily basis.[5]

Even after the Soviet regime had settled from its early, revolutionary days, and there appeared a routinization and rationalization of power after the Stalin dictatorship, the press was assigned important functions by the Soviet leadership. For those still committed to the belief that socialism could metamorphose humanity, the press was to play a transformative role, helping to 'mould' a new society.[6] Even for the many who had lost their ideological fervour, the press theoretically served the important function of mobilizing the population, albeit for the purpose of attaining short-term aims in areas such as industrial production or alcohol consumption.[7]

While the press enjoyed limited success in these transformative and mobilizing roles, it did help to perpetuate the Party's rule. First, it contributed to the imposition of a limited discourse on society. The press was used as a means of instructing people not simply about what they could say in public, but about how they were to express themselves.[8] It set an example which others were supposed to follow. In helping to impose this language, the press aided the Party by shielding it and the ideology which justified its rule:

> The continued use of Marxist-Leninist language, even after the genuinely Marxist content of the language had largely decayed, is to be explained by its function of excluding other modes of expression and thought. If everything has to be expressed in a stilted, formalised and alien political vocabulary, it makes criticisms and alternatives far more difficult to articulate.[9]

Second, it helped to legitimate the Party's rule.[10] By portraying the Soviet Union as socially and materially ahead of the West, or at least poised to catch up with and pass its capitalist rivals,[11] the press implied that even if the Party could not achieve the cherished goal of communism it could still provide for the population better than any alternative.[12] It also reinforced the Party's legitimacy by suggesting that the Party was the best guarantor of security and sovereignty given the ubiquitous external threat.

The continuing demands of the Party, particularly the requirement that the press perpetuate Newspeak, meant that even with a decline in belief in the system the press continued to be consciously identified with the Communist Party and the ideology espoused by it.[13]

In order to ensure that the press fulfilled its duties, the Communist Party established an elaborate system of supervision through which it exercised both positive and negative control over the press. Indeed, the press served as little more than an extension of the Party's ideological apparatus.[14] As one journalism handbook put it, 'mass media are not independent, "autonomous" elements of the political system. Journalism is subordinate to the aims laid down for it by the political forces governing it.'[15] The system included the creation of organizational biases and pre- and post-publication controls which deserves some elaboration.

ORGANIZATION

The Soviet press was dependent upon the Party for its existence. The Party controlled all elements of the publication and distribution process. There was no private ownership. Publications were either sponsored by the Party or the Party-dominated government, or by public organizations subjugated to the Party.[16] There were no private publishing houses, nor was there an independent distribution system. Even possession of a photocopier was forbidden without Party approval.

It was far easier for the Soviet Communist Party to regulate the press than it was, for example, for the National Socialists in Germany or the Fascists in Italy, where the continuation of private ownership served as an important barrier to government control.[17]

Sponsorship and ownership, however, were insufficient guarantors of journalistic compliance. In order to ensure that journalists co-operated with Party demands, an elaborate system of vetting of personnel and positive and negative incentives were established to ensure co-operation amongst journalists.

The most important means was through its control over personnel appointments. The Ideology Department of the Central Committee, often under the guidance of the Politburo, approved candidates for editors-in-chief, editorial boards, heads of departments and political commentators of all major publications.[18] It was also consulted on appointments of reporters.[19] The more important the publication, the tighter the control over personnel. Regional publications were overseen at the corresponding Party level.

Journalists at key publications were almost invariably Party members whose recruitment was largely contingent upon their loyalty. Many had been educated in university journalism departments which taught the proper, party-minded approach to journalism.[20] Still others, particularly at central publications, came directly from the Party apparatus. That was especially the case for editors-in-chief of major publications, the most important of whom also served on the Central Committee.[21] This process not only minimized the potential for opposition to the regime in higher press organs, it further ensured the integrity of the entire system by encouraging journalists in lower and middle level publications to demonstrate unnatural levels of loyalty if they hoped to advance professionally.[22]

As a final guarantee of co-operation, a number of incentives were offered to journalists to comply with Party demands. Payment was largely based on the amount of work which journalists published, but publishing was contingent upon supporting the Party line. Advancement up the journalistic hierarchy to the top publications (and an apartment) in Moscow could not be achieved through iconoclasm, but through fealty. Standards of loyalty were particularly high for foreign correspondents who enjoyed the perquisites of living abroad.[23]

PRE-PUBLICATION AND POST-PUBLICATION CONTROLS

Although it took several steps to create a co-operative disposition amongst journalists, the Party did not solely rely on self-regulation. It constructed an elaborate system of pre- and post-publication controls to offer guidance and to ensure that press content did not stray far from Party policies and ideology.

The day-to-day operations of the Soviet press were primarily overseen by departments of the Central Committee of the CPSU. Prior to the Gorbachev period, international press coverage was governed by no less than three departments: the Propaganda Department, the International Department and the International Information Department. The Propaganda Department was concerned with questions of ideology and culture, including domestic developments in foreign countries. The International Department primarily dealt with issues concerning international relations, communist parties, and international history. The International Information Department, created in 1978 in response to the inefficacy of Soviet communications policy, had a more ill-defined role, overseeing a variety of issues concerning international relations and culture.[24]

In the pre-publication phase, the departments' role was to promote coverage and the 'correct interpretation' of issues, while discouraging the discussion of others.[25] They used a variety of means to fulfil their obligations. One common means of influence was through the regular dissemination of information at meetings between the editors and members of the Party apparatus. The most important editors, including those of *Pravda* and *Izvestiya*, attended weekly meetings of the Party's Secretariat and the *Pravda* editor sat in on select Politburo meetings. At these meetings editors received information about policy decisions and guidance on how the press could lend support for their implementation.[26]

More focused directives occurred during the regular weekly sessions for editors-in-chief at the Propaganda Department, which played the most important institutional role in media management.[27] Its weekly meetings were described by one editor as 'brainwashing sessions' at which 'all became clear; what to write on, what one could write on, what one could not write on, what to criticize and what never to criticize'.[28] Propaganda campaigns were discussed and occasionally articles written by department members were given to editors for publication.[29]

The other two departments also held regular meetings. The International Information Department held meetings every two or three weeks for editors and other leading officials of central media organs. The meetings primarily focused on 'correct' interpretations of international issues.[30] The International Department also held periodic meetings, primarily with foreign editors. They also met with foreign correspondents during their periodic visits to Moscow.[31] Again, the latest interpretations of foreign events were discussed and articles occasionally submitted for publication.[32]

For periods between meetings, or for those who were not invited, other mechanisms existed which gave the Party apparatus direct control over the media. Editors and journalists received regular telephone calls about appropriate press coverage[33] from the Central Committee departments, representatives of the Ministry of Foreign

Affairs[34] and Politburo members.[35] Indeed, one interesting element of the Soviet press system was that all major publications had telephone lines leading directly to the General Secretary. Although the frequency with which those lines were used was probably rare, their very existence illustrates the degree to which the press was integrated into the political power structure of the regime.

In spite of these unifying links, the Party was sufficiently vigilant that it maintained other systems of control to ensure that unwanted information did not find its way into the press. One means was through pre-publication verification of political commentaries. Representatives of both the Ministry of Foreign Affairs and the Ideology Department regularly read commentaries and initialled them before publication in order to guarantee that the commentaries did not compromise the Soviet Union's foreign relations or relent in the war of ideas with the ideological enemy.[36] More important was the ubiquitous presence of the state censorship agency, Glavlit (the Administration for the Protection of State Secrets in the Press). Although the agency was technically under the auspices of the Council of Ministers, it was in fact the most consistent means through which the Central Committee, through the Propaganda Department, oversaw the press.[37]

Glavlit representatives situated at publications read every issue prior to printing. They were empowered not only to prohibit the publication of material which might 'damage the country's interest', but also to prevent 'the use of the press for purposes of undermining the established socialist system of the USSR'.[38] This left a tremendously broad range of materials subject to the censor's knife. Glavlit representatives not only could act to prevent the publication of state secrets, as in any country (although there was an unusually strict definition of state secrets in the Soviet Union), but could censor material for ideological reasons. The latter meant the prohibition of material ranging from portrayals of the General Secretary which were not sufficiently respectful (such as publishing photographs revealing Gorbachev's birthmark)[39] to non-ideologized references to political and artistic dissidents.[40] Any items found in violation of their 'Talmud,' the list of officially prohibited materials, were censored. For material which was not specifically prohibited, but which seemed to fall outside the accepted ideological interpretation of Marxist-Leninism, the Glavlit representatives could appeal to outside Party and state bodies to prevent publication.[41]

The combination of organizational biases and pre-publication controls meant that objectionable material rarely found its way into the press. However, on the rare occasions when undesired information appeared, the Party possessed a number of post-publication mechanisms to ensure that it did not happen again. These included criticism behind closed doors at the Propaganda Department and the Ministry of Foreign Affairs, published criticism, dismissal, imprisonment and even exile. During the Stalinist period the dangers were greater.[42]

The important point about post-publication controls is that they rarely had to be employed. The combination of the vetting of personnel and positive and negative incentives bred within journalists an internal censor and a predisposition to co-operate which were far more effective means of control than regular intrusions into the editorial room. The Party apparatus was rarely forced to intercede to ensure that Party policy was supported. A fairly peaceful relationship existed between the Party and the press. However, as we shall see later, that relationship was strained during the Gorbachev period.

PRESS CONTENT

Through its oversight of the press, the Party went to great lengths to ensure that it and its ideology were respected above all else. The Party instructed journalists that press content should follow six basic principles: *partiinost'* – party mindedness; *ideinost'* – ideological correctness; *pravdivost'* – truthfulness; *narodnost'* – being for, by and close to the people; *massovost'* – serving mass interest and allowing for participation of the masses; and *kritika/samokritika* – criticism and self-criticism.[43] However, in actual practice these tenets were not applied equally. There was great tension between *partiinost'* and *ideinost'*, which were to serve the Party as socializing and controlling influences over the masses, and *narodnost'* and *massovost'*, which were supposed to allow the masses to be heard and thus theoretically have greater influence over decisions.[44] Throughout most of Soviet history, the press overwhelmingly promoted socialization and control at the expense of mass interests.[45] In the process, it sacrificed truth and avoided criticism.

The Soviet press was dogmatic and didactic, uninteresting and frequently untruthful. There were no limits to the glorification of the Party and its ideology. The press almost exclusively touted Party policy. It inflated achievements through the 'propaganda of success' while ignoring manifest deficiencies.[46] There was rarely criticism in the press, and when there was it was almost invariably manufactured by the regime in the form of propaganda campaigns. Strict guidelines meant that meaningful criticism was effectively precluded.[47] They also meant that the press had to be imbued with the discursive values of Newspeak. Alternative terminology was unacceptable.

For the Soviet press, information was not important in its own right. Rather, it was a closely guarded tool used to promote Party policy. According to the former head of TASS news agency:

> News should not merely be concerned with reporting such and such a fact or event. News or information must pursue a definite goal: it must serve and support the decisions related to the fundamental duties facing our Soviet society, our Soviet people marching on the road of gradual transition from socialism to Communism. . . .[48]

This left no room for Western standards of objectivity.[49] It also meant that even the most innocuous of articles, be they on economic production or whales, were supposed to reflect the Party ideology and support Party decisions.[50]

Nowhere was the dogmatism felt more powerfully than in foreign press coverage, particularly coverage of the West and its leader the United States. Writing about the West was governed by one overriding criterion: it had to show the superiority of Soviet socialism over American capitalism. From the mid-1970s onwards, as the ideological battle between the Superpowers intensified, counter-propaganda and disinformation spread.[51] The Soviet press contained numerous mirror image charges of human rights violations, with frequent references to political prisoners and even US government-run concentration camps.[52] The tone of the coverage might have altered during periods of particularly bad or good relations, but the foundation remained the same.

SANCTIONED DIVERSITY

In the post-totalitarian phase, the Soviet press did not always perfectly reflect the Party's formal guidelines. The regime tolerated varying levels of diversity in the press, depending on political conditions. It permitted some writers to produce ideologically neutral articles and even tolerated a level of dissent.[53] Conditions were certainly different from what they had been under most of Stalin's reign.

However, the press was still clearly imprinted with its totalitarian experience. The scope for dissenting and ideologically neutral articles was limited and there was rarely a consistent pattern of either. Such articles generally appeared in publications with relatively small circulations, normally only touched peripheral issues and did not contain outright attacks on the official ideology. Often, they were so laden with official discourse, or so constrained by it, that the arguments were largely obfuscated and incomprehensible to non-specialists.[54]

The important point is that the vast majority of the Soviet press continued to function largely as if it were in the totalitarian period. Although the Party tolerated some level of ideological neutrality and even mild dissent, it had created conditions in which the press was predominantly compliant and actively supportive of it and its ideology. Moreover, it still retained the capacity to take coercive measures if necessary.[55]

EFFICACY OF THE SOVIET PRESS

The problem with the Soviet approach to press content was that it lacked efficacy, or *effektivnost'*, as a socializing and mobilizing agent. The press simply did not fulfil the role assigned to it by the Party.

Soviet communications policy had largely assumed the efficacy of what Western researchers call the 'hypodermic effects' model of media, that is, 'the immediate and unaltered reception of all new information carried by the media system, much as a hypodermic needle inserts its dosage into the human organism'.[56] In other words, it assumed that people would almost automatically internalize messages. While faith in the hypodermic effects model might have proved comforting to Soviet policy makers and to Western cold warriors who tended to assume the worst of the Soviet system,[57] sociological studies conducted after the reintroduction of sociology in the Soviet Union in the 1960s and 1970s showed otherwise.[58]

The studies provided ample evidence of shortcomings. An examination of television habits of viewers with less than fourth grade education (which described 40 per cent of the rural population) revealed that 93 per cent could not understand programmes on social/political topics.[59] Another study in Taganrog, an industrial city in Russia, indicated that a large proportion of the population did not understand key words used in the press. Forty-six per cent did not know what 'imperialism' meant, 68 per cent did not know the meaning of the word 'reactionary' and 73 per cent did not understand the term 'liberal'.[60]

While this clearly posed a problem for those who wanted to transform Soviet society, it was not necessarily indicative of as great a failure as Mickiewicz asserts.[61] While it may be true that the population did not understand some important terms, other evidence suggests that it did absorb some of the broader messages conveyed by those terms.[62] If an important role of the media was to legitimate Party rule by convincing people of the superiority of socialism over the capitalist alternative, then the press might have been more successful than the evidence above indicates. The Taganrog study demonstrated that even if people did not understand the common words used in domestic and international propaganda, they seemed to at least incorporate desired images and connotations associated with specific countries. For example, in identifying the country with the highest living standard, almost three times more respondents named Czechoslovakia than the United States. No one listed the United States as among the most democratic countries, whereas Czechoslovakia again was the most positively received, followed distantly in order by Bulgaria, the German Democratic Republic, Poland and Yugoslavia. The US was also rated second to Britain in violations of workers' rights. No respondents named a socialist country in this category.[63]

The attitudes expressed in the Taganrog study were confirmed elsewhere. One nation-wide study in 1977 showed that respondents ranked the Soviet Union 4 on a 5 point scale regarding quality of life versus an average of only 2 for Western countries.[64] Studies of Soviet émigrés and travellers to the West also found fundamental hostility towards many crucial elements of Western democracy.[65]

This survey information points to the unique nature of international propaganda. Western studies have demonstrated that readers show more confidence in stories which are distant from them, in those stories which are not independently verifiable by their own experience or by word of mouth.[66] For international propaganda this has generally meant a greater level of trust and belief. This was confirmed in the Soviet Union where one survey indicated that newspaper readers were 'four to six times as likely to be critical of

articles on domestic problems as they are to be on articles in international relations'.[67] The same study demonstrated general support
for Soviet foreign policy positions. This meant that if a key aim of
the Soviet leadership was winning the ideological war with the West
then the media was enjoying some success.

Even with the measure of success enjoyed by Soviet propagan-
dists in creating positive views of socialism *vis-à-vis* the West, there
were other underlying problems in the system of ideological education. Simply put, the system was beginning to rot. The most acute
of the problems involved the more educated groups in society and
the young. Soviet studies revealed an inverse correlation between
the amount of education and satisfaction with media messages.
Indeed, as Mickiewicz points out, 'the highly educated were not
likely to be more persuaded; quite the contrary, they were more
likely to disagree with official communications'.[68] This dissatisfaction extended to international press coverage, which opinion surveys
consistently pointed to as being of the most interest to the readership.[69] Young readers and the highly educated especially expressed
the desire for more varied international information.[70] The dissatisfaction amongst the intelligentsia was so great that, according to
interviewees for the Rand study of former Soviet journalists and
editors, it was one of the main reasons for the creation of the
International Information Department in 1978, one in a long line
of failed leadership attempts to increase media efficacy.[71]

One result of such scepticism (and it was not simply caused by
foreign press coverage) was that it led people to seek other sources
of information. Samizdat (illegal, citizen-operated press) was one
possibility, but difficulties with production and distribution limited
its influence.[72] More important was the tendency of people to seek
foreign sources of information, the most prominent of which were
radio broadcasts. One Soviet study revealed that 21 per cent of
older school children listened to foreign broadcasts. This was not
simply done for entertainment reasons, but because, according to
one Soviet author, 'If they fail to get satisfactory answers at school
to questions which concern them, they turn to other sources with a
hostile ideological orientation.'[73] This penchant amongst the young,
who were far more educated than previous generations,[74] was perhaps reflected in the Taganrog study, where younger respondents
rated aspects of Western life significantly higher than their elders.[75]

The search for alternative sources of information, however, was
by no means limited to the young and highly educated. The number

of Soviets listening to foreign broadcasts appears to have been substantial. The Voice of America estimated in 1987 that it had more than 30 million Soviet listeners, while Radio Liberty claimed 50 million.[76] Even if these figures are inflated, the numerous references to foreign broadcasts in the speeches of Soviet leaders, the frequent denials in the press of charges levied by foreign broadcasters and the amount of manpower and money put into jamming the broadcasts[77] indicate that the Soviet leadership perceived them to be a substantial threat in the battle for control over the minds of the masses.[78] That the phenomena existed at all indicates that the Soviet press not only failed in its task of moulding the New Soviet Man, but that it was in some ways counter-productive, pushing the young and well educated to the ideological opponent's sources of information.

The problem of citizens seeking alternative sources of information only promised to get worse. In the 1970s and 1980s, Soviet citizens were increasingly gaining access to radios which let them receive foreign signals.[79] Soviet leaders also repeatedly expressed concern over plans by the United States Information Agency to beam television broadcasts to the Soviet Union.[80] The third technological revolution, which fostered and necessitated broad and easy access to information, was even more of a threat.[81] The Soviet leadership was faced with a difficult problem: How could the press remain so dogmatic and uninteresting when new technologies would provide easy access to alternative sources? What could they do when their main area of success in the press, building hostility towards the outside world, was under threat?

With these problems in mind, we shall now examine some of the dimensions of Soviet communications policy in the period leading to the accession of Gorbachev.

COMMUNICATIONS POLICY: HISTORICAL RESPONSE AND FAILURE

The Soviet leadership seems to have paid increasing attention to the problems of ideological work, including communications policy, from the mid-1970s. However a review of the statements and actions of Gorbachev's three predecessors, Brezhnev, Andropov and Chernenko, reveals a common pattern: they all spoke of the need to change but none took steps to implement significantly new policies.

If there was one main theme running through all of their speeches concerning ideological education and the press it was that the ideological war with the West was a dominant priority. In the end, this effectively precluded significant innovations.

BREZHNEV, ANDROPOV AND CHERNENKO

In the late 1970s and early 1980s there was a flurry of meetings and speeches devoted to ideological education work. Although over the years of Soviet rule there had been periodic criticism of the efficacy of the press in ideological upbringing, this activity seemed to indicate a heightened concern.

In terms of the media, the 'Party Resolution on Ideological and Political Upbringing'[82] of May 1979 was the most significant statement to come from the leadership in this period. The resolution was, in all likelihood, the product of a special Politburo commission established in November 1978 with the express purpose of studying the Party's work in this area.[83]

The resolution contained significantly more powerful language than Brezhnev had used in his speech to the XXVth Party Congress three years earlier. While at the Congress Brezhnev had spoken vaguely of improving the media's 'co-ordination and operational efficiency',[84] the resolution took on a more direct and critical tone, pointing to 'quite a few weaknesses and shortcomings, some of them substantial'. In elaborating these shortcomings, two main points were made: first, the press's failure to take into account the 'growing educational and cultural level' of Soviet citizens; and second, its failure to give sufficient consideration to the 'nature of the aggravated ideological struggle in the international arena'.[85]

These two points are important to bear in mind because they represent incompatible sides of the leadership's approach to the press: efficacy versus ideological struggle. Increased efficacy was supposed to be produced by, among other things, the exploration of more diverse subject matter and the employment of better style and language.[86] However, attempts to introduce such innovations were ultimately rendered useless by the demands of the ideological struggle. Indeed, the resolution concentrated so much on 'imperialist propaganda' which was 'continuously conducting a fierce offensive against the minds of the Soviet people,' to 'poison their consciousness,' that it seems that combating such propaganda was its primary aim.[87] The problem was not simply that Soviet propaganda was ineffective, that the masses were not sufficiently 'inculcated' with proper Soviet thought or that mass activeness was waning. More importantly, it was feared that 'bourgeois' propaganda might succeed where Soviet propaganda had failed.

Similar sentiments were expressed by Brezhnev in his speech to the XXVIth Party Congress two years later, in a section labelled 'The Party's Ideological and Political Upbringing Work'.[88] Brezhnev began by listing the glorious achievements of the Soviet Union in the information and education spheres. He then pointed out the main concern, warning, 'On the other hand, the class enemy's propaganda media have become more active, and its attempts to exert a demoralising influence on the minds of the Soviet people have increased.' He claimed that the Soviet Union could improve its propaganda, and that the basis of such improvements could be found in the 1979 Party resolution. Referring to the resolution, he called for the restructuring (*perestroika*) of 'many sectors and spheres of ideological work', then, again warned, 'It is very important that propaganda not shun crucial issues,' because 'if we do not answer them, the foes of our country try to take advantage of this to slander socialism.'[89] It was against these slanderers that the policy was intended to work.

The Andropov and Chernenko general secretaryships did not produce any significant changes. The specific policies of the two leaders are difficult to distinguish because the clearest articulation of ideological policy and the mass media during Andropov's general secretaryship was made by the then Secretary of Ideology, Chernenko. However, there seems to have been continuity between the two, at least as far as ideological war with the West was concerned.[90]

Chernenko's speech at the June 1983 plenum, entitled 'Urgent Questions of the Party's Ideological and Mass Political Work,' was similar to the 1979 resolution and Brezhnev's speech at the XXVIth Party Congress. In the introduction, he made it clear that the Party would continue to guide Soviet society. He mentioned the Soviet goal of creating a 'new man' and spoke of the weapons at the Party's disposal for effecting proper ideological moulding. He then moved to the theme of ideological confrontation. He claimed that 'imperialism', particularly the American variety, was concentrating 'attacks of an unprecedented scale on our social system and Marxist-Leninist ideology'. 'The two ideologies', he said, 'are waging an intense and truly global struggle.' Later, Chernenko returned to the same theme, warning of the influences of 'foreign artistic and intellectual products' which lacked 'proper ideological content'. He spoke of the need for Party committees to 'deliver a prompt re-buff' to the West, which was attempting to 'organise outright inform-ational and propaganda intervention' against the Soviet Union.[91]

Chernenko did not simply attack the misanthropic West. He went into greater detail about means of promoting press efficacy than the 1979 resolution. He called for the press to pay more attention to the young, to provide more timely information and to end overly dogmatic coverage. However, these suggestions were accompanied by warnings of the threat of imperialism.[92]

Andropov voiced similar views in his speech to the plenum on the following day. He reaffirmed the Party's leading role and the need for the 'moulding of consciousness of communists and of all citizens'. He also made clear his view on ideological competition. His final introductory point on the Party's 'principal tasks in ideo-logical work' stated:

> All upbringing and propaganda work should constantly take into account the specific features of the historical period in which man is living. It is marked by a struggle, one that is unprecedented in the entire post-war period in terms of its intensity and acute-ness, between two diametrically opposite world views and two political courses – socialism and imperialism. A struggle is under way for the hearts and minds of billions of people on our planet. The future of mankind depends, to a considerable extent, on the outcome of this ideological struggle.[93]

Andropov touched on other subjects, like the need for greater mass activity, particularly in economic processes. Indeed, his frequent talk of the need for economic improvement in this speech and others is more akin to Gorbachev than to Brezhnev.[94] However, for press coverage as a whole, and international press coverage in particu-lar, the fundamental problem remained: the ideological battle was the number one priority.

EFFECT OF THE RESPONSE

While the leadership resolutions and proposals and the creation of the 1978 Politburo Commission and the International Information Department indicate a growing leadership concern with the press, the impact, particularly on international press coverage, was minimal.[95]

The failure of successive leaders to respond to the deteriorating situation reflects less a lack of concern than fear of the impact which reforms might have had on the system of ideological education: changes which might have produced results would have meant too many compromises with established priorities.

On the one hand, freeing the press from party control was apparently out of the question. If anything, the creation of the International Information Department suggests the leadership felt that more, rather than less, bureaucratic control was necessary. Journalists were thus tightly constrained within the boundaries of Party policy, precluding change from below.

On the other hand, static policy priorities prohibited change from above. The capacity for reform was not simply limited by the top priority given to the ideological struggle, but by the leadership's narrow interpretation of what such a struggle entailed. Typical of the conservative attitude was an authoritative *Pravda* editorial in 1981 which, while acknowledging problems associated with delays in reporting international events, expressed greater concern over 'a superficial, or still worse, a wrong interpretation', which might lead to 'the loss of important positions in the battle of ideas'.[96] As far as press coverage of international affairs was concerned, the sharpening of the ideological war only meant an increase in counterpropaganda and more fierce and unrelenting criticism of the West.

The ideological struggle also restricted the potential for change in domestic press coverage. If the Soviet Union was intent on demonstrating that its system was superior to the West, then how could real criticism occur or the disastrous reality of the Soviet economy be revealed? If it wanted to hide embarrassing errors and accidents, then how could it have timely responses? The answer was that as long as the battle remained the top priority of the leadership, significant change was impossible.[97]

A few changes did appear in response to the increasing concerns. For example, in 1984 *Sovetskaya Rossiya* began a column which allowed for greater reader participation.[98] There was also a greater turnover in press personnel in 1984 than there had been in the recent past, including at *Izvestiya*, where Ivan Laptev, who would be their relatively progressive editor throughout the *glasnost'* period, took over as editor-in-chief.[99] In his work on the newspaper *Pravda*, Angus Roxburgh claimed that the Soviet response to the KAL 007 downing was quicker than that to past disasters, although this might have been to counteract the West in the propaganda battle that would follow. It is possible that at least the former two changes were influenced by Gorbachev, who was serving as Secretary of Ideology at the time and chairing for an ailing Chernenko at Politburo meetings.[100] However, according to most testimony of journalists, change was insubstantial and rare. Moreover, international press coverage was still dictated by the overwhelming demands of ideological orthodoxy: attack and counter-propaganda reigned. Substantial change would not occur until Mikhail Gorbachev became General Secretary.

GORBACHEV: ECONOMY VS. THE IDEOLOGICAL ENEMY

The most crucial task for Gorbachev if he hoped to make his reforms succeed was to reorient policy makers and the masses away from concerns about the external threat and ideological competition with the West, towards internal problems facing the Soviet Union. This was especially true if he hoped to revivify the press and make it an effective tool to promote reform.

Initial indications of new approaches under Gorbachev were set out at an Ideology Plenum held in December 1984, in a speech entitled 'The Improvement of Developed Socialism and the Party's Ideological Work in Light of the Decisions of the June (1983) Plenary Session of the CPSU Central Committee.' In spite of the fact that he was nominally under the ailing Chernenko at the time, this speech espoused many of the fundamental ideas and goals which Gorbachev would later pursue in his roles as General Secretary and President. Interestingly, some of his ideas were stressed more strongly in 1984 than in his early speeches as General Secretary.[101]

In his speech, Gorbachev clearly identified his main priority: the Soviet economy. Although other leaders had spoken of the need for the press to assist with economic reform, they had always subjugated that desire to their concerns over ideological competition. In speeches at Party Congresses and Ideology Plenums, Brezhnev, Andropov and Chernenko had all made the need to rebuff Western enemies the dominant priority for the press. They all addressed this issue in the opening sections of their speeches.[102]

In 1984, Gorbachev offered a new approach, seeking to raise economic issues above ideological warfare. Gorbachev discussed the ideological battle only in the fifth section of his six-section speech and even then asserted:

> Comrades! Socialism's primary influence on world development was and remains through its economic politics, through success in the socio-economic sphere. Each new step forward on this road is the most convincing argument in favour of the socialist system and the Soviet way of life.[103]

The point is not that Gorbachev failed to see the ideological struggle as existing. Indeed, when he mentioned the West, particularly America, he was nearly as vitriolic as his predecessors.[104] What is important is that he was more concerned with the Soviet Union itself, particularly its economy, than with its ideological opponents. Indeed, the speech as a whole, which was supposedly devoted to ideology, was remarkably un-ideological, at least by Soviet standards. As Gorbachev said: 'the most important field for exerting effort in ideological work, as in all activity of the Party and people, was and remains the economy'.[105] In other words, Soviet success would ultimately be tested by deeds rather than words.

This shift in emphasis was of crucial importance for the press because it cleared the way for significant changes designed to support the economic and political reforms of the Gorbachev leadership. It permitted the press to take a more critical view of Soviet society. Gone was concern over giving 'bread' to the ideological enemy. Although it did not mean an end to ideological competition (as exhibited by Soviet secrecy concerning Chernobyl), and it did not initially extend to international press coverage, it was an important first step towards what would ultimately be a fundamental re-evaluation of capitalism and relations with the West. In short, it removed the chief obstacle preventing a real liberalization of the Soviet press.

CONCLUSION

The pre-Gorbachev Soviet press reflected all of the key traits of a post-totalitarian press system. Access to the press and the freedom of information were limited and the press did not enjoy autonomy from the Communist Party. The press educated the population and mobilized it, when necessary. The Party, although exercising a large degree of negative and positive control over press content, did allow some measure of diversity and even dissent. Most importantly, the press continued to propagate through the discourse of the official ideology. Many in the Party might have given up hope of a fundamental transformation of mankind, but even if the regime slipped into a more conservative form of authoritarianism, the press was still to speak to the population in the language through which it had always spoken. People could believe or not believe, but what was most important was that they understood that in public expressions they could not challenge the regime, or the ideology which justified its rule.

The Soviet press also appeared to help the regime in terms of its influence on people's beliefs. Although it did not successfully transform humanity as had once been hoped, it did help to imbue the population with hostility towards the West and comparatively positive views of socialism. This was of unlimited benefit to a regime which in part legitimated its rule with as many references to its enemy's failures as to its own successes.

This partial success (of imbuing hostility) did not outweigh a great danger. The one-sided, cliché-ridden press framed and imposed a limited discourse on the population, but it was incapable of mobilizing the population, falling short of its potential to assist the regime implement policies.[106] Worse yet, it was turning off key segments of the population, particularly the highly educated and the young, impelling them to seek information from other, hostile sources. Gorbachev's predecessors recognized the problems but they were too focused on an ideological war with the West to make the necessary changes to revivify the press. They settled for conservatism and certainty; in short, stagnation. It took the Gorbachev leadership, with its commitment to reform in all elements of Soviet society, to make real changes.

3 *Glasnost'* vs. Freedom of the Press

> The project of Liberalisers is to relax social tension and to strengthen their position in the power bloc by broadening the social base of the regime: to allow some autonomous organisation of the civil society and to incorporate the new groups into the authoritarian institutions. In light of this project, liberalisation is to be continually contingent on the compatibility of its outcomes with the interests or values of the authoritarian bloc. Thus, liberalisation is referred to as an 'opening' (*apertura*), 'decompression' (*distensao*), 'renewal' (*odnowa*) or reconstruction (*perestroika*). . . . These are terms with strong conditions of limits to reform.
>
> Adam Przeworski[1]

National media systems are not static. The press is both an agent and object of change and its fate is closely linked with that of the political system in which it operates. When regimes liberalize, the press frequently becomes a tool, a battleground and a prize.

In the Soviet Union, the Gorbachev leadership took a calculated risk. It believed that a liberalized press could be used to support its reform programme and to help revitalize socialism. At the same time, it believed that the process could be controlled and limited. In the final instance it lost its wager. Forces outside its control took over the liberalization process and pushed change in the Soviet polity and in the press beyond the boundaries which anyone had imagined.

The purpose of this chapter is to examine changes in the Soviet press in the Gorbachev period. Change will be examined from above, that is, from the view of the leadership, and from below, from the vantage point of the press. The chapter begins with an exploration of Gorbachev's communications policies. Special attention is devoted both to how his policies differed from those of his predecessors and the aims and limits of *glasnost'*. It then examines how and why *glasnost'* moved beyond the limits originally foreseen by the regime. Finally, the special role of international press coverage is addressed with particular reference to Soviet ideology.

Although the chapter focuses on changes which took place in the Soviet Union, evidence is drawn from other cases of press liberalization, particularly those in Spain and Eastern Europe in the 1950s and 1960s. These liberalizations, while clearly different from the Soviet experience, point to revealing patterns of change.

Before moving to an examination of the Soviet press, it will be helpful to clarify what is meant by liberalization.

LIBERALIZATION

In studies of regime transitions, liberalization generally refers to a partial opening of an authoritarian system. This opening can potentially include the expansion of individual and collective liberties (including freedom of the press), diminishing coercion and institutional changes which notionally or actually allow the population to play a greater role in political processes.[2] In the case of socialist-state systems, the process generally entails 'humanization', or limits on the 'scope and level of unpredictability of repressive measures', and the introduction of 'a style of ruling . . . more sensitive, more humane and, sometimes, more responsive to basic needs'.[3] Liberalization can be an integral part of an articulated regime programme, a by-product of an unplanned series of compromises within the leadership or a haphazard process forced upon the regime by opposition emanating from the political sphere and society.[4]

What does liberalization mean for press systems? Using the outline of the illustration from Chapter 1 which classifies press content according to three concentric circles – the sphere of consensus, the sphere of legitimate controversy and the sphere of deviance – we can say that liberalization means any change in the government/press relationship which produces an expansion of the sphere of legitimate controversy, or which minimally produces a significant deepening of discussion within the sphere of consensus such that issues are pushed towards legitimate controversy.

The most radical form of liberalization would entail government abandonment of negative and positive controls and the institutionalization of guarantees of press freedom.[5] However, more typical are smaller, incremental steps. The most basic liberalization may involve little reduction in government control: the political centre can maintain strict negative and positive control over the press while manufacturing a significant broadening of debate and encouraging the publication of new information. Another likely scenario is a reduction in the scope of positive control and a small increase in sanctioned diversity. However, even mild steps can have significant resonance because they can metamorphose beyond the original limited goals into a fundamental transformation of the press and press/government relations.

COMMUNICATIONS UNDER GORBACHEV

Communications policy under Mikhail Gorbachev was markedly different from that of his predecessors. His policies not only led to important changes in press content, they also, perhaps unintentionally, altered the relationships through which the media were traditionally controlled.

Gorbachev's communications policy has traditionally been characterized with reference to the Russian word *glasnost'*. However, there has been confusion over the meaning of this word and its significance for the press. Western analysts have not only had to cope with debates in the Soviet Union between political leaders and journalists about the purpose and limits of *glasnost'*, they also have been trapped by the difficulties of translating an abstract term (literally meaning voice-ness), expressing it alternately as openness and publicity, words with tremendously different connotations. To avoid some of this confusion, communications under Gorbachev will be approached from two directions: change from above and change from below. The former was a leadership policy (*glasnost'*) which implied controlled change, that is liberalization within relatively well-defined guidelines that were established by the Party. The latter was a more dynamic process, largely initiated by journalists, who extended liberalization beyond the boundaries originally foreseen by the leadership.

CONTROLLED CHANGE

The controlled change of the press under the policy of *glasnost'* took two primary forms, both intended to support the Party and its reform policies.

First, there were press campaigns, or what have been termed 'organized pseudo-controversies', which involved Party use of the press as a tool to promote specific policies.[6] Although the campaigns might have appeared to demonstrate a growing tolerance of debate and a substantial widening in the sphere of legitimate controversy, they were more indicative of changing consensus. The diversity represented by them was largely manufactured by the regime. Pre-determined policy outcomes were supported while old approaches were discredited.[7] In spite of this highly instrumentalist approach, these changes can be considered a form of liberalization. The campaigns in the Gorbachev period were often different from past campaigns in that they addressed issues of fundamental importance to the regime. As such, they represented a significant change in the depth of coverage, moving once superficially discussed consensual issues towards the sphere of legitimate controversy.

A second component of the policy of *glasnost'* involved a more substantive liberalization in the form of a widening of sanctioned diversity. These were not directed publicity campaigns or manufactured differences in press coverage designed to satisfy different audiences, but a limited opening of the press which permitted it to cover a wider variety of issues with some degree of varying interpretation. These changes reflected a diminution of the Party's scope of positive and, to a lesser extent, negative control, and concomitantly a growth in the sphere of legitimate controversy. As we will discuss below, these steps were taken largely as a means of mobilizing the population to support the reform programme. The leadership was willing to take the risk in the hope that the changes would pay dividends in the reform process.

THE AIMS OF *GLASNOST'* AND LIBERALIZATION

Mikhail Gorbachev was candid about the purpose of *glasnost'* and the role of the press in the restructuring process:

> The main task of the press is to help the nation understand the ideas of restructuring, to mobilize the masses to struggle for successful implementation of party plans...We need *glasnost'*, criticism and self-criticism in order to implement major changes in all spheres of social life....[8]

Following in the paths of the Spanish and Czechoslovakian press liberalizations in the 1960s, the policy of *glasnost'* was designed to buttress the Gorbachev reform programme.[9] Although it is impossible to reconstruct the exact aims of the policy, and it is certain that different people who contributed to its formation had different goals, there are at least five which need discussing.

First, press liberalization, particularly the widening of sanctioned diversity, was designed to assist the reform process by revitalizing propaganda and attracting people back to the Soviet press. If the regime was counting on using the press as a tool to support reform, it was necessary that people read it. As was discussed in Chapter 2, many, especially the highly educated and the young, were dissatisfied with the press and had begun to turn to alternative sources of information.[10] Underground publications, which predominated in Spain and had an important role in Eastern Europe, were present but less prevalent in the Soviet Union.[11] More worrisome for Soviet leaders were foreign radio transmissions which were attracting a substantial number of Soviet listeners.[12]

The problems promised to worsen. Transmission equipment was improving and the threat of satellite television loomed. Moreover, if the Soviet Union was to modernize its economy, as foreseen by the reform programme, it would have to allow an increasing number of citizens access to modern communications technologies.[13]

With these new threats looming and the need to enjoy the fruits of the communications revolution, the old solutions of jamming[14] and counter-propaganda were not promising. They were also of little help to a regime planning on harnessing the press to support its reforms. The only way to compete effectively with other sources of information was to make the domestic press more dynamic in the hope of attracting more readers.[15] This would minimally involve covering a wider array of issues of interest to the population, especially the educated and the young. The same stale clichés would not do: 'We have seen for ourselves that such (one-sided) propaganda is not believed and given the diverse means of obtaining information today ... the Soviet people ... will simply choose alternative sources of information, and not ours.'[16]

A second and related way in which press liberalization was to assist the reform process was by helping to foster a new relationship between the government and the governed. In authoritarian and totalitarian systems, the passage of time, changes in education and economic levels and a loss of revolutionary fervour can result in the population tiring of a shallow, sermonizing press. The public suffers from cognitive dissonance, that is, a sharp discrepancy between what they hear and read and the reality of the world which surrounds them.[17] A press which patently ignores society's interests[18] alienates the population, contributes to scepticism about the press and government, and makes countries like the Soviet Union fertile ground for rumour.[19] It particularly alienates the intelligentsia, whose support is normally viewed by liberalizers (including Gorbachev) as critical for the success of reforms.[20]

Gorbachev recognized that the population was disenchanted and disinterested, and that a new approach was necessary for reform to succeed. He wrote in his book *Perestroika*, 'One of the prime political tasks of the restructuring effort, if not the main one, is to revive and consolidate in the Soviet people a sense of responsibility for the country's destiny.'[21] For Gorbachev, part of the solution lay in actually increasing the role of the masses in economic and, to a lesser extent, political processes.[22] More important for our concern, he also recognized that the mass media could play an important role in overcoming mental barriers to such participation:

> *Glasnost'* is an integral part of socialist democracy and a norm of all public life. Extensive, timely and candid information indicates trust in people and respect for their intelligence, feelings and ability to comprehend events on their own. It supports the activeness of workers.[23]

Gorbachev was not the first to draw such a link between the press and the involvement of the masses. The 1979 resolution on the need to reform ideological education stressed that a lack of '*kritika/samokritika*' and 'insufficient *glasnost'* in public affairs' damages the 'activeness of the masses', which itself is 'an important source of the socialist system's strength'.[24] Previous leaders had spoken in a similar vein. Nonetheless, the frequency and force of such assertions were almost negligible compared with those of Gorbachev. The others tended to speak of 'moulding' a new man while Gorbachev spoke of using the press as a means of recognizing the 'human factor'. He seemed to believe that by treating the population as rational beings who can think for themselves and be trusted with more diverse information and views, rather than as 'imbeciles' who require constant supervision, the press could encourage support for and a will to participate in the reform process.[25]

A third reason for press liberalization was to offer incentives to the population to support change. This reflects more the utilitarian side of *glasnost'*, but was crucial for the liberalization process in the Soviet Union. The press offered incentives by exposing flaws in

Soviet society. Numerous Soviet journalists revealed the failures of past Soviet policies and the ulcers of contemporary Soviet life. Articles appeared damning everything from the environment to health care, from agricultural production to sports training.[26] While the ideological war would have previously made it impossible to publish such material, it now served to demonstrate that some form of change was necessary.

The press also offered a form of carrot to the population, showing what Soviet society could be like if it supported the reforms. Foreign press coverage was particularly important in this regard because images of foreign countries were used to suggest that if the Soviet Union learned from Western experience, it could approach the West's material wealth while at the same time preserving the social and economic justice associated with socialism. The implicit caveat, however, was that the population had to support the reform path proposed by the leadership.

The fourth way in which the liberalization of the Soviet press fostered political and economic reform was by educating the population about specific means of assisting the reform programme.[27] Here we are not speaking of motivation, but of actual teaching. Again, images of foreign countries were important because they were used to demonstrate new political and economic processes to an ignorant population. The Soviet press in the *glasnost'* era continuously presented previously banned images of Western experience in a didactic fashion, teaching the population about everything from efficient methods of food production and the advantages of co-operative ownership to institutions which could help promote a more efficient and stable government.[28] Many articles were presented as parts of propaganda campaigns, designed to support specific government programmes and policies and thus representing the utilitarian nature of *glasnost'*.

A final reason for the leadership to liberalize the press was to assist policy makers in instituting effective reforms. Leaders in countries with totalitarian and mobilizational authoritarian media systems are frequently victims of a combination of the propaganda of success and government secrecy. Instead of acting as a critical fourth estate, the press simply celebrates achievements, trumpeting overblown claims of accomplishments.[29] At the same time, middle-level government and Party officials are often unwilling to admit failure, and, because of the press's lack of autonomy, are able to silence rare attempts at media criticism.[30] This not only

means that policy-makers lack the necessary information to institute effective reform, but that they do not have access to feedback
mechanisms necessary to test the efficacy of reforms.[31]

As a response, and perhaps as a means of circumventing bureaucratic interference, the press can be marginally liberalized in
order to gather and publish information which reflects more accurately the contemporary situation. For example, the Czechoslovakian
press under Novotny in the early 1960s was charged with the task
of gathering economic and social data to reveal true economic
conditions and the attitude of the population towards reform.[32]
Similarly, the Gorbachev leadership was hopeful that feedback would
help the reform process. As Gorbachev wrote in *Perestroika*, 'We
won't be able to advance if we don't check how our policy responds
to criticism, especially criticism from below.'[33] He also said in 1985,
'We are particularly in need of objective information that depicts
not what we would like to hear, but what really is.'[34] A military
writer put it more succinctly, asserting, 'we need information not
for the sake of information, but as a basis of decision-making'.[35]

LIMITS OF *GLASNOST'*

The more active role of the press and masses in society engendered by the reforms and press liberalization did not mean that
under *glasnost'* the Party would give up its role in the press or
otherwise as the ultimate arbiter of policy. It might allow for a
relatively wider sphere of legitimate controversy, but it was still to
determine where the boundaries of deviance lay. Diversity was always to be sanctioned in accordance with the priorities of the
government.

Gorbachev made very clear both his instrumentalist view of the
mass media and his commitment to continued Party control in his
frequent talks with media representatives. In early 1987, he described the primary role of the press as being to 'help the nation
understand and assimilate the ideas of restructuring, to mobilize
the masses to struggle for successful implementation of Party plans'.[36]
In July 1987 he told editors that '*glasnost'* and democracy do not
mean that everything is permitted. *Glasnost'* is called upon to
strengthen socialism and the spirit of our people . . . *glasnost'* also
means criticism of shortcomings, but it does not mean the undermining of socialism and socialist values.'[37] In 1988, he described

he media as 'an instrument of restructuring', and claimed that the Party's role in guiding society, and thus the press, would increase during the reform process.[38] Even in March 1989 he told media leaders that the work of the mass information media was 'not separate from the work of the Party'.[39] Then in October of the same year he claimed that 'The main purpose and highest purpose of journalistic work and journalistic creativity' was to 'uphold our socialist values, advance the ideas of restructuring, and affirm positive, progressive trends, and to overcome everything negative.'[40]

Certainly journalists understood the limited nature of *glasnost'*. As one reporter said in 1990, '*[G]lasnost'* ... is measured in doses by ruling quarters ... [T]here is still a long way to go to real openness let alone to freedom of speech.'[41] Another called *glasnost'* a temporary certificate' granted by leaders who had the right to revoke it at will.[42]

However, in spite of the limited nature of *glasnost'*, the government demonstrated an unmistakable pragmatism in its relations with the mass media, pragmatism which formed a stark contrast with the unyielding conservatism of the Brezhnev, Chernenko and Andropov periods.[43] Although not giving up the leading role of the Party or the requirement that the press support Soviet ideology, the leadership injected measured doses of real openness to satisfy and inspire the masses and the intelligentsia. Particularly in its efforts to appeal to the interests of the population, it acted more as a regulator of the press than as a totalitarian controller of content, giving the press a greater degree of autonomy. The key problem for the government, however, was how to manage the forces which it had set free.

CHANGE FROM BELOW: THE SNOWBALL EFFECT

Although it is impossible to know how far *glasnost'* strayed from the leadership's original intent,[44] one can deduce from the leadership's periodic attacks on reporters and editors that the press went beyond the circumscribed version of *glasnost'* originally envisioned.[45] Changes in press content were not restricted to information designed to promote policy goals. The press went further, even reaching the point of questioning the reform programme itself and the Gorbachev leadership's right to rule. The Soviet leadership, like other 'third wave' liberalizers, soon found that 'liberalised authoritarianism is not a stable equilibrium; the halfway house does not stand'.[46] A variety of factors accelerated the liberalization process, allowing the press an ever greater amount of autonomy. This process, termed the 'snowball effect',[47] was the product of several interrelated factors, the most important being pressure from the press itself.

PRESSURE FROM THE PRESS

In liberalization processes in all of the countries studied there was at least a core of journalists which led the push for the expansion of the boundaries of the sphere of legitimate controversy.[48]

Journalists' motivations in agitating for further liberalization of the press varied. In the Soviet Union, as in other liberalizing countries, some simply wanted to shed the psychological burden of the self-censor and express themselves more freely.[49] Others wanted to please readers in order to redeem themselves and their profession's legitimacy after years of serving as mouthpieces for the Party.[50] Still others wanted to have a direct impact on the reform process, and hoped that their views could ultimately affect government policies. Some sought to use their exposure as a springboard to the newly formed and at least partially elected political institutions which emerged in 1989.[51] This increased politicization sometimes coalesced in the emergence of inchoate interest groups, usually centred around individual publications, leading to more distinct editorial lines.[52]

On a more practical note, journalists were in some cases moved to press for greater freedom in response to market forces. The result was typical for countries undergoing a liberalization process: the seemingly exponential growth of the prurient, the scandalous and the bizarre.[53]

Regardless of whether journalists changed for creative reasons, because of guilt, a genuine interest in their readership, for commercial or political reasons, or for various combinations thereof, many consciously moved away from their Party orientation, in effect challenging the Party to stop them.

Journalists were fortified in their challenge by an emerging professional and corporate identity. They co-operated, building off each other. If a reporter wrote about a previously prohibited subject or presented a controversial new interpretation, and they were not subject to excessive Party sanctions, others would follow and take the challenge one step further.[54] Indeed, at times there seems to have been a competition to see who could print the most controversial material.[55] Editors, who had once been viewed by reporters as 'the number one danger,' began to encourage journalists to push limits. They were also willing in many cases to shield journalists from potential repercussions. Of course, the editors themselves still had to be wary, but a supportive editor could galvanize a publication and give confidence to reporters and commentators to push new heights.[56]

Journalists also publicly agitated for greater collective freedoms. They conducted this battle both with their pens and through their journalist/politician representatives and sympathizers in the Party and in newly empowered political institutions.[57] As in Eastern Europe, several referred to Western press freedoms as a justification for the extension of their rights.[58] International journalists, the *mezhdunarodniki*, in particular seemed to band together to express their dismay at being left behind by their domestic brethren in terms of their capacity to question traditional dogma. Beginning in 1987 and continuing through 1990, there were frequently individual and group articles by the *mezhdunarodniki* lamenting the special limits placed on international journalists and calling for greater freedoms.[59]

Not all journalists shared this collective identity and many, regardless of how they identified themselves professionally, did not actively agitate for greater freedoms: self-censorship, the most ubiquitous form of control in all media systems, continued to thrive.[60] The silent majority passively waited to see how things developed, letting others be the risk-takers. They would take steps after it was certain that all was safe. Some even took the opposite approach, calling for more restraint,[61] reflecting the degree to which journalism had been intertwined with the Party and government.

For those journalists who were able to push aside the internal constraints of self-censorship, several paths were pursued. In rejecting Party-imposed interpretations of news, some tried to move to American standards of objectivity.[62] Indeed, some publications, like *Argumenty i Fakty* (a journal which was once devoted more to arguments than to facts) went a step further by becoming sources of volumes of raw data which were left for the reader to interpret. For its editors, information had become important in its own right. Others chose a more European approach, using the press as a platform to advocate specific policies and interpretations, albeit, different from those of the government.[63] This occurred both on an individual and editorial level, with some publications adopting distinct editorial lines espousing views different from those of the leadership. Another group took a less serious approach and focused on popular culture, including the latest trends sweeping the West. Some even took up the practices of the Western tabloids, publishing the absurd ('Stalin is still alive') and the racy (stories about grisly murders and pornography stars).[64]

The key point, however, is not the exact path which these journalists followed, but the simple fact that many began to reject the traditional relationship between the Party and the press. Many were no longer predisposed to follow the Party line. More worrying for the Party, they were willing to agitate individually and collectively to subvert Party controls. This placed the Party apparatus responsible for controlling the press in an alien position. It could no longer count on many journalists to regulate themselves through self-censorship and therefore if it wanted to retain control it would be forced to be more intrusive. However, this was increasingly difficult at a time when Party lines were not as clear and the Party's administrative infrastructure was beginning to decay.

One does not want to overstate the degree of press freedom in the Soviet Union under Gorbachev. There were strict standards throughout the Gorbachev period and the looming threat of reinstituted restrictions and nightmarish punishments. However, by the same token, it is important to recognize that the constant pressure applied by journalists helped to accelerate the process of liberalization.

A final and important point about pressure from journalists is that they also challenged the restrictions imposed by Newspeak. Because it was so difficult to communicate ideas through the traditional, evaluative terms of the Soviet lexicon, journalists (as well as politicians) searched for symbols which could express new ideas in support of change. Some looked back into Soviet history, to the NEP period. Others looked to the Tsarist period, back to a time of supposed Russian greatness. However, these were of limited appeal to people living in the 1980s. More poignant were the new images of capitalist countries. Increasingly, positive images of Western experience were used to communicate ideas which otherwise would have been difficult, if not impossible, to express. How, for example, was a reporter to explain the advantages of a system of checks and balances and constitutional separation of powers when such concepts had regularly been dismissed in Soviet writing as bourgeois rubbish? How could a journalist criticize traditional Soviet approaches to human rights and offer an alternative, when all official propaganda had so long insisted that theirs was the only just approach? The way to break through the linguistic and ideational barriers was to find new reference points. Many found them in the experience of the traditional ideological opponent. As one *Izvestiya* reporter said, 'Now, America is a kind of model for the Soviet Union. When you want to make a point and you want to make sure your point is going through, you just have to make a reference to the experience in the United States.'[65] It did not matter if the image was accurate. Indeed, the United States was frequently portrayed in overly flattering terms. What was important was that in using these images, journalists were able to escape and undermine the barriers of Newspeak. They may not have been intentionally attacking the ideology and its protective shell. Nonetheless, in finding alternative ways to communicate that which their present vocabulary would not permit, they undermined Newspeak and the ideology which it perpetuated.

Crucial to the journalists' capacity to press for greater reforms was the new political environment in which they found themselves. Indeed, many of the most 'liberal' journalists of the Gorbachev period, like *Ogonyok*'s celebrated editor Vitaly Korotich, wrote tremendously malicious and dogmatic material prior to their reincarnation as reformers.[66] Several factors aided journalists in their fight for expanded freedom and helped make possible change from below. As has been noted, some in their own right created pressure on the government for greater liberalization. However, the important factors of society, leadership policies and divisions and the decay in the Party apparatus need further discussion.

PRESSURE FROM SOCIETY

The opening of the press is generally greeted enthusiastically by people who are accustomed to being exposed to images which bear little resemblance to the objective realities surrounding them.[67] However, when society is afforded even a glimpse of an informative, lively press, potentially for the first time in decades, significant elements demand more.[68] Pressure emerging from the population may be particularly acute when the liberalization process entails revisions of history which suggest that past claims by the ruling party were deceptive.[69] In a country like the Soviet Union where a single party long claimed a monopoly on truth, such revelations led to fundamental distrust in the regime and concomitant demands for more 'objective' information.[70]

Popular demands promoted liberalization in two ways. On one level, they helped protect journalists who pushed the boundaries of legitimate controversy. This was apparently the case in late 1989 when *Argumenty i Fakty*'s editor-in-chief steadfastly refused to resign under Party pressure, which stemmed in part from his decision to publish a survey raising doubts about Gorbachev's popularity. The fact that he ultimately retained his position where previous editors had not was almost certainly because his publication had a circulation of over thirty million.[71]

On another level, society actually pushed journalists to new boundaries. Readership satisfaction became such an important concern to journalists that they attempted to cater their reporting to their audience's interests. This inspired journalists to publish new types of material on subjects ranging from popular culture to the Party's right to rule.[72] It also pushed some to take one-sided approaches to issues which, if not crossing the letter of Party policy, certainly undermined the intent. Such was the case with press coverage of the United States. As one reporter insisted:

> Now it is almost a taboo to write anything negative about the United States of America, because almost immediately you will get a very strong reaction from your readers in the Soviet Union who will tell you that they are tired of hearing everything negative about the United States. So, you write something positive.[73]

The growing respect for the readership also had significant professional consequences for journalists. Previously, many were content to censor themselves while actively promoting orthodox positions because they hoped to climb the career ladder to prestigious publications, like *Pravda* or *Izvestiya*.[74] However, in the *glasnost'* period many preferred to write for 'lesser' publications which were both more innovative and popular than their 'prestigious' counterparts.[75] In some situations things had become inverted: journalists were inspired sometimes to challenge limits in order to make themselves attractive to the editors of the more radical publications. The liberalization process was thus accelerated.

DIVISIONS AND CHANGING PRIORITIES

The swift changes in Party policies assisted journalists to expand the limits because they made for less certainty about Party expectations. In other words, there was less certainty about consensus values. Although some journalists tried to move blindly to new formulas, it was not always so easy. Perestroika was a dynamic process with the leadership continually zigzagging as it searched for effective but politically tenable policies. Policy lines changed so quickly that it was frequently unclear where the boundaries of consensus, legitimate controversy and deviance lay.[76] The result was that the black and white certainty of stagnation dissipated and with it went journalists' tightly defined purpose.

The capacity of reporters to challenge limits in the Soviet Union was further enhanced by increasingly open divisions within the leadership itself. A cohesive leadership can serve as a dam, effectively controlling the pace of liberalization and resisting pressures for acceleration. However, as events in several liberalizing countries have demonstrated, when divisions above become sharper, opportunities for change from below expand.[77] The press can serve as an arena for the different positions. When divisions are sufficiently deep, important actors turn to the press in an attempt to gain political advantage by discrediting their opponents and their opponents' policies, and by attempting to attract public support to be used as a weapon in inter-elite competition.[78]

Under Gorbachev, the Soviet press nearly from the beginning served as a weapon in the battle for policies, power and authority. However, in the early stages it was largely the possession of one side, with Gorbachev and his allies using the press to help discredit rivals like Viktor Grishin and Dinmukhamed Kunaev, during the course of the immense personnel changes which took place during his first years in office.[79] From early 1988 onwards, the divisions within the leadership increasingly surfaced in the press. The real turning-point was the publication of Leningrad chemistry lecturer Nina Andreeva's letter in *Sovetskaya Rossiya* in March 1988.[80] Her letter combined rabid anti-Semitism, an attack on 'left wing intellectuals' and criticism of the values of the young, with a defence of Soviet history, including Stalinism. The important point, however, was not simply that the letter was published, but that it was identified with the positions of conservative Politburo member Yegor Ligachev.[81] Although the article was summarily attacked in an

authoritative, unsigned *Pravda* editorial a few weeks later, it opened
the gates for more public disputes, including an open debate on
Soviet foreign policy which broke out a few months later in the
summer of 1988 between Ligachev and Politburo liberals Aleksandr
Yakovlev and Eduard Shevardnadze.[82]

The divisions had important unintended consequences for the
press, blurring party lines. Journalists traditionally based reporting
primarily on the speeches of the political leadership.[83] To be sure,
they looked for the most official line, that is, the position of
Gorbachev and, for foreign affairs, Shevardnadze.[84] However, when
someone with considerable authority, like 'second secretary' Ligachev,
entered into public disputes with other leaders, and remained in
office, it must have offered journalists greater choices. They had
increasing opportunities to seek out like-minded leaders for protection. Moreover, those leaders, less encumbered by the requirements
of formal expressions of unity, were freer to provide such protection.[85]

DECAY

The decay in the Party apparatus which controlled the press was a
source of further opportunity for change from below. Practices which
were crucial to the creation of organizational biases in favour of
journalistic promotion of Party lines were often eliminated or
watered-down significantly.

The main area of decay of controls on foreign press coverage
was in the International and Ideology Departments of the Central
Committee.[86] The weakening occurred on several fronts. By early
1990, the Party no longer controlled appointments at many publications. For example, the early 1990 appointment of Fedor Burlatsky
as new editor of *Literaturnaya Gazeta* occurred without first consulting
the Ideology Department.[87] *Moscow News'* foreign editor indicated
that by the beginning of 1990, the Party no longer controlled *Moscow News'* appointments. That had not been the case a year and a
half earlier.[88] An editor at *Mezhdunarodnaya Zhizn'* (*International
Affairs*) claimed that his 1989 appointment was approved a full six
months after he had begun work in his new position.[89] When asked
in the spring of 1990, most people indicated that they were uncertain about the current parameters because they were changing so
quickly. It seems that the system was coming to an end, at least
for the less 'official' publications.

There was also considerable weakening in the pre- and post-publication controls. Meetings in the International and Ideology Departments began to lose their force. As of late 1988, the meetings in these departments were supposed to have become informational and advisorial only. Journalists indicated that they no longer received continual orders (*zakazi*) as in the past[90] and that the atmosphere was less rigid.[91] The same was true for orders over the telephone. Although calls continued throughout the period (indeed, the assistant editor of *Sovetskaya Rossiya* received a call from the International Department while I was in his office in April 1990), they were considered to be of a less dictatorial tone.

This is not to say that all orders ended. However, even when they were made, the press was, by early 1990, able to reject them. One *Moscow News* editor explained in early 1990 that when he received orders from the Party to cover a topic a certain way, or to publish articles sent from the Central Committee departments, he was no longer obliged to follow: 'Now, I can argue, then do what I consider to be necessary. And two years ago, I could not do this.'[92] This points to the key period of change somewhere in late 1988 or 1989.

As far as the initialling of political commentaries is concerned, the Foreign Ministry ceased this function by 1990 and, although the process continued in the Ideology Department, it was no longer mandatory. The decision to send articles for approval was then at the discretion of the editor(s) and writer(s) involved: some publications patently refused to send articles.[93]

Pre-publication changes also occurred in the operations of the state censorship agency, Glavlit. Two changes in particular were of significance. First, the role of Glavlit as an ideological censor declined significantly. Although it still censored material on state secrets, numerous journalists pointed to this as one of the most important changes in the *glasnost'* era.[94] Their claim should not be surprising, given the pervasive influence of the war of ideas on the Soviet press in the pre-Gorbachev period. According to Volovets of *Moscow News*, the final peak of ideological censorship was late 1987 and early 1988.[95] By 1989, the concentration had moved more to state secrets.

Second, Glavlit's capacity to censor was weakened. While earlier, Glavlit rejection of an article for any reason meant that it could not be published barring successful appeal to a higher authority, in the year to year and a half prior to the new press law, a publication could print an article and take responsibility upon itself for any repercussions.[96] In this period before the press law came into effect,[97] some publications were already outside its control. Some newspapers in the far reaches of the empire simply did not submit materials to Glavlit representatives.[98] Other more central newspapers ignored it. One editor at *Argumenty i Fakty* indicated in 1990 that his editors sometimes did not show the Glavlit representatives articles which they felt might be rejected, giving the representative an edition with a blank space, then placing the article in after the review.[99]

LIMITS TO CHANGE FROM BELOW

In spite of the decay which occurred in the mechanisms of Party control over the press, it is important to realize that what had occurred was decay, not dissolution. Throughout the period, the Party still possessed the desire and, in the final resort, the capacity to take significant repressive measures against those who stepped beyond the boundaries of what it perceived to be permissible. This was reflected not only in the statements of Mikhail Gorbachev about *glasnost'*, but also by the concrete actions taken against *Argumenty i Fakty*'s editor-in-chief.

Perhaps the most candid testimony comes from an actual member of the apparatus. In February 1989, the Head of the Ideology Department claimed that the main task of its mass media sub-department was 'the implementation of the CPSU Central Committee guidelines on the leadership of the mass media and on increasing the efficiency of their work'.[100] Similarly, he claimed that the sub-department on foreign political information and international ties was not only supposed to support 'The needs of restructuring of the foreign policy sphere and the advancement of the priority of general human interests and values,' but it was also to 'sharply redirect . . . informational and ideological activity in the international arena and to place all aspects of the new political thinking at the centre of this work'.[101]

These statements, and the fact that they were made in 1989, highlight two important factors concerning the Central Committee departments. First, they were still committed to imposing Party policy on the press. They were attempting to make the press a more effective tool, not, as some would claim, simply advising journalists what to publish, as might a public relations department of any political party. Second, the admission that changing Party priorities in the Gorbachev period forced them to 'sharply redirect' their work indicates that the sudden and dramatic transformation of the international press coverage in the Gorbachev period might not simply have been a matter of a freer press, but of changing Party priorities.

The Party's continued pretension as overseer of the press frightened journalists. Given the long history of Party rule and an uncertain future, this had an understandably constraining effect on some. Many reporters and commentators continued to censor themselves and editors blocked publication of controversial material.[102] They also continued to show subservience to the Party. Some treated 'requests' and 'suggestions' made by the Central Committee departments like orders and acted accordingly.[103] Many editors chose to continue sending political commentaries to Central Committee departments for review when they were concerned that articles deviated too far from the official line.[104] Again, the former relationship between the Party and press was weakened, but powerful connections continued to exist.

The position of journalists was well illustrated by an assistant editor of *Argumenty i Fakty* who, when asked in the spring of 1990 whether he could criticize by name the Minister of Foreign Affairs, responded, 'I am on the edge of it, I am on the way.'[105] He was on the way, but not sure when he would be there. At some point he would have to go out on a limb and risk a reprimand or wait for a colleague to do so. He was by no means free to do as he desired.

MORE AND LESS OFFICIAL PUBLICATIONS

Although all publications experienced continuing limits on their ability to publish material, the extent of limits varied. In some ways it was dependent upon personnel and the risks which they were willing to take. However, of equal importance was the position of the publication within the hierarchy of the Soviet press. The 'more official' publications, normally official organs of higher Party and state institutions, enjoyed considerably less freedom than the 'less official' ones, which were normally sponsored by non-party organizations. Although they had all previously been subject to Party diktat, significant changes began to emerge in the *glasnost'* period, particularly from late 1987 when ideological censorship began to weaken.

Publications like *Pravda*, the official organ of the Central Committee, and *Izvestiya*, the organ of the Praesidium of the Supreme
Soviet, were much more accountable to Party demands than, for
example, *Moscow News*, which was joint-sponsored by the Union
of Friendship Societies and Novosti Press Agency.[106] While the latter had effectively severed its relations with its sponsors,[107] the former
two, despite some assertions to the contrary, were still largely required to demonstrate loyalty to their sponsors and ultimately the
Party. For example the head of the American desk at *Izvestiya* claimed
that his newspaper was free to publish what it pleased, yet at the
same time it was 'more official' than *Moscow News*. When asked if
his newspaper could criticize the policy of President Gorbachev in
international affairs, he answered, 'In the final instance we can.
However, in principle we support exactly the course of the President . . . there are simply no subjects to criticize.'[108] Each of these
statements might be independently true, but put together they seem
to indicate a more than casual link between the newspaper, the
President and the policies of the Soviet Union.

INTERNATIONAL PRESS COVERAGE: CHANGE FROM ABOVE VS. CHANGE FROM BELOW

International press coverage posed special difficulties both for the
policy of *glasnost'* and for Soviet reporters. It was initially difficult
for the government to encourage change in the international sphere.
Relations with the West in 1985 and 1986 were better than in the
early 1980s, but they were still bad. Although the Gorbachev leadership demonstrated a boldness on the domestic front and a willingness
to reign in some of the more extreme manifestations of the ideological war, it was at that point too much to ask for significant
changes in the way in which the West was depicted. Indeed, at the
XXVIIth Party Congress in 1986 Gorbachev decried the West's
'information imperialism' and called on ideological personnel,
including the press, to aid the Soviet Union in 'the struggle for
people's minds, for their world view and for their reference points
in life, both social and spiritual'.[109] Gorbachev might have been
more concerned with the economic situation in the Soviet Union
than the battle with the enemy, but either he was unable or unwilling to change the old formula concerning the West.

The continued commitment to the ideological struggle was best illustrated by the Soviet press's response to the Chernobyl accident. The accident occurred only three days after Gorbachev had announced: 'We categorically oppose those who call for releasing public information in doses; there can never be too much truth.'[110] However, after the accident the information was delivered in tiny morsels. Not only were revelations about the accident delayed for 65 hours while children near the accident zone were out on the streets celebrating May Day, but when the press finally acknowledged the accident it was apparently more concerned about attacking the West than revealing what really occurred. In keeping with the imperatives of the ideological struggle, it took a mere forty minutes after the initial TASS statement revealing the accident for a second dispatch to be issued criticizing the American nuclear power industry.[111] In the following weeks, numerous articles appeared highlighting past American accidents and a variety of mishaps at American civilian and military nuclear reactors.[112] A number of sub-themes also emerged, including attacks on Western press coverage of the accident, claims that the accident demonstrated the dangers of modern technology, particularly those found in the Strategic Defense Initiative, and assertions that Chernobyl showed the need for the US to join the Soviet nuclear test moratorium.[113] The combination of a fierce counter-propaganda campaign directed at the West and the relatively sparse accurate information about the accident given to Soviet citizens indicated that in spite of some preliminary changes in the Soviet press, the war of ideas was still powerful.

The abject failure of the Soviet response to the Chernobyl accident, and the adverse domestic and international repercussions which followed, did have important consequences for the press. It appears that the accident caused the leadership to accelerate its re-evaluation of Soviet communications policy.[114] Significantly for our concern, the ensuing debate extended into the sphere of foreign press coverage.

The most substantial sign of the beginnings of a new approach to international press coverage was an article in *Pravda* on readers' complaints about Soviet television. After describing readers complaints concerning Chernobyl, the author said:

> Repeatedly (readers) drew special attention to (the need for) improvement of international information, to the necessity for rapid response and deep analysis of world events . . . Information about the capitalist world is monotonous. The journalists' clichés

migrate from broadcast to broadcast. Mainly they show political meetings, demonstrations and protests. Rarely do they discuss the achievements of science and technology, about how, under conditions of capitalism, they turn out for simple workers, about economic and cultural collaboration, about problems of women, old people, the growth of crime and terrorism in the western world . . .[115]

Although the letter is an important indication that changes were being considered, one must be careful in assessing its significance. It did call for more information about the West, but many of the main issues of concern could easily have been integrated into the war of ideas (conditions of workers, problems of women and the elderly, crime and terrorism). Moreover, the article was relatively isolated, without comment from the leadership. Chernobyl was not a turning-point in terms of policies towards international press coverage, but rather a catalyst for the reconsideration of past policies. Certainly at the time the print media did not show substantial signs of change.[116]

More significant indications of changing Soviet policies towards international press coverage were manifested in the first half of 1987. In this period several articles appeared in the Soviet press justifying the publication of more information about life in the West and attitudes of Western leaders.

The most prominent articles were associated with a propaganda campaign centring on tele-bridges (satellite television broadcasts which linked Western and Soviet audiences), three of which had been broadcast in the two preceding years.[117] The campaign began with a letter to *Izvestiya* editor from a Soviet citizen, G.N. Bochevarov. Bochevarov complained about a dialogue between tele-bridge hosts American Phil Donahue and Soviet Vladimir Pozner which appeared in *Izvestiya* in February 1987 and more generally lambasted tele-bridges and trends towards increased contact with the West.[118] He criticized Pozner and called Donahue a 'political provocateur and ideological saboteur'. The tele-bridges were termed 'harmful to our country and to our people'.[119]

The letter, however, was not printed to show the leadership's point of view, but for the opposite reason, namely, to start a discussion campaign aimed at justifying a different approach to the West. The initial rebuff came in the form of an article accompanying the letter written by *Izvestiya*'s experienced political commentator

Aleksandr Bovin. Bovin criticized Bochevarov's approach to the United States and called for further understanding of all aspects of America, its 'pluses' as well as its 'minuses'. While he was not sympathetic to America as a whole, criticizing 'racism, militarism and spiritual emptiness', his comments were very revealing of the incipient Soviet policy concerning tele-bridges and, more generally, information about the West:

> Each tele-bridge is only a small part, an element, of our general policy of improving the international psychological atmosphere, which means the political atmosphere as well, and forming public opinion that favours an easing of international tension and disarmament.[120]

The fact that Bovin was confident enough to speak of a new, if nascent, policy points to the changing approach to the ideological war and explains the need for the propaganda campaign.[121]

The campaign grew more powerful with time. Other articles supporting Bovin's view appeared in *Pravda*, *Izvestiya*, *Argumenty i Fakty* and *Moscow News*.[122] A little over a month later ten letters commenting on the Bovin–Bochevarov debate appeared in *Izvestiya*. An editorial preface to the letters set the tone, indicating that of the approximately five hundred letters received on the subject, only about forty supported Bochevarov. This proportion was reflected in the letters which appeared below, nine of the ten supporting Bovin's position.[123] The tone of the letters and the way in which they were presented was typical of the controlled form of debate that characterized the policy of *glasnost'*. A semblance of debate was created but the arguments were funnelled towards a specific end, an emerging government policy.[124]

In the following months, other articles in a number of publications called for new approaches to international press coverage.[125] They developed the themes of the new 'policy' of easing international tensions, and also expanded on the idea of portraying capitalism's 'pluses' as well as its 'minuses'. It would seem that at this point the journalists advocating changes were following the initiative of the leadership rather than setting their own course. That is why Bovin spoke of a new policy.[126]

Press content reflected the emerging policy with some sympathetic portrayals of domestic America and with articles exposing Soviet audiences to American views on international issues. However, at this point the policy was still inchoate and timid. The ideological struggle still dominated international press coverage. Indeed, after the failure of the Reykjavik summit in late 1986 the United States was portrayed in particularly hostile images. At this point, it was Bovin and other commentators speaking of new policies, not Gorbachev or Shevardnadze. However, following the INF agreement reducing nuclear arms there would be more substantial calls for change.

Although Gorbachev had stated several times that there was a need for *glasnost'* in all areas of press coverage, prior to 1988 his speeches almost always implicitly referred to the domestic sphere. For example, in the important January 1987 Party Plenum, Gorbachev cited the need for the press to present information concerning 'topical problems involved in the acceleration of the socio-economic development of the country and affecting the most diverse aspects of life in our society'. Even though he said later in the speech that 'no zones are closed to criticism', he concentrated solely on press coverage of domestic issues.[127]

However, the INF agreement (reached in September 1987) seemed to free him, as it did the entire Soviet press, of fear of pressing *glasnost'* into the international arena. In early 1988, Gorbachev directly linked the policy of *glasnost'* with international affairs, stating at another plenum:

> Soviet people have a natural desire to look into everything themselves, to get a better understanding of what is taking place and especially to participate knowingly in the nation-wide struggle against the danger of war and in international relations. This is why all the necessary conditions are being created to resolutely raise the informational and intellectual level of foreign policy propaganda and of work to explain and comment on international questions.[128]

This call was repeated by Gorbachev at the XIXth Party Conference in June 1988,[129] and by Shevardnadze at an important conference in the Ministry of Foreign Affairs in July 1988.[130]

This is not to say that there had been no changes in the press prior to these announcements. There had been timid steps towards change in 1987. However, the INF accord seems to have permitted the leadership and the press to take *glasnost'* to another level. Indeed, Soviet reporters and members of the Party apparatus pointed to the post-INF period as a key turning-point for change.[131]

In spite of these announcements and changes in the press, the policy of *glasnost'* was still restrictive *vis-à-vis* international press coverage. For example, Eduard Shevardnadze, who repeatedly spoke of the need for a more open press, also asserted that the press should support Soviet foreign policy efforts. In 1989 he told one interviewer: 'If you and I are politicians or political figures – and public affairs writing is undoubtedly a kind of politics – then we have no right to argue for an unlimited monopoly on independent opinions.' In the same interview he spoke of the 'union of diplomacy and journalism' and how journalism was an effective tool to 'correlate public opinion with planned foreign policy actions'.[132] What he was speaking of was not simply the press showing some sympathy and understanding for the intricacies of international diplomacy and concerns over national security, but of the press actively working with the government to promote its policy positions. This vision of the press/government relations is typical of the policy of *glasnost'* and is very different from traditional notions of freedom of the press.

Part of the problem for politicians like Shevardnadze, and thus for the press itself, was the perceived 'officialness' of the Soviet press by foreign countries. The Soviet press, especially the major newspapers and TASS, had for so long reflected to the very last detail the position of the Soviet government, that foreign countries found it difficult to accept that what was written in *Moscow News*, let alone *Pravda* or *Izvestiya*, was the opinion of individual reporters and commentators, not the 'official view of the Soviet government'. The result was that foreign countries protested to the Soviet Ministry of Foreign Affairs (MFA) when controversial articles appeared. This in turn led the MFA and embassies abroad to complain to newspapers that they were interfering in government affairs and risking the well-being of the Soviet Union.[133] It became a vicious circle because such MFA interference in turn lent credence to the original premise.

Reporters and editors openly acknowledged that these difficulties particularly constrained the larger, 'more official' newspapers. A fundamental problem on this level is how a newspaper can represent a political organ yet divorce itself from the official views of that organ. *Novoye Vremya*'s Pumpyansky wrote that the situation was 'absurd'. 'It would never occur to anyone to complain to the "Iron Lady" about *The Times*, or to the State Department or the Republican Party headquarters about *Time* magazine. But you may complain about a Soviet newspaper or magazine any time as loudly as you can.'[134]

This complaint might have been justified for *Novoye Vremya*, which was associated with Novosti Press. But Pumpyansky, and other writers with similar views, miss an important point concerning the likes of *Pravda* and *Izvestiya*. If a publication of the United States Information Agency or an organ of the Republican or Democratic Party published controversial material there would be legitimate complaints. Indeed, complaints about the activity of the United States Information Agency were regular fare in Soviet publications.

Moreover, the 'absurdity' which Pumpyansky spoke of was not so far from reality. An article in *Pravda* from March 1989 did just that. The article attacked a cartoon in *The Times* of London which depicted Lenin in Nazi vestments. The justification for the criticism is crucial here: the newspaper was portrayed as 'the unofficial voice of ruling circles of Great Britain, including the current Conservative government'. The cartoon was thus considered to call into doubt London's 'readiness to develop political dialogue' with the Soviet Union.[135] This highlights the difficulties. If a *Pravda* reporter attacked the British government because of the statements of an 'unofficial mouthpiece', and *Pravda* editors approved such an article, then how did they perceive their own newspaper which was supposed to be the official mouthpiece of the CPSU? And how were foreign governments supposed to interpret this? The answer is that the continued 'officialness' hampered writers at all publications at the end of the period, but particularly those at *Pravda* and *Izvestiya*.

It should not be surprising that there was greater controversy concerning coverage of international relations; international affairs are treated with more circumspection than domestic in all media systems.[136] There are good reasons for this: journalists do not want to be accused of harming their country's national interest. Indeed, as citizens of one country they might simply want what is best for them and for their families. These concerns and fears, when coupled with traditional Soviet journalistic practice, led many in the press to be cautious in their approach to international relations. For example, even in mid-1990, one *Moscow News* journalist called for 'restraint' in the coverage of Soviet–Chinese relations so that 'we' can 'hold on to what we have so far achieved through so much pain'.[137]

The same restrictions, however, did not apply as much to press coverage of domestic life in foreign countries. In this sphere there was tremendous change in the Soviet media. Reporters used images of Western experience to agitate for change in the Soviet Union.

They also focused on important figures in popular culture, ranging from Elvis and Madonna to Sylvester Stallone and a star of pornographic movies. This information in part reflected the changes in news values taking place within the press, particularly the growing respect for audience interests. They were typical of the way in which change from below was contributing to the transformation of the Soviet press.

CONCLUSION

Mikhail Gorbachev's policies towards the press were significantly different from those of his predecessors. He took a radical turn in emphasizing the economy over ideological competition, undermining an important pillar of Party rule. He then attempted to revitalize the press. The policy of *glasnost'*, or change from above, did produce a limited liberalization of the press. Although much of the change involved a shifting consensus and very focused criticism designed to assist the reform process, other changes allowed for deeper analysis and a limited widening of the sphere of legitimate controversy. These changes, encouraged and controlled by the government, began to alter the balance between the principles which traditionally guided the press, allowing journalists to address the interests of the masses which had for so long been ignored. While the changes were introduced to serve an instrumental end, they still breathed life into a complacent press. They showed a flexibility and boldness which previous leaders avoided in their desire to retain power at all costs, even if it meant slow decline.

However, the Gorbachev leadership, like others before it, failed to take into account the snowball effect; pressures emerged which caused a controlled liberalization to expand beyond the boundaries originally foreseen by its initiators. The press, with the support of the population, pushed for change from below, exploiting the limited freedoms of *glasnost'* and growing chasms in the leadership itself. Many reporters looked at *glasnost'* the same way that radical economists looked at the policy of perestroika, they believed that what was necessary was not restructuring but dismantling of the old system and construction from the ground up. Specifically they wanted legally guaranteed freedom of the press instead of a licence granted from above. Although they did not get those guarantees for a variety of reasons many succeeded in pushing the limits of reform. They also undermined the restraints imposed by the linguistic structure of the official ideology. In the name of their profession and their readership many refused to be easily cowed by the Party apparatus. Some even took up independent editorial lines which challenged the government.

This is not to say that the most important changes in Soviet press content happened because of pressure from below. In the coming chapters on Soviet press coverage of the United States, it will be important to remember that in 1987, and to a large degree in 1988, the Party still had a strong grip on the press, particularly international press coverage. Gorbachev did not even speak of *glasnost'* in the context of international affairs until after the INF accord was signed in late 1987. Even after that, the policy of *glasnost'*, at least as far as international relations was concerned, was always more circumscribed than domestic coverage. Indeed, in 1990 the *mezhdunarodniki* were complaining about the strong constraints imposed on them.

Many of the important changes in the Soviet press happened as a product of changing government policies towards the United States and capitalism. However, before examining the press coverage of the United States, it is first necessary to see how the leadership approach to the United States changed in the Gorbachev period.

Part II: Soviet and Russian Images of the United States

4 'Otherness', Enmity and Envy in Soviet Images of the United States

The purpose of this chapter is to provide a critical basis for understanding Soviet and Russian identities, particularly as they impact upon Soviet and Russian press coverage of the United States. Within this context, I begin to explore a second important theme of this work, changing Soviet and Russian perceptions of the United States in the Gorbachev and post-Soviet eras.

DIFFERENTIAL IDENTITY: THE SOVIET VIEW OF THE UNITED STATES

Identity is inherently relational and determined by a socially constructed world. Whether on an individual basis or in the context of 'imagined communities', identity is not only rooted in a notion of the self, but is contingent upon a sense of the 'other', the image against which the self is measured.[1] 'Otherness' is thus integrally related to individuals' and communities' world-views.

Otherness has the capacity to translate into antipathy. Social psychology demonstrates that from an early age people have a tendency to divide the world into coupled, easily identifiable polarities, or what psychologist Charles Pinderhughes calls 'paired differential bonding'. Paired differential bonding entails both 'affiliative' bonding – like me – and 'differential' bonding – not me. The former is reflected by closeness and affection, the latter by distance and, in the extreme, by hostility and aggression.[2]

The relationship between the United States and the Soviet Union is an extreme example of differential bonding between states.[3] Citizens and especially leaders of both countries had a propensity to identify the other as 'the enemy', and to seek self-affirmation by comparing themselves favourably to that enemy. It did not matter whether the images were distorted, nor if accuracy was sacrificed for clarity, because such images gave people certainty and with it a form of unity and comfort. Witness the statement by former US President Richard Nixon: 'It may seem melodramatic to treat the twin poles of human experience represented by the United States and the Soviet Union as the equivalent of Good and Evil, Light and Darkness, God and the Devil. Yet if we allow ourselves to think of them that way, even hypothetically, it can help to clarify our perspective on the world struggle.'[4]

While the system of enmity helped to shape identity for both sides of the cold war, the Soviet Union was particularly in its thrall. As a multi-ethnic, supra-national state, it lacked the strong unifying identity associated with nationality.[5] Although there existed a form of civic identity which engendered pride in Soviet scientific, military and athletic achievements, and there were many symbolic forms through which the polity was represented, Soviet identity was always precarious. It had to compete with pre-existing and legally institutionalized national and ethnic identities. Moreover, attempts by ideologists to construct such unifying concepts as the 'new Soviet Man' and 'the Soviet people' were never successful.[6]

In keeping with precepts of identification theory, Soviet leaders attempted to create trans-national unity through appearing to be both 'materialistically beneficent' and 'protective in the face of an external threat'.[7] The guiding Soviet ideology, Marxism-Leninism, lent itself perfectly to this identity-building task. According to Marxism-Leninism, socialism was an inherently more just and ultimately more efficient socio-economic system which according to the laws of history would ultimately supersede capitalism.[8] These two systems were clearly juxtaposed, with no 'middle course' possible.

This competition between rival socio-economic systems was extended to an interstate level by Lenin's interpretation of imperialism which posited an inherent conflict between socialist and capitalist states.[9] Soviet ideologists viewed foreign affairs as a mirror of the internal socio-economic order of states and thus international relations became a larger arena for struggle between the proletariat and the bourgeoisie.[10]

The Soviet Union's leading role in the socialist world and the United States' position as capitalism's most potent economic and military power meant that these two states were situated closest to the axis upon which the battle between the 'two world systems' turned.[11] The United States was thus the logical choice as the prime Soviet enemy.

In applying role theory to US/Soviet relations, international relations scholars describe the US/Soviet relationship in terms of 'negative identity', which suggests that each state constructs its identity so that 'the ego's gain is the alter's loss'.[12] While such a conclusion accurately describes much of the zero-sum game which existed in the international sphere until the late 1980s, it does not capture the breadth of the inter-subjective relationship between the leading capitalist and socialist powers. The associations produced by differential bonding are not purely negative: there may be positive characteristics associated with the enemy, albeit ones which may be masked through hostile rhetoric. It is for this reason that I prefer to use the term 'differential identity' when describing the way in which Soviet identity was constructed *vis-à-vis* the United States.

The reality was that the Soviet view of the United States was always a mixture of hatred and envy. The United States was not only the object of scorn, it was the measuring stick of Soviet progress.[13] Khrushchev's claim that the Soviet Union would make the transition to communism by 1980 was coupled with assurances that it would outstrip the United States in a variety of production figures by the end of the 1960s. In the late 1950s, signs everywhere proclaimed 'We shall overtake and outstrip the USA, in per capita production of meat, milk and butter!'[14] Such envy is relatively harmless when coupled with confidence of success. Khrushchev's promise to 'bury' the United States was a statement of certitude of the social and material progress of the USSR (as well as the internal contradictions of capitalism).[15] However, when the Soviet economy turned for the worse in the late 1970s and early 1980s, it had an immense impact on Soviet identity and, concomitantly, the Soviet Union's image of the United States.

CRISIS IN IDENTITY

The crisis in Soviet identity emerged when it became clear that the Soviet Union would fall short of Khrushchev's promises and, if anything, was threatening to fall further behind the socio-economic system which it was pre-ordained to replace. Because the Soviet state itself emerged on the promise of social and economic progress, the legitimacy of the state and thus the unifying strength of Soviet identity were to a large extent contingent upon performance.[16] The growing gap with its competitors/enemies thus posed an enormous threat. As Ernest Gellner explained in referring to dissidents such as Sakharov,

> It was the conclusive defeat in the technological and economic race which persuaded men of good will that change was essential. Had Soviet Marxism been able to continue to persuade them that the sacrifices, however terrible, were worth while, because they would eventually lead to a better life, first for Soviet man and then for all mankind, many of them would have continued to accommodate themselves to the horrors.[17]

As was discussed in Chapter 2, the leadership was particularly worried that the country's most educated and young were becoming disillusioned with Soviet society and, with the advent of modern communications technologies, would fall under the sway of the capitalist opponent.

In response to this fear, Soviet leaders called to reinvigorate the system of ideological education and heighten attacks on the capitalist enemy.[18] Such steps were designed to achieve three ends: first, to promote unity in the face of a threatening adversary; second, to create a mentality which would turn people away from Western information systems; and third, to use a monopoly on mass communications to continually demonstrate the superiority of the Soviet Union materially and socially *vis-à-vis* the United States.

There was an explosion of anti-American rhetoric in public expressions in the late 1970s and early 1980s.[19] Successive General Secretaries, Brezhnev, Andropov and Chernenko, painted a Manichaean battle which, in the words of a *Pravda* editorial, featured a struggle 'unprecedented in the entire post-war period in terms of its intensity and acuteness', between 'two diametrically opposite world views and two political courses – socialism and imperialism . . . for the hearts and minds of billions of people on our planet'.[20] While there might have been periodic improvements in US/Soviet relations, as far as Soviet ideologists were concerned the underlying tension between the two systems remained. Indeed, peaceful co-existence was viewed as a 'specific form of class warfare'.[21]

Soviet leaders made it very clear that the United States in particular was the primary opponent in the world-wide class struggle. Yuri Andropov claimed that 'US imperialism' headed aggressive 'ultra-reactionary forces' which were attempting to 'reverse the course of development at any price'.[22] Konstantin Chernenko called the US a 'class enemy' which was attempting to 'liquidate the socialist system'.[23] Mikhail Gorbachev, in 1986, described the United States as the 'mother country of imperialism' and the 'locomotive of militarism'.[24]

Interest in American actions bordered on obsession. Nowhere was this more evident than in the Soviet press, the prime medium of official discourse. One survey of Soviet newspapers in the first half of 1984 found that there were almost twice as many references to US President Ronald Reagan than to Soviet General Secretary Konstantin Chernenko.[25] Newspapers were saturated with articles attacking the United States and all things American, depicting an uncompromisingly racist society in which human rights violations were the norm. The US was even portrayed on a semi-regular basis as the heir to Nazi German policies, something of immeasurable emotive quality for the Soviet Union. Two reporters looking back on the pre-Gorbachev era stated succinctly that 'The function of Soviet propaganda was promoted by its main procedural principle – it compared and contrasted "our" socio-political and ideological precepts to those of "others". As a rule, "other" became synonymous for enemy.'[26] Indeed, by the late 1970s, what the Soviet Union was not – the United States – was perhaps its most defining feature, at least as far as public discourse is concerned.

5 US/Soviet Relations in the Gorbachev Period

The purpose of this chapter is to analyze how Mikhail Gorbachev's policies undermined the system of enmity between the United States and the Soviet Union. In doing so, it will begin to form a chronology linking quantitative and qualitative changes in press content, namely in political cartoons, with changing Soviet policies *vis-à-vis* the US.

The interaction between changing policies and press content is important to establish because the sources of new Soviet images of the United States cannot simply be understood by analyzing media content: the press in the Gorbachev era was not so free as to be an autonomous actor. The only means of understanding the nature of the changes in press content is to examine such changes in light of changing policies.

RE-EVALUATION OF THE UNITED STATES

The Soviet approach to the United States of America fundamentally altered during the Gorbachev period. In fits and starts, the Soviet leadership, and concomitantly the press, changed the way in which it characterized the United States. Although many of the ideas of the Gorbachev period had been expressed previously by Soviet experts and former Soviet leaders, they had never been adopted on the scale or with the fervour of this period. In the words of Alex Pravda, 'Gorbachev (was) the first Soviet leader to see the salvation of the Soviet Union in a strongly Westernizing strategy rather than a temporary tactic.'[1]

The primary impetus for a re-evaluation of the United States was the Soviet leadership's open acknowledgement of the impending economic crisis. The optimism of catching and surpassing the West, which had been at least supported rhetorically by previous Soviet leaders, disappeared to be replaced by despondency over a stagnant economy and fear of losing more ground. Gorbachev openly acknowledged Soviet failures at the June 1987 Central Committee plenum when he derided the Soviet economic performance of the 1970s and 1980s and claimed that in that period 'the gulf in comparison with the most developed countries began to widen – and not in our favour'.[2] For a country whose *raison d'être* was based on social and economic progress, this was a critical blow.

The crisis facing the Soviet Union required a broad-based response. The Gorbachev leadership came to realize that administrative-bureaucratic methods, like its initial policy of *uskorenie* (speeding up), could not produce the desired results. The solution was sought in a programme of economic, social and political renewal which came to be known under the general rubric of perestroika. However, for perestroika to succeed, the Soviet Union could not simply look within; if domestic reform was to move forward, a truly global approach was required. This meant that Soviet foreign policy had to be altered to promote domestic needs.[3]

Chief amongst Soviet priorities was the creation of a calmer, more co-operative international environment, and in particular good relations with the United States.[4] As Gorbachev said, 'We must try to reach a situation where interrelations among states encumber our economy as little as possible and create a stable psychological atmosphere in which Soviet people can work peacefully.'[5] It was hoped that a calmer international environment would permit the Soviet Union to reduce its massive military expenditures, allow it greater access to much-valued Western technology and know-how, and lead to the removal of barriers blocking trade and access to international trade and economic bodies.[6] Finally, new relations could help to remove the psychological barriers about which Gorbachev spoke. As long-time *Izvestiya* commentator Stanislav Kondrashov put it,

> By admitting that the causes of our troubles lie in our system's imperfect nature, not in the intrigues of imperialism, and getting down to the capital repairs needed on our own home, we have gained greater internal freedom and begun to feel like masters of the situation rather than impotent victims of 'dark forces'.[7]

Kondrashov summed up the new Soviet approach very clearly: 'The new relations of cooperation and interaction, particularly with the USA, are now seen as one of the chief levers of lifting us out of the crisis.'[8]

The specific foreign policy which emerged in response to the demands of domestic reform came to be known as new political thinking. New political thinking, an amorphous collection of new prescriptions and old ideas reshaped for a leadership committed to real change, concentrated on lessening international tensions and promoting cooperation in the international sphere.[9] The three pillars of new political thinking which most helped to undermine the system of enmity between the United States and the Soviet Union included a movement towards interdependence in the military and security sphere, a re-evaluation of capitalism and the 'de-ideologization' of interstate relations.

At the foundation of the conception of interdependence was a willingness to seek political solutions to a range of world problems, be they social, ecological, economic or military.[10] The move towards interdependence was accompanied by new military and security doctrines[11] which allowed for asymmetrical arms agreements. The view of US/Soviet relations as a zero-sum military game was discarded for one which stressed that security had to be mutual if it was to succeed.[12]

The changing Soviet view of capitalism which emerged with new political thinking entailed re-evaluations of its internal capacity to survive and the nature of its external aggressiveness. Soviet thinking shifted away from a focus on the imminent collapse of the capitalist world to an examination of how capitalism had successfully adjusted to modern realities, particularly through the use of technology, and how it successfully overcame many of the social ills with which it was traditionally associated.[13] New political thinking also questioned the inherent link between capitalism and militarism, instead suggesting that hostility was conditional, a matter of choice rather than historical law.[14] It also opened the door to new evaluations of the potential roles of capitalism and socialism in the developing world, leaving open the possibility that capitalism could lead to a superior form of development.[15]

These shifts in focus were of fundamental importance for US/Soviet relations. The expectation that capitalism would survive into the distant future meant that temporary tactics and 'breathing spaces' would not do; long-term solutions were needed and these required approaches which would be prosperous for both sides. The shifting evaluation of the relation between capitalism and militarism justified the Soviet Union's stress on interdependence and its willingness to make compromises with the West. Without such a re-evaluation there would be little chance that Gorbachev could express an 'optimistic view of the future and the prospects for creation of an all-embracing international security system'.[16] Finally, the new view of capitalism made it a more acceptable model from which the Soviet Union could learn. As we will see in Chapter 7, this had a tremendous effect on the press.

Closely related to the promotion of the concept of interdependence and to the re-evaluation of capitalism was the Soviet effort to 'de-ideologize' interstate relations and eliminate the so-called 'enemy image'. The de-ideologization of interstate relations was an attempt to reduce tensions between East and West by eliminating intertwined ideological and psychological barriers which stood in the way of increased cooperation. The policy was designed to undermine the long-held two-camp view of international relations in which the international arena was viewed as a zero-sum game between capitalism and socialism.[17] In Soviet terminology, it postulated that the idea of peaceful coexistence should be cleansed of notions of class struggle when applied to interstate relations.[18] Previous interpretations of peaceful coexistence had seen it more as a breathing space, or a temporary order, in which class conflict would continue to thrive. This placed impossible barriers in the way of long-term cooperation, because, to paraphrase Shevardnadze, it is impossible to 'make friends with a person' and simultaneously 'carry on an implacable struggle against him'.[19] This is to say nothing of the higher level of cooperation envisioned by the Gorbachev leadership.

The implications of the removal of class struggle from interstate relations were enormous. It meant not only that class struggle was no longer the defining feature of the international arena, but also that the United States and the Soviet Union were no longer situated at the focal point of international tension. In place of class struggle the Soviet leadership shifted focus to the idea of 'universal human values', a concept which transcended belief systems.[20] This meant that shared values were stressed instead of differences.

These changes constituted important steps towards better relations with the West. However, regardless of restated intentions, the leadership still faced the difficult task of convincing people at home and abroad of the virtues of change. One of the key means through which that was to be achieved was the elimination of the so-called enemy image (*obraz vraga*).

The enemy image in the context of Soviet theorists referred to a psychological projection of hostility.[21] This image was seen as being created in public expressions both by political figures and the press.[22]

On the domestic front, the elimination of the enemy image was supposed to help prepare the path for internal renewal by diminishing the fear of the 'external threat,' a fear which had so long served to justify conservatism and the status quo. The changes were also designed to prepare the Soviet public, as well as government and military officials, for the compromises which the Soviet Union would be required to make in order to promote its foreign policy based on new political thinking.[23]

For the foreign audience, both policy makers and the public alike, the elimination of the enemy image was to remove barriers to improved relations which the Soviet Union needed for its domestic reform programme.[24] Soviet leaders realized that the tense international environment would not improve as long as the attitudes underlying the hostility remained.[25] As Gorbachev told a *Time* interviewer in 1985: 'It is a fact that even now it is very difficult for the United States and the Soviet Union to reach an agreement, to take any steps toward each other. The mutual distrust is so great.'[26]

The Soviet leadership took several concrete steps to remove the enemy image, or at least to diminish its impact. These ranged from more conciliatory speeches to placing younger ambassadors abroad who had better knowledge of native languages and public relations. It also meant changes in the Soviet press.[27]

The leadership believed that less hostile portrayals of the United States in the Soviet press would not only prepare Soviet citizens for concessions to come, but that they would convince American policy-makers that the Soviet Union was serious about reform. Soviet specialists realized that their domestic propaganda influenced their image abroad. This was particularly the case in the *glasnost'* era when many in the West viewed the apparent opening of the press as an indicator of change.[28]

Perhaps more importantly for this study, Soviet leaders hoped that changes in the Soviet media would result in reciprocal actions that would help to eliminate the enemy image of the Soviet Union in the West. The Soviet leadership had long been concerned with the country's demonization in the foreign media.[29] Although their hope for reciprocity might have been based in part on a misperception of how the Western mass media operate (coming from the belief that Western leaders could manipulate the press as easily as Soviet leaders),[30] it was clear that they were expecting the West to follow their lead. Fedor Burlatsky, a well-connected journalist and editor, indicated that the Soviet Union expected 'parity' from the West in efforts to change international press coverage and remove the enemy image.[31] Even more telling was a letter to the *New York Times* from Georgi Arbatov, head of the Institute for the Study of the United States and Canada, in which he literally challenged the American press to follow the Soviet example and refrain from hostile 'cold-war' style criticism.[32] Later, in meetings between US and Soviet media representatives in Moscow, Ideology Secretary Aleksandr Yakovlev repeated the same message.[33]

POLITICAL CARTOONS AND A CHRONOLOGY OF CHANGE

In order to develop a chronology of change in the Gorbachev period, we will now offer a brief quantitative analysis of the depiction of the United States in Soviet political cartoons. Political cartoons are a useful starting point because they provide easily decipherable messages which appeared regularly in the press through much of the Gorbachev period. Changes in the volume of anti-American political cartoons will be linked chronologically with policy changes.

Political cartoons played a prominent role in communicating communist ideas since the Bolshevik Revolution. The *Bolshaya Sovetskaya Entsiklopediya* describes them as a 'sharp weapon of political agitation' which was 'one of the most important forms of socio-political satire'.[34] This visual weapon was wielded particularly fiercely when aimed at foreign adversaries. Indeed, after studying the cartoons appearing in *Pravda* and *Izvestiya* from 1947 to 1964 one observer concluded that: 'The apparent objective of cartoons was to implant, repeat and reinforce a negative image of the West in the minds of readers.'[35]

The Gorbachev era witnessed profound and fundamental changes in the role of international political cartoons in the Soviet press. In order to evaluate these changes, I have relied primarily on content analysis because it can provide a concise view of change over time.[36] The publications to be examined are *Pravda, Izvestiya* and *Krokodil.* The former two have been chosen because they were the most important Soviet dailies. The latter was selected because it was the most important Soviet journal devoted to political satire.

The most important quantitative change was the tremendous decline in the number of anti-American cartoons. This decline is illustrated below in Figures 5.1 and 5.2.

While at the beginning of the period anti-American cartoons appeared almost on a daily basis in *Pravda* and on roughly two out

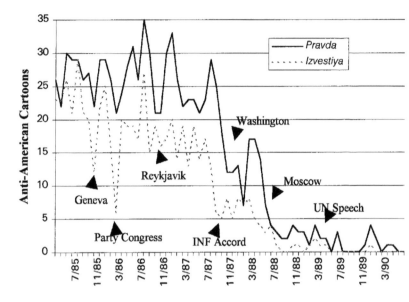

Figure 5.1   *Pravda* and *Izvestiya*: Anti-American Cartoons

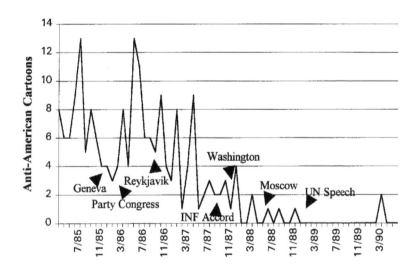

Figure 5.2   *Krokodil*: Anti-American Cartoons

of every three days in *Izvestiya*, by the end of the period they practically disappeared. *Krokodil* experienced a similar decline. Although
the figures fluctuate more, probably because *Krokodil's* thrice monthly
appearance made it more susceptible to the vagaries of editorial
decisions, the volume of cartoons declined from six per month early
in the period to almost none during the last year and a half.

More interesting analytically than the overall trend towards fewer
anti-American cartoons were the sharp declines and alternating
plateaus found in all three publications. Some changes were short-
lived and associated either with internal events (such as the XXVIIth
Party Congress of March 1986) which filled Soviet papers and left
little room for editorial cartoons or with the early US/Soviet sum-
mits, when the press attempted to help build an environment
conducive to successful negotiations.[37]

Of greater significance than these ephemeral declines were the
plateaus, outlined in Figure 5.3, which signified more lasting reductions, usually linked with turning-points in US/Soviet relations
(the INF agreement, reached September 1987; US Senate passage
of INF treaty/Moscow Summit, May/June 1988; and Gorbachev's
United Nations speech, December 1988). These plateaus provide
us with the opportunity to examine a careful chronology of changes
in Soviet approaches to capitalism and its leading power. Below
we will analyse four periods as outlined in Figure 5.3.

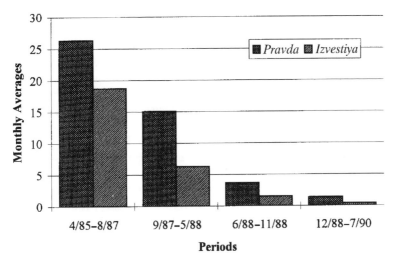

Figure 5.3   *Pravda* and *Izvestiya*: Anti-US Cartoons by Period

APRIL 1985 TO AUGUST 1987

In the period from April 1985, the first full month of Gorbachev's general secretaryship, through August 1987, the United States was the object of heavy criticism. In this period, *Pravda* averaged over 26 anti-American cartoons per month and *Izvestiya* had nearly 19 per month. *Krokodil*, which is not represented in Figure 5.3, averaged just under six anti-American cartoons per month.

The volume and nature of cartoons reflected the fundamental hostility of the leadership towards capitalism and the United States. Views expressed by the leadership about the United States were unyieldingly critical. America's political system was seen as being controlled by 'right wing circles'.[38] At the Reykjavik Summit in October 1986, Gorbachev asserted that the 'military-industrial complex' was 'in power', and that the President was 'not free to make decisions'.[39] He claimed that American workers were suffering worse than ever, because the 'most intransigent reactionary groupings of the ruling class have, on the whole, gained the upper hand'. He assailed technological modernization because it was 'throwing millions of people onto the streets', and attacked American culture, insisting that mankind must reject imperialism's 'unrestrained hucksterism', its 'cult of violence', 'preaching of racism' and 'propagation of base instincts and the morals of the criminal world'.[40]

US foreign policy was viewed in an equally negative light. Gorbachev called the United States the 'mother country of imperialism', and implied a necessary connection between imperialism and militarism, asserting that 'because of its social nature, imperialism continually generates aggressive, adventuristic policies'.[41] He extolled the virtues of national liberation movements, while assailing America's 'neo-colonialist' policies, its 'exploitation' of the developing world and its attempt to 'halt the course of history' by blocking the advancement of socialism. He also pointed to the sharpening of 'inter-imperialist contradictions', criticizing US attempts to bully its allies, while lauding those in Western Europe who questioned US policies.[42]

Gorbachev's overall view of the West was summed up in a statement at the XXVIIth Party Congress: 'Bourgeois ideology is an ideology of service to capital and the profits of monopolies, of adventurism and social revenge, the ideology of a society with no future.'[43]

While the rhetorical onslaught against the United States was the

norm, it is important to note some indications of doctrinal innovation, particularly with reference to relations with capitalist countries.
Eduard Shevardnadze, the new foreign minister,[44] spoke in late 1985
of 'separating carefully ideological differences from inter-state relations'.[45] The Party Programme at the XXVIIth Congress concurred,
stating that the Party considered 'the spread of the ideological
contradictions between the two systems to the sphere of inter-state
relations [based on peaceful co-existence] to be inadmissible'.[46]
However, such statements, when surrounded by the vitriol described
above, did not at the time offer any substantive indication of long-
term and meaningful change in doctrine or in policy.

More substantial indications that the leadership was considering
new approaches to the United States and capitalism came in the
wake of the thrice delayed January 1987 party plenum.[47] The plenum, which marked what Gorbachev called 'a real revolution' in
the Soviet Union, was marked by significant criticism of the Soviet
Union's economic performance and was followed in the June party
plenum with the unequivocal recognition that the Soviet Union was
falling further behind capitalist countries.

Following from this, leading figures began to tentatively re-evaluate
capitalism. The most important statement was prepared by party
secretary and candidate politburo member Aleksandr Yakovlev, a
key Gorbachev ally, and appeared as the lead article of the authoritative journal *Kommunist* in May 1987. In the article, Yakovlev
decried the 'oversimplification' and 'dogmatism' which tainted Soviet
studies of capitalism, causing analysts to underestimate the capacity of capitalism to adjust and survive, and called for new approaches
in order to attain a better understanding.[48] While there had been
some previous calls for a re-evaluation of capitalism in the Gorbachev
era, they were never made by anyone with the authority of Yakovlev.[49]
Significantly, he was promoted to full Politburo standing the following month and, as ideology secretary, was given guardianship
over the press.[50] An article by such an authority was certainly designed to draw the attention of the entire ideological apparatus,
including the press.

The steps towards a re-evaluation of capitalism were accompanied
by practical and theoretical changes in the foreign policy sphere.
In late February and early March 1987, the Soviet Union began to
offer previously unthinkable concessions which ultimately paved
the way for the INF accord on nuclear arms reductions.[51] In May,
the first articles on 'reasonable sufficiency' in the military sphere

began to appear in the professional literature.[52] In June, Eduard Shevardnadze emphasized the need to 'economize' Soviet foreign policy, foreshadowing a new emphasis on arms concessions and attempts to promote trade.[53]

An indication of how these changes might have impacted on the press comes from *Krokodil* which averaged only two anti-American cartoons per month in the final three months of the period under consideration (June–August 1987). While this change might have been one of its regular fluctuations, it was more likely that it was part of an editorial policy. *Krokodil*, unlike *Pravda* and *Izvestiya*, the official newspapers of the party and state, was not perceived as an official representative of Soviet positions, and thus it had greater, albeit limited, flexibility. It was likely to have been expressing emerging policies at a time when the INF negotiations seemed likely to bear fruit, yet had not reached the point where optimistic results could be recognized by the more official publications.

SEPTEMBER 1987 TO MAY 1988

The period from September 1987 to May 1988 marked a key turning-point in the depiction of the United States in Soviet political cartoons. The number of anti-American political cartoons in *Pravda* declined 43 per cent compared with the first period to 15 per month, *Izvestiya* fell by two-thirds to 6.3 per month and *Krokodil* had a decline of 74 per cent to 1.6 per month.

The changes clearly emerged with the signing of the INF treaty in September 1987, the first US/Soviet agreement to provide for a reduction of nuclear missiles. After the agreement, many of the remaining barriers to change were swept aside and, as we will see in Chapters 6 and 7, press coverage shifted dramatically.[54]

The agreement saw other significant changes in Soviet approaches to capitalism and its leading power. The most important theoretical changes in this period related to the Soviet assessment of capitalism. In his speech at the LXXth anniversary of the October Revolution, Gorbachev called into question two important assumptions which had played vital roles in Soviet approaches towards capitalist countries. First, he questioned the link between imperialism and militarism. Second, he raised doubts about previous assumptions concerning capitalism's capacity to survive.[55] Although he did not offer any firm conclusions, suggesting that previous assumptions be re-examined, there is little doubt that these signified an important new approach to the West.[56]

This period also witnessed the Soviet Union beginning to make more concrete attempts to eliminate the enemy image. This was the period when Georgi Arbatov wrote to the *New York Times* challenging the US press to follow the Soviet lead in removing the enemy image. Similar sentiments were found in Gorbachev's book *Perestroika,* released in November 1987, which was directed primarily at Western audiences.[57] Indeed there were so many articles about the deleterious effect of the enemy image in 1987 and 1988 that it was deemed a 'fashionable term' by *Izvestiya*'s Aleksandr Bovin.[58] This undoubtedly had important implications for the Soviet press, for, if the Soviet challenge were to be real, then it too would have to change. Certainly that was the implication of Arbatov's letter.

JUNE 1988 TO NOVEMBER 1988

The period from June to November 1988 witnessed further declines in the hostile portrayal of the United States. Change was so dramatic that the period represents the effective collapse of political cartoons as a weapon of ideological struggle and, perhaps, the struggle itself. In this period, *Pravda* saw a decline in anti-American cartoons to an average of only 3.7 per month, an 86 per cent decline from the first period, *Izvestiya* fell 92 per cent to only 1.5 per month and *Krokodil* fell to 0.34 per month, a decline of 94 per cent from the first period.

The changes coincided with the Moscow Summit (29 May–2 June 1988), by which time the INF agreement had been formally ratified by the US Senate and further treaties seemed possible. So positive were feelings that in late July 1988 Eduard Shevardnadze asserted that 'the struggle between the two opposing systems is no longer the defining tendency of the contemporary era'.[59]

The period also witnessed further steps towards the re-evaluation of capitalism amongst the leadership, most prominently signified by a call for borrowing from Western experience. In October 1988, newly named Secretary for Ideology Vadim Medvedev asserted that the Soviet Union should not simply study the 'scientific and technical achievements of the system opposing us', but that it should also explore 'the many forms of the organization of public life and the economic process, including large- and small-scale production, co-operative forms of activity, international economic integration etc.'.[60]

Finally, the period saw further attempts to improve the Soviet image abroad when, at the joint meeting of American and Soviet media representatives in October 1988, the American journalists were challenged to follow the Soviet lead in eliminating the enemy image.[61]

DECEMBER 1988 TO JULY 1990

The period from December 1988 to July 1990 saw anti-American cartoons become the rare exception. While at the beginning of the period they appeared almost every day, by this point they rarely appeared more than once in any publication in a given month, and then they were borrowed from foreign publications. In comparison with the first period, those in *Pravda* had declined by 95 per cent to 1.35 per month, in *Izvestiya* by 98 per cent to only 0.2 per month and in *Krokodil* by 97 per cent to 0.15 per month. The changes corresponded to the Reagan/Gorbachev/Bush meeting in Washington and Gorbachev's United Nations speech (December 1988) in which he outlined for the first time significant unilateral reductions in Soviet conventional forces.

Again, the decline in negative depiction of the United States corresponded with significant policy and theoretical changes in the Soviet leadership. In the UN speech Gorbachev echoed Medvedev's views on the future of socialism, asserting that the Soviet Union would not 'shut itself within (its) own values', because that would mean renouncing 'a powerful source of development', namely, 'sharing all the original things that are being created by each nation independently'.[62]

This speech was important, because it signalled to journalists that learning from the West was not only legitimate, but that it was to be encouraged. Moreover, the leadership was not simply speaking of science and technology, as had been the case periodically in the past, but of a wide range of affairs, from business practices to governmental structures. It was also directed at the general Soviet population, not the rarefied world of specialists as had been the case in the past.

In terms of foreign policy, this period witnessed a continuation of a series of Soviet efforts to foster better relations. In his UN speech, Gorbachev offered unilateral troop reductions of 500,000 men. In January 1989, he announced moves to reduce military expenditures. Moreover, in this period the leadership asserted more firmly than ever a commitment to de-ideologization. In July 1989, Gorbachev spoke of the rights of any people to 'choose a social system as it sees fit' and claimed that 'any interference in internal affairs of whatever kind, any attempts to limit the sovereignty of states, both of friends and allies, no matter whose it is, is impermissible'.[63] This meant an end to the zero-sum game with the United States.

DISCUSSION AND CONCLUSIONS

There were enormous changes in leadership policies concerning the United States in the Gorbachev period. The leadership made a conscious effort to undermine the system of enmity which had so long served as a barrier to improved and sustainable long-term relations between the Soviet Union and the West. In doing so, it moved from a permanently critical approach towards the West and all things capitalist, to policies calling for a de-emphasis on the capitalist threat, a re-evaluation of capitalism and learning from the Western experience.

That is not to say that all criticism of capitalism ceased. You could still hear occasional criticisms from Gorbachev later in his rule, as he attempted to salvage socialism in the Soviet Union. Criticism was louder from those who were opposed to reforms, or at least reforms which would have involved the large-scale adoption of Western methods. However, the entire environment had changed. Criticism became the exception instead of the rule. The primary policies of the leadership stressed movement towards better and more positive relations with the West. *Rapprochement* with the West was not a tactic but a policy.

The implications of the changing policies were felt in the press. International political cartoons, whose official role was to 'mercilessly expose imperialist warmongers and their collaborators',[64] ceased fulfilling this function. International cartoons rarely appeared[65] and the content of those cartoons which did appear were less biting. The worst of the cartoons, including those linking the United States symbolically with Nazi Germany, ceased appearing by the end of 1986.[66] Towards the end of the period, there even appeared what

Table 5.1   Average international cartoons per month and anti-American cartoons as percentage of international cartoons

	Pravda		*Izvestiya*		*Krokodil*	
Period	Avg int/mo.	% anti-US	Avg int/mo.	% anti-US	Avg int/mo.	% anti-US
4/85–8/87	29	90.5	22	84.8	7.5	79.4
9/87–5/88	21.8	69.9	10.9	57.1	2.7	56
6/88–11/88	8.7	42.3	5.5	27.3	1.7	20
12/88–7/90	4.7	23.7	2.3	15.6	0.65	23.1

can be termed anti-Soviet, pro-American cartoons. One of these bemoaned the inconvertibility of the ruble while celebrating the strength of the dollar.[67] Another maligned Soviet bureaucrats for obstructing trade with honest-looking Western businessmen who seemingly had nothing in common with the 'capitalists' who were so long demonized.[68] It is difficult to imagine a more radical transformation.

In response to a query about the decline in anti-American cartoons, one *Pravda* satirist said in the spring of 1990, 'The reason we no longer have cartoons about America is because we want friendship. We no longer want the enemy image.'[69] Other Soviet cartoonists, satirists, writers and editors apparently took the same view. With their move away from the enemy image towards universal human values, Soviet international cartoons ceased to meet their billing as a 'sharp weapon of political agitation'. Indeed, the observer's comment that the purpose of cartoons was to implant, repeat and reinforce a negative image of the West in the minds of readers, which could have applied in 1985 just as in 1950, was no longer accurate.

6 Changing Images of American Military and Foreign Policy

This chapter examines the evolution of images of the United States' military and foreign policy in the Soviet press during the Gorbachev period and attempts to identify sources of change. The study has been divided into four sections. The first section examines changing discourse. Content analysis has been used in order to explore chronological changes in the use of key evaluative terms traditionally used to describe the United States. The second section explores the evolution of disinformation campaigns designed to paint a negative image of the US in the Soviet Union and to discredit the US world-wide. The third section examines press coverage of US relations with the developing world and includes a comparative case study of press coverage of the US attack on Libya in 1986 and its invasion of Panama in late 1989. The final section looks at US relations with its allies, particularly those in Western Europe and Japan. Special attention is devoted to coverage of the Group of Seven's annual meetings from 1986 to 1990.

US FOREIGN POLICY AND THE SOVIET PRESS

In the beginning of the Gorbachev period, Soviet press coverage of US foreign policy manifested three critical characteristics. First, Soviet obsession with the United States meant that coverage of foreign policy was seen through the prism of US/Soviet competition. The press either focused on 'fraternal countries' or those countries loyal to, or victimized by, the United States. Second, practically every step which the United States took in the foreign policy sphere was portrayed in a negative light. Co-operative initiatives of individual citizens, which fell under the general rubric of cultural diplomacy, might prove exceptional, but overall the press reflected a Manichaean battle between the Superpowers. Finally, the press primarily presented uncomplicated, propagandistic images.

Complex analysis, albeit with a strong ideological bent, was left to theoretical and specialty journals. The popular press's role, as far as its coverage of US foreign policy was concerned, was to legitimate the regime by creating fear of the United States and demonstrating the appropriate language for public communication. It was also supposed to show Soviet allies and prospective allies that the United States was a dangerous and tangible threat, and that the Soviet Union was sympathetic. Implicit in press coverage was the Leninist argument that America's aggressive foreign policy was a product of its unjust socio-economic system. With time, however, all three pillars would change.

CHANGING DISCOURSE

Language used in the Soviet press was not chosen haphazardly. This was especially the case for press coverage of international relations, where even a typographical error might cause the Soviet Union to lose ground in the 'war on ideas' by conveying the wrong impression to friends or enemies.[1] Terms used to describe other countries were both descriptive and evaluative and were intended to express solidarity or opposition. Significant changes in word usage, therefore, can be important indicators of change.

In order to evaluate such changes, I have examined the usage of two key terms used to describe the United States which were essential to the pre-Gorbachev discourse on foreign policy: 'imperialism' and 'militarism'. Both are evaluative in the sense that neither could have been used to describe the United States without critical connotations.

Table 6.1 summarizes results taken from a cross-section of articles from *Pravda*, *Izvestiya* and *Sovetskaya Rossiya* in the period from March 1985 to July 1990. It reflects the weekly average number of articles in which the chosen terms were used to describe the United States and its actions in the foreign and military sphere.[2] The periods have been divided largely in accordance with the chronology used for political cartoons in Chapter 5.[3]

Table 6.1 points to a few interesting developments. There was a dramatic decline in the usage of critical terms in the period under consideration. As was the case with the political cartoons, the INF treaty, agreed to in September 1987, appeared to be a turning point, and was followed by a new approach to the language used to describe the United States.

Table 6.1   Average weekly appearance of key terms in articles on military/international relations

| Period | | Imperialism | | | Militarism | |
	Pravda	Izvestiya	Sov. Rossiya	Pravda	Izvestiya	Sov. Rossiya
4/85–8/87	7.5	4.13	2.5	6.38	5.38	3.38
9/87–5/88	1	0	0	0.75	1.5	0
6/88–7/90	0.13	0.13	0.5	0	0.13	0

This is not to say that the use of the terms disappeared completely once the INF treaty had been signed. As we will see below, Soviet authors used the terms immediately following the US invasion of Panama in December 1989, a period which did not coincide with any of the sample weeks. However, even then usage was more abstract, referring to 'a reversion into imperial thinking', as opposed to characterizing the incidents as a sign of the inherent evils of US imperialism.[4] Moreover, in the final period, when the terms were used, they often appeared in articles written by or quoting foreign authors. For example, *Pravda*'s only reference to US imperialism in the last period of the survey was made by English author Graham Greene. This followed the trend in political cartoons, where most anti-American cartoons in the period from June 1988 onwards were taken from foreign artists, suggesting that they could do what Soviet authors could not: freely criticize the United States.

MISINFORMATION AND ACTIVE MEASURES: AIDS AND BABY PARTS

While the Gorbachev period witnessed a decline in the appearance of words and pictures which perpetuated the enemy image, that decline was not linear. An irony of the Gorbachev period, and an indication of the depth of anti-American passion, was the emergence of anti-American disinformation campaigns, the most important of which accused the United States of 'manufacturing' the AIDS virus as part of its biochemical weapons programme.[5]

The AIDS campaign apparently began in 1983 with a letter to the editor of the Indian newspaper *The Patriot*, a publication which, according to a KGB defector, was established by the KGB in 1962 'in order to publish disinformation'.[6] The letter was purportedly written by a 'well-known American scientist and anthropologist' desiring to remain anonymous. It charged that the virus was 'believed to be the result of the Pentagon's experiments to develop new and dangerous biological weapons'. The charge was not substantiated.[7]

The campaign lay dormant for over two years but resurfaced in October 1985 in the Soviet weekly *Literaturnaya Gazeta*. In an article entitled 'Panic in the West or What is Hidden Behind the Sensation around AIDS', the accusations made by the 'well-respected Indian newspaper *Patriot*' were repeated verbatim, including claims that the virus was a new type of biological weapon. However, the author, Valentin Zapevlov, failed to acknowledge that the original source of the claim was an anonymous letter.[8]

In the following year, the charges were repeated in the Soviet press and Soviet radio, and in TASS for abroad and Radio Moscow World Service for redistribution through foreign media. The campaign reached its peak in the months following the Reykjavik Summit, when the Soviet leadership was bitterly disappointed at perceived American intransigence. A United States Information Agency report found eight AIDS-related charges in the Soviet print and wire media in the year after the *Literaturnaya Gazeta* article appeared in October 1985, but a total of 29 in the eight months following the October 1986 summit.[9] The charges appeared in several publications, including *Pravda*, *Izvestiya*, *Sovetskaya Rossiya* and *Moscow News*.[10] Also, according to the design of these campaigns, they were distributed by TASS for abroad and repeated in media throughout the world.

The campaign began to wind down in late summer–fall 1987, when the call for the elimination of the enemy image grew. Then, in August 1987, with the INF treaty in sight, Soviet representatives promised US officials that the Soviet media would cease to publish the AIDS charges (they had been a point of contention with the United States since it first appeared). This was followed by a substantial decrease in these charges in the Soviet media as well as client media throughout the world.[11] On 30 October 1987, *Izvestiya* published a disavowal of the accusations by two leading Soviet academicians, both of whom criticized the Soviet media for spreading rumours which 'no serious scientist' supported.[12] However, on the same day, *Sovetskaya Rossiya* repeated the charge, citing a story of 'foreign origin' and claiming its duty to 'report different views'.[13] Nonetheless, the accusations rarely appeared after that. In July 1988, after the US Senate's approval of the INF treaty, *Sovetskaya Rossiya* published an interview with the President of the Soviet Academy of Medical Science in which he not only issued the strongest denial yet of the possibility of the US having created the virus, but also lambasted Soviet journalists for the 'damage' produced by 'unfounded accusations' about the United States and the origin of the virus. He concluded, 'not a single Soviet scientist, not a single scientific institution, shares this position'.[14] This delay suggests that, as in the case of political cartoons and the use of terms 'militarism' and 'imperialism', Soviet officials did not want to give up the campaign until tangible progress in relations with the United States had been achieved. By the summer of 1988, with the INF treaty signed, the campaign ended.

A similar pattern was witnessed in the Soviet press in its circulation of reports accusing American (and Israeli) families of purchasing babies in Latin America in order to dismember them for organ transplantation. The stories tended to mix fact, that there was an international trade in babies for adoption, with fiction, that numerous babies were butchered for profit.

Although the origin of the story, which first appeared in Honduras and Guatemala in early 1987, has not been conclusively linked to Soviet sources, the Soviet press played an important role in propagating the charges. In the Soviet Union, the charges appeared in numerous publications, including *Pravda*, *Izvestiya* and *Sovetskaya Rossiya*. They were also spread by Radio Moscow International. After distribution by Soviet sources, the charges were quickly disseminated throughout Communist Party publications in France, Finland, India, Cuba and Nicaragua. After Western protests, Soviet media reports on the subject declined following the pattern of the AIDS campaign in the fall of 1987. There were occasional references after that, but according to the USIA, they disappeared from the Soviet media by the spring of 1988.[15]

The AIDS and baby parts campaigns are important for a number of reasons. First, they demonstrate the length to which the Soviet media demonized the United States. Both campaigns sent very clear messages about the United States and its foreign and military policy: the US was an irresponsible power which violated international conventions (concerning weapons and adoption) and which exhibited barbaric, indeed, cannibalistic behaviour *vis-à-vis* the developing world. The campaigns were probably geared more towards foreign rather than Soviet audiences and were by all accounts successes; they were perpetuated in foreign media long after they ceased appearing in the Soviet Union.[16]

Second, the timing reinforces suggestions about links between the evolution of US/Soviet relations and changes in Soviet press coverage of the United States. In both cases, the Reykjavik summit failure played an important role: in the case of the AIDS campaign, the period after the summit saw a significant acceleration of the campaign; in terms of the baby parts charges, it witnessed the Soviet Union and its press, if not initiating, then at least propagating the charges. Again in both instances there were significant reductions in accusations after the INF agreement and the concomitant calls for an end to the enemy image. Finally, after the INF treaty was approved by the US Senate and formally put into effect at the Moscow Summit, the charges disappeared totally. This certainly reinforces suggestions of the existence of central directives influencing the press. Indeed, the fact that the Soviet officials could offer assurances to US representatives that the charges would cease suggests a significant measure of control over the press and lends credence to US assertions that the International Department of the Central Committee was responsible for initiating and perpetuating the campaigns.[17]

THE UNITED STATES AND THE DEVELOPING WORLD

Until the middle of 1987, with the signing of the INF accord, the Soviet press depicted the US as inherently and, for the most part, uncontrollably militaristic in its relations with the developing world. The United States was constantly portrayed as a 'neo-colonial' power governed by a policy of 'state terrorism'. A host of evils, including genocide, were not beyond it.[18] The period since Ronald Reagan had become president was painted in particularly critical terms, the conflict between imperialism and developing countries being described as 'the sharpest in the entire period since the collapse of the colonial system'.[19] One writer in 1985 noted 'a new stage of the crusade by American imperialism against all peoples and countries fighting for peace'.[20]

In early 1986, the Soviet press became even more critical of US foreign policy, describing it with a new term, 'new-globalism'. New-globalism, a particularly harsh manifestation of imperialism, was defined as America's self-determined right 'to interfere in the affairs of sovereign states on a global scale, to wage undeclared war against them and to conduct covert and overt operations as well as to carry out a policy of state terrorism'.[21] It was closely interlinked with the Reagan Doctrine which was 'a doctrine of world-wide counter-revolution'.[22] Numerous articles in 1986 and early 1987 were devoted to US new-globalism, although references to it all but disappeared after the INF treaty.[23]

The brutality of American foreign policy was frequently highlighted through articles depicting American efforts to 'destroy' national liberation movements. Aggressive actions were often portrayed as simple manifestations of US ruthlessness; the United States attempted to quash national liberation movements in the same instinctive way a cat attacks a mouse.[24] Other times, the US was seen as more calculating and governed by more obvious manifestations of self-interest. Regardless, the US would go to any lengths to stop countries from asserting their independence, including invasion, as in the case of Grenada,[25] or though covert and overt acts of state terrorism, as in Libya[26] and Nicaragua.[27] Its favourite targets were the Arab world[28] and Latin America,[29] although no developing country was safe.

Many of the most brutal images of US foreign policy towards the developing world contradicted images of the United States found in the context of articles on US/Soviet arms negotiations.[30] Here, the United States was primarily seen as an aggressive power, but one which could at least contain its militaristic inclinations. After all, the Soviet leadership could not be portrayed negotiating long-term agreements with an uncontrollably aggressive partner.

However, such competing interpretations were not uncommon in the Soviet press. The seemingly contradictory messages were the products of attempts to communicate different signals to different audiences. Images of the United States as capable of controlling its instincts, and, after the INF treaty, as a 'normal' partner, were intended to show to Soviet audiences that the United States could be trusted to abide by its agreements. Press coverage which depicted the United States as insatiable in its lust to dominate the developing world was directed at leaders of developing countries, demonstrating the threat posed by the United States and the need of developing countries to align themselves with the Soviet Union. Consistency was not paramount. More important was the instrumental objective which the press was supposed to help achieve.

The success of the INF agreement and Mikhail Gorbachev's direct questioning of the link between imperialism and militarism in November 1987 led to some important if subtle changes in the portrayal of US relations with the developing world. Generally, there was a tendency towards depicting the United States as more in control of its aggressive instincts. The image improved further with the signing of the Geneva accords on the conflict in Afghanistan in April 1988, the US Senate's passage of the INF treaty and Gorbachev's speech at the United Nations in December 1988 in which he called for the de-ideologization of interstate relations.

Changes were manifested in a number of ways. Terms used to describe American aggression were altered. Instead of 'imperialism' and 'militarism', which had broad and deterministic connotations, the press started to use phrases like 'hegemony', and 'aggressive acts'.[31] This change reflected the government's adoption of similar terms in its official pronouncements.[32] There were also more references to 'reversion' to imperial activity or 'imperial thinking', rather than to imperialism itself. This was important because it ran counter to Leninist theory by suggesting that imperialism was a state of mind rather than a historical fact. Such expressions had occasionally been used in earlier periods, but they were comparatively rare and, given that they were surrounded by repeated references to American imperialism, they did not appear to offer a revision of Soviet theory of international relations.

Two other changes emerged towards the end of the period which were significant indications of new approaches. First, the developing countries against whom the US demonstrated hostility were not always portrayed as innocent victims of US machinations. For example, some journalists revealed that Panama's Manual Noriega was a despised dictator and others spoke of problems in Nicaragua, including Sandanista corruption.[33] Such articles placed US actions in a different light; if not legitimating them, they at least made them seem more understandable. Second, some articles began to show that it was possible for the United States to have relations with the developing world that were marked neither by aggression nor exploitation.[34] This would have been impossible at the beginning of the period.

These changes were indicative of the movement away from the view of the world as an arena for the Manichaean battle between the United States and the Soviet Union; it was no longer necessary to pretend that the friend of your enemy was your friend because the enemy was no longer. The world thus became much fuller of different shades, not simply black and white. This move away from America-centrism was also reflected in a dramatic decline in the amount of coverage devoted to US relations with the developing world and, indeed, to the United States as a whole. US activities in the developing world simply ceased to be a critical topic because the United States and the Soviet Union were no longer in a constant state of opposition.

There were varying degrees of change in the different publications examined with a few trends emerging. *Pravda* and *Sovetskaya Rossiya* continued, on the whole, to present a relatively high level of criticism of the United States, highlighting aggressive tendencies with a significant amount of coverage reflecting old, ideological formulas. *Izvestiya* moved away from such interpretations and tended to show the United States as more of a changed partner, albeit one which could still slip back to its old ways. In 1990, it made several references to international problems caused by developing countries, as opposed to forces of imperialism, and to the possibility of mutually beneficial relations between the US and the developing world. However, it still contained occasional references to America's propensity for militarism. *Moscow News* and *Argumenty i Fakty* almost entirely ceased coverage of US relations with the developing world, except in reference to questions of aid. This silence in itself represented significant change and was indicative of the publications' shift in focus to internal events and to their editorial lines which held the United States up as a model for domestic reform.

The changes, however, were slow, indefinite and uneven. There were still occasional references to US imperialism, still uses of the term militarism and still occasional portrayals of the United States which suggested an inherent desire to repress. There was an overall change in emphasis, but not a radical reversal as in the case of political cartoons. The press still played to the developing world. One *Izvestiya* author lambasted the US for showing 'realism' in the sphere of arms control, and yet still viewing regional problems 'through the prism of new-globalism', and seeing the world 'like a chess board for the conflict of two superpowers'.[35]

The ambivalent way in which the Soviet press approached US relations with the developing world reflected the government's own uncertainty. Although significant improvements had emerged in US/Soviet discussions of regional conflicts, problems still remained. There might have been a need to re-evaluate the relationship between

imperialism and militarism, but that did not mean that no relationship existed. The battle between the two world systems may
not have been the 'defining tendency of the contemporary era', as
Eduard Shevardnadaze said in 1988, but the leadership and the
press both recognized that competition still existed.[36] There was
an overall trend away from the most brutal images of the United
States in both leadership statements and in the press, however criticism, even with 'ideologized' overtones, did not cease.

LIBYA VS. PANAMA

In order to underline changes in the Soviet press's portrayal of
coverage of American foreign policy, with particular reference to
the developing world, we can examine coverage of the two most
significant American military actions in the period under consideration, the 1986 bombing of Libya and the 1989 intervention in
Panama.

The most obvious indication of change is the volume of coverage devoted to both incidents. *Table* 6.2 examines the space devoted
to the two attacks in a number of issues (seven for the dailies and
four for the monthlies) following the assaults.[37]

In each publication there was a significant decline in the volume
of coverage. The greatest decreases were in *Moscow News* and
Argumenty i Fakty, where the invasion of Panama received no direct press coverage. Although there were a few references to the
invasion in articles on other issues, there were no descriptions of
the invasion and there was no coverage of the response to the invasion
in the Soviet Union or abroad. This contrasted sharply with coverage
of the attack on Libya in 1986, to which *Moscow News* devoted ten
articles and *Argumenty i Fakty* three articles, one of which was a
full-page survey of the international response to the aggression.[38]
The absence of articles devoted to the invasion of Panama is particularly noteworthy when compared with the other three publications
under consideration. While all demonstrated significant declines,
Pravda's and *Izvestiya*'s declines were 65 per cent and 60 per cent
respectively, with coverage in *Sovetskaya Rossiya* decreasing relatively little at only 23 per cent.

The decrease in the volume of coverage of the invasion of Panama
vis-à-vis the attack on Libya is indicative of the Soviet press's shift
away from America-centrism and a bi-polar view of the world. At

Table 6.2   Press coverage of US attacks on Libya and Panama

	Pravda	Izvestiya	Sov. Rossiya	Argumenty i Fakty	Moscow News
Libya 4/86	992*	823	328	142	332
Panama 12/89	346	323	251	0	0

* All figures in column centimetres

the same time, the different approaches of the selected publications also suggests that divergent editorial lines were emerging. The decision of *Moscow News* and *Argumenty i Fakty* to downplay the invasion of Panama is in part a product of their 'democratic' and pro-market editorial lines in domestic affairs and the symbolic importance of the United States for such a position. The reverse is possibly true for *Sovetskaya Rossiya*, whose editors were beginning to assert a more nationalist line while at the same time remaining cognizant of and honouring the government's desire for improved relations with the US.

Qualitative changes in press coverage, as well as emerging differences between reporters and between publications, can be further illuminated by examining descriptions of the attacks and analysis of their implications for US/Soviet relations.

The attack on Libya was largely viewed as a typical manifestation of American imperialism. For example, a *Pravda* reporter described the bombing as 'yet another shameful page' in the 'history of violent crimes of imperialism'.[39] A commentator in *Sovetskaya Rossiya* claimed that the 'regular militaristic raid' against Libya was a typical 'fit of imperialist rage'.[40] An *Izvestiya* commentator asserted that the assault showed that the 'hypocrisy of American imperialism knows no bounds'.[41] A *Moscow News* editorial said that the attack typified the Reagan administration's aggressive policy of new-globalism.[42] Several articles predicted future acts of American aggression.[43]

The Reagan administration's hostility towards national liberation movements and Libya's role in the 'anti-imperialist struggle' were viewed as the impetuses for the attack.[44] The official US explanation that the assault was a justified response to Libyan-led terrorism was dismissed out of hand.[45] Indeed, in partial response to US accusations of Libyan terrorism, numerous writers charged the United States with a policy of 'state terrorism'.[46]

The raid was also interpreted as a blow directed at the Soviet Union and its attempts to improve the international climate. 'Ruling circles', particularly the 'military industrial complex', were seen as attempting to derail US/Soviet relations.[47] Such charges were typified by a *Pravda* writer who claimed that the attack was 'a link in the chain of provocative US acts carried out in response to the Soviet Union's peace-loving initiatives and aimed at . . . extinguishing the positive trends and hopes which emerged as a result of the Geneva meeting'.[48]

In spite of this criticism, journalists did not take the next step of questioning the Soviet leadership's policy of pursuing *rapprochement* with the US. The journalists' approach was, in fact, very close to that of the government. The government statement on the attack began with an assertion that 'American imperialism has committed a new criminal action fraught with a serious threat to world peace and security'. It saw the attack as a 'confirmation of the United States' essentially aggressive approach to independent developing countries', and claimed that the US was 'becoming more bellicose and more dangerous to the developing world day by day'. It also noted that the US actions 'cannot help but affect relations between the US and the USSR'.[49]

The government statement on Panama three and a half years later was substantially different. The official statement on the invasion did not mention US imperialism, nor did it venture analysis on US attitudes towards the developing world. Instead, it criticized America's 'act of outright international lawlessness', which was 'a violation of the fundamental principles of the UN Charter and of the norms of governing relations among states'. It did not analyze the reasons for the attacks and made no mention of developing countries: it only dismissed US assertions that it was restoring democracy. It also did not comment directly on how the invasion would affect US/Soviet relations, although it criticized the United States for actions 'at variance with the positive trends that are gaining strength in world politics and with the policy of dialogue and political and diplomatic methods of resolving complex issues'.[50]

This weaker and more vague declaration left far greater room for debate amongst reporters about the meaning of the US actions. Accordingly, the press coverage of the invasion of Panama, although universally critical, demonstrated a far greater variety of images. The focus was not on America's inherent militarism nor on its desire to punish countries for their pursuit of national liberation, as was the case with Libya. Instead, most reporters saw the attack as a return to past behaviour, or a 'relapse of imperial thinking'.[51] This implies that the attack was more an error than a manifestation of an inherently aggressive socio-economic system.

In analyzing the reasons for the attack, most reporters and commentators concentrated overwhelmingly on causes unique to Panama, rather than on forces of historical and socio-economic development. The primary explanation put forward was that the attack reflected America's desire to prolong its control over the Panama canal.[52] Here the emphasis was geo-strategic as opposed to ideological. Other analyses pointed to psychological factors, such as America's preoccupation with villains and President Bush's desire to assert himself after his failure to show support to an earlier coup attempt in Panama.[53] Significantly, at least three articles pointed out that Noriega was an unloved dictator and that his ouster was very popular amongst Panamanians.[54] These approaches were different from the Libyan analysis, which focused on America's inherent and seemingly immutable commitment to aggression and Libya's noble role as defender of national liberation movements.

Some reporters were not so kind, suggesting that the actions reflected normal and regular American aggression impelled by imperialism, rather than a 'reversion to aggression' or 'imperial thinking'.[55] Others suggested that other Latin American countries, particularly Nicaragua, would have to be aware of the potential of future US actions.[56]

Also interesting were the different approaches which reporters took to the potential impact of the attack on US/Soviet relations. While in the Libyan case there was little comment on this subject, and that which appeared suggested that it could only cause harm, in the case of Panama there were not only differing opinions about its potential impact, but implicit suggestions of how it might affect relations.

One school believed that the action was not likely to have an effect on the overall positive movement of US/Soviet relations. For example, a *Pravda* writer asserted that 'Restructuring of the world will continue and as far as the reversion to interventionism demonstrated by the United States is concerned, it will become an episode of history, not doing justice to this great country.'[57] A *Moscow News* journalist, in an article on US/Soviet relations at the end of the year, put forth a similar view. After acknowledging that the invasion was a 'relapse of imperial thinking', he asserted in the next sentence that in spite of this, 'in the main, confrontational bipolarity is giving way to cooperation'. Moreover, throughout the article he was very optimistic about trends in international relations and future possibilities, particularly in US/Soviet relations.[58] Although neither author went so far as to suggest how the Soviet leadership should respond to the invasion, their suggestions that good relations would continue seemed to imply faith in the United States as a long-term negotiating partner.

The writers at *Sovetskaya Rossiya* took a more hostile line. The two commentaries which appeared after the invasion were both amongst the most critical in all of the publications consulted. The first raised very pointedly the possibility of further US action and suggested that, despite American claims, the United States did not abide by the principles of détente and cooperation.[59] The next article took criticism to another plane. Yuri Subbotin, *Sovetskaya Rossiya*'s foreign editor, not only lambasted US actions in Panama, but used the opportunity to raise broader questions about the Soviet Union's relationship with the United States. He asked rhetorically 'Aren't we at times hurrying to the desired instead of the real in declaring that all stereotypes of the past have been thrown on the ashheap of history'. He then addressed the US/Soviet relationship, asserting that the Soviet Union was being far too obliging to its 'good overseas uncle, who exchanged his aggressiveness for goodwill'.[60] While he claimed to be supportive of better US/Soviet relations, he also called for caution: 'Let's not fall into euphoria, hurry events, or place the facts into a pretty design. We did this for too long and the results are well known'.[61] Although Subbotin applauded the realism of the Soviet government's statement on the invasion, one cannot help but see the thinly veiled criticism of the official Soviet policy towards the United States. His portrayal of the Soviet Union as a weak and obliging partner left no doubt as to his intent. However, as significant as his attacks were, it is also important to note that at that time they still had to be slightly veiled. He made no references to any officials or specific government policies and even praised elements of the government response. It was different from the more assertive criticism that would appear eight months later after the US military actions in Iraq.[62] In other words, even as late as the beginning of 1990 the press held back from explicit, broad-based criticism of government policy.

The comparison of the attacks highlights many important trends for changing press coverage of the developing world and foreign and military policy as a whole. While there were significant changes from the start to the end of the period, they were ultimately limited and not universal. Most of the images of the United States as an implacably hostile imperialist power had disappeared, but the overall portrayal of US foreign policy towards the developing world remained distinctly negative. Whether it acted as an inherently aggressive imperialist power, or it had 'reverted' to imperialist behaviour, US actions in most cases were still portrayed in a critical light. For those sympathetic to the United States it was almost better not to comment at all, as was the case for *Moscow News* and *Argumenty i Fakty*. Furthermore, the changes seemed to be partly linked with the government's approach to the invasion; vaguer responses to the Panama invasion left greater room for interpretation. This was typical of the government's emerging ambivalence towards the developing world.

Writers availed themselves of this opportunity and not only offered different analyses of the sources of US actions, but also took it upon themselves to suggest what the actions would and should mean for US/Soviet relations. *Sovetskaya Rossiya*'s implicit criticism of government policy demonstrated how publications were beginning to take different perspectives. However, its criticism of the government was still veiled, and it was even made while praising the official government response. This seems to support statements of the interviewed journalists that, as of the spring of 1990, they were not free to criticize the Soviet government directly on matters of foreign affairs.

Finally, all publications demonstrated a shift away from the bipolar view of the past. The invasion of Panama was seen as having little to do directly with the Soviet Union. The world was no longer seen as a zero-sum game between the two dominant superpowers, therefore the actions of the United States did not warrant the attention accorded to previous acts of aggression.

US/ALLY RELATIONS

The portrayal of US relations with its leading Western allies went through subtle but significant changes in the period under consideration. In the beginning of the period, the dominant and consensual image of US/ally relations was that such relations were governed by 'inter-imperialist contradictions'. Market competition meant that the 'three centres of imperialism', the US, Western Europe and Japan, were constantly engaged in conflict in both the economic and political sphere. Although there were occasional bi- and multilateral agreements, the competing powers could rarely work out lasting solutions. Conflict between the different powers was seen to be 'deepening' and, despite gaining valuable resources through the enslavement of the developing world, the international system of capitalism was seen to be heading towards inevitable collapse.[63]

There was not as powerful a consensus on the dynamics of specific bi- and multi-lateral relations between capitalist powers. The dominant picture was America-centric, seen through the bi-polar lens of the battle between the United States and the Soviet Union. America, capitalism's leading power, 'the mother-country of imperialism', was almost invariably seen as a condescending and aggressive protagonist, attempting to pressure its allies into supporting policies which were to its benefit and often their detriment.[64] Economically, the US attempted to force one-sided trade concessions and pressed allies to finance its aggressive foreign policy.[65] Politically, it sought support for an uncompromising anti-Soviet line and 'interfered' in allies' internal affairs.[66] Militarily, it sought co-operation for its aggressive weapons programmes, agitated for permission to place weapons of mass destruction on allied territory and encouraged allies to join in its exploitation of the developing world.[67]

The depiction of the allies in the dynamic of relations with the US varied. By far the most dominant image was that of victim of US machinations. It was a paradoxical image for capitalist rivals of the Soviet Union, but was indicative of the importance of the United States in the Soviet psyche; the overwhelming concern of the Soviet press was its chief enemy, not the 'satellites' of that enemy. Again the intended audience was important. Through the press, the Soviet government attempted to speak to allied governments and citizens,[68] using the image of victimization to implicitly and explicitly encourage them to reject pro-American policies.[69] When allies rebuffed US proposals, the Soviet press acted like a cheerleader, lauding their actions.[70] When they followed US policies, there were a variety of reactions. Often, the allies were depicted as having been bullied by the US into supporting its policies and lacking the will to take another course. In such cases the allies were usually spared the venom directed at the United States, but their leaders were derided and challenged to choose a different path.[71] At times, they were treated more harshly and portrayed as willing co-conspirators, joining the United States because of the common class interests of the ruling elites.[72] Occasionally, they were even shown as protagonists. It should also be pointed out that allies were singled out without reference to the United States for their own actions which were viewed as opposing the Soviet Union and the developing world.[73] However, insofar as the dynamic of inter-capitalist relations was concerned, the United States was almost invariably the main focus.

These images dominated through late 1987 when changes began to appear. The most important changes occurred in the dominant image of 'inter-imperialist contradictions' leading to inevitable conflict and the decline of the capitalist system. With the new evaluation of the viability of capitalism which began to emerge with the Yakovlev articles in May 1987 and Gorbachev's speech in November 1987, competition between capitalist countries was decreasingly viewed as an inevitable and fatal consequence of capitalism. Although 'contradictions' still existed between capitalist powers, their capacity to adjust to modern conditions and to cooperate allowed governments (and their ruling elites) to bridge potential conflicts and to prolong the life of the world capitalist system, perhaps indefinitely.

After the signing of the INF treaty in late 1987 the dynamic of relations changed. Although the United States was still seen as the dominant capitalist power, it was no longer almost automatically seen as the aggressor and source of tension in inter-ally relations. At that point, the evaluation of other capitalist countries became more nuanced, and allies were increasingly depicted as individual actors rather than as objects of American manipulations.

The changes, however, were ultimately limited. Even towards the end of the Gorbachev period, images of American domination were still the most prominent, especially amongst correspondents based in allied countries and the developing world. However, the image of American domination did not prevail as much as it had done in the past. Indeed, press coverage of international issues as a whole began to lose its America-centrism, with increasing coverage devoted to European powers, especially West Germany, and the Soviet Union's former socialist brethren in Southern and East-Central Europe.

GROUP OF SEVEN

The depiction of evolving relations between the United States and
its capitalist allies can be illustrated by examining the evolving press
coverage of the annual meetings of the world's leading capitalist
powers, the Group of Seven (G7). The coverage of the meetings
generally focused on four areas: US/ally relations, Western relations with the Soviet Union, Western relations with the developing
world and the capacity of capitalism to survive.

Coverage of the G7 meetings in May 1985 and 1986 followed
similar patterns. At both meetings, relations between G7 members
were portrayed as conflict-ridden in both the economic and political spheres. Although the meetings were designed to produce 'if
not harmony . . . then restraint in the growth of contradictions',[74]
economic conflict between the leading capitalist countries was seen
to be sharpening. Indeed, because of the nature of imperialism,
and the concomitant inter-imperialist contradictions, conflict was
seen as unavoidable.[75] In assessing the search for solutions to the
economic problems facing the G7, the United States was continually portrayed as both aggressive and dictatorial, and the Europeans
and Japanese as victims. The US encouraged its allies to adopt
reactionary social and economic policies to boost the world capitalist system,[76] imposed unfair trade concessions,[77] and demanded
that allies support its foreign aggression.[78] European leaders were
depicted as being wary of such demands, and were applauded by
the Soviet press for 'successfully repulsing America's diktat'.[79] The
end result, according to the Soviet press, was the failure of the
meetings, largely due to American intransigence.[80]

With economic divisions irreconcilable, the United States searched
for points of compromise elsewhere, the most successful area being anti-communism which was viewed as 'a kind of political cement
whose function is to unite these competitors'.[81] Here again, the
United States was portrayed as aggressive and Europe, and to a
lesser extent Japan, were seen in a more sympathetic light, at least
partially rejecting America's militaristic overtures. The Western
European countries were seen as more amenable to Soviet peace
initiatives.[82] Many also rejected America's SDI proposals and were
thus lauded for their desire to cling to their 'military, political and
economic independence' while refusing to become 'American satellites', and 'subcontractors' of America's military-industrial complex.[83]
The same scenario held true for the developing world; the other

G7 countries were seen to reject the US policy of new-globalism and its unlimited aggression.

The portrayal of US/ally relations at the June 1987 G7 meeting demonstrated continuity with 1985 and 1986 meetings. The United States was still seen as the clear leader of the capitalist world.[84] It remained the biggest obstacle to economic agreements[85] and attempted to inveigle its allies into new militaristic adventures, this time in the Persian Gulf.[86] Most commentators viewed the meeting as another in the long line of failed G7 meetings which would not resolve the ultimate conflicts between the leading capitalist powers: 'The Venice conference . . . represents the same thing as all previous similar meetings of the Western leaders – the irreconcilability of inter-imperialistic contradictions and competition in the battle for markets and political influence.'[87]

There were, however, two areas of subtle change. In the political sphere, there was little criticism directed towards the United States on the subject of US/Soviet relations. In the wake of the INF negotiations, relations with the Soviet Union were singled out as an area of great success.[88] In the economic sphere, there were signs of the first small steps towards the re-evaluation of capitalism and inter-imperialist contradictions. One author noted recent economic growth in several capitalist countries. Although he also indicated that this success was threatened, the piece represented a change from the constant stream of pessimism articulated in the past.[89] More importantly, *Izvestiya*'s Aleksandr Bovin suggested that while meetings could not change capitalism's ultimate fate, they did have the potential to prolong significantly its lasting power.[90] This was an important turn away from the previous focus on the ever-growing contradictions facing the capitalist world. Although he still foresaw the ultimate collapse of capitalism, Bovin's recognition that capitalist countries could group together to effectively (and seemingly indefinitely) delay that collapse was indicative of an emerging re-analysis of capitalism and its capacity to survive. His claims echoed Aleksandr Yakovlev's assertions in May 1987 about capitalism's potential to sustain itself.

The coverage of the G7 meeting in June 1988 marked a key turning-point in the depiction of inter-capitalist relations. It reflected the improvements in East–West relations after the ratification of the INF treaty and the Moscow Summit, and the new evaluation of capitalism emerging after Gorbachev's speech at the LXXth anniversary of the October Revolution.

In a radical departure from the past, none of the papers consulted mentioned inter-imperialist contradictions. On the contrary, the meeting was seen as 'one of the least conflictual' which had ever taken place.[91] Ideas about the sustainability of capitalism, which had previously been only hinted at in coverage of the 1987 meeting, were loudly trumpeted in 1988. Capitalism was no longer seen to be in a state of terminal decline. Instead, it was seen as thriving. Even in the wake of the stock-market crash of October 1987, there was a 'triumphant mood', and 'everyone was happy with the stable situation in the world economy'.[92] Economic growth was up and unemployment was down.[93] Indeed, one writer suggested that, after the difficulties of the 1970s, a 'new stage' in the development of state monopoly capitalism was possibly emerging.[94] Flowing from this, the G7 meetings were in themselves seen in a positive light and viewed as contributing to capitalism's stability.[95]

In terms of the dynamic of inter-ally relations, the United States was no longer portrayed as a predatory protagonist which was attempting to impose policies on its allies. At the same time, the other members of the G7 were no longer presented primarily as victims of America's aggressive policies. Instead, the relationship was seen as one largely conducted between equal partners. Differences of opinion were acknowledged, but they were seen to be only that. The United States was neither singled out for attempting to impose its diktat, nor was it seen as being primarily responsible for existing conflicts.[96]

Relations between the G7 countries and the Soviet Union were also painted in a positive light.The entire atmosphere was 'dominated by optimism' over the agreement between the US and the Soviet Union, with universal support shown for the INF agreement.[97] There were even some signs of positive coverage directed towards the relations between the G7 countries and the developing world, with reports of progress in debt relief for African countries.[98]

If there was a discordant note in the overall positive spin of the meeting, it was in *Sovetskaya Rossiya*. Its reporter continually stressed the downside of events, emphasizing the tremendous security surrounding the meeting, economic problems facing the Seven and American obstinacy and isolation over its refusal to approve the sale of high-technology goods to the Soviet Union. The author was also sceptical of the ultimate results of the meeting. Although he did not speak of inter-imperialist contradictions, the overall sentiment was very negative, distinguishing it from that which appeared in other publications.[99] Many authors had mentioned elements which he referred to, but none had done so in such a concentrated and negative fashion.

The coverage of the July 1989 meeting was not infused with quite as much excitement, the celebrations of the Washington Summit being in the distant past. However, it did not fall back to the level of earlier criticism. Again, there was no mention of inter-imperial contradictions, although some authors spoke of 'inevitable antagonisms', but even then cooperation was stressed. The body was seen to be 'increasingly influential' and acting on the basis of 'consensus and common interests'.[100] *Sovetskaya Rossiya* again offered criticism, but even its author acknowledged that the meeting produced positive and tangible results.[101]

Coverage also reflected the shift away from a strictly bi-polar view of world events. Although there was some discussion of differences of opinion between the G7 countries, the United States was not singled out any more than France or the United Kingdom.[102]

The area where the most significant differences emerged between publications was in their analysis of the dynamic of G7/Soviet relations. Here, the *Izvestiya* authors tended to stress the potential benefits of Soviet cooperation with the G7 and even encouraged possible Soviet membership.[103] *Pravda* writers, on the other hand, highlighted the threat of the meeting. Although not criticizing the Soviet attempt to increase cooperation with the West, its journalists tended to point out the dictatorial approach which the United States in particular took to Soviet initiatives and the threat that success at the meeting represented in terms of creating greater opportunities for Western 'diktat' throughout the world.[104]

CONCLUSION

The depiction of United States' foreign and military policy in the Soviet press changed in the period from March 1985 to July 1990, but changes were uneven, conspicuous in some areas, subtle in others.

An examination of press content suggests that the most obvious area of change was in the language used to describe the United States. The use of evaluative terms central to Soviet ideology, such as imperialist and militarist, declined sharply from the end of 1987 onwards. Concomitantly there was a decrease in ideologically deterministic images and in mechanistic explanations of US foreign policy. This increasingly 'de-ideologized' approach meant that US relations with its allies were no longer portrayed as fundamentally conflictual, resulting from inter-imperialist contradictions. It also meant that by the end of the period, the United States was rarely portrayed as driven to oppress the developing world. It might at times demonstrate 'imperialist thinking', it might revert to an 'imperialist mentality', but it was rarely shown as inherently and uncontrollably militaristic.

A related area of change was in the extreme enemy images which were, according to one analyst, reminiscent of war propaganda. These images, which portrayed the United States as a country whose people dissected poor, innocent children and whose scientists created the AIDS virus, were eliminated. Similarly, images of the United States as insatiable in its drive to oppress the developing world declined. By 1988, the United States was no longer seen as a country intent on world domination; it was no longer the second coming of the Third Reich, as some articles and political cartoons had suggested in 1985 and 1986. The press still pointed to imperialist 'hegemonic' tendencies, especially in relation to the developing world, however the worst and most malevolent images had disappeared.

Towards the end of the period, United States' foreign and military policy was still treated more negatively than positively. However, alternative images of it being a reliable and trustworthy partner also emerged. While prior to INF, the US was alternately described as uncontrollably militaristic or as naturally aggressive, but capable of containing itself, in the post-INF period, especially from late 1988 onwards, it was portrayed alternately as capable of controlling itself and reformed and essentially unmilitaristic. In the final period there was much greater variation, with both critical and positive assessments sometimes appearing in the same publication. In short, while the tendency was towards less harsh criticism, there was no strict line and no consensus as before.

Another important development was the dissipation of the press's obsession with the United States. By the end of the period, the United States had to share more space on the international pages with stories about Eastern Europe, Europe, Africa and Asia. Competition between the United States and the Soviet Union was no longer seen to be the axis upon which world politics turned. Although the United States was still the single most important actor, America-centrism dissipated. Indeed, some publications did not even cover its 1989 invasion of Panama, something unthinkable a few years earlier.

In explaining why changes in press coverage occurred, we must look first to changes in Party policy. When the Party said that the Soviet press would stop spreading disinformation, charges dwindled, then stopped. When the Party leadership questioned the link between imperialism and militarism, the use of those terms declined sharply. When the Party called for the end of the enemy image, many of the most hostile images ceased. When government statements concerning US aggression in the developing world used less ideological terminology, so did the press's descriptions of US actions. Conversely, when the government grew particularly hostile after the Reykjavik Summit's failure, the press followed suit.

This is not to say that through the end of the period, the press blindly followed the government and the Party. A key defining factor in the period was the Party's loss of focus concerning the United States. Although no longer the chief enemy in the ideological war, it was still not a close ally. This meant the position concerning the United States was vague and that the area of legitimate controversy was wider.

With this freedom, publications moved in different directions. *Moscow News* largely refused to criticize the United States, most likely because that would have interfered with its domestic, pro-market line. *Argumenty i Fakty* did the same, although this was probably in part because of its overwhelming concentration on domestic events. *Izvestiya* often stressed the positive, but contained a wide variety of perspectives. *Pravda* also voiced different views, but its authors tended towards the negative. *Sovetskaya Rossiya* took this a step further. Although it did not devote a substantial amount of press coverage to the United States, that which it did devote was invariably amongst the most hostile. *Sovetskaya Rossiya* also voiced criticism of government policy in relation to the United States. Nonetheless, it is important to note that even in early 1990, criticism was still veiled. Sufficient controlling mechanisms remained so that the press was still not free in its evaluations.

7 Images of Domestic America

> Uncritically held, the stereotype not only censors out much that needs to be taken into account, but when the day of reckoning comes, and the stereotype is shattered, likely as not that which it did wisely take into account is ship-wrecked with it.
>
> Walter Lippmann[1]

In this Chapter I will explore changes in Soviet press images of domestic America[2] in the Gorbachev era and attempt to explain why those changes occurred in specific periods.

The main questions to be addressed include: How were changes in the portrayal of domestic America manifested in the Soviet press? When did significant changes occur? How were changes in press content related to changes in leadership policy? To what extent were there differences between reporters and publications and what does this say about the government's control of press coverage of domestic America?

SOVIET PRESS AND DOMESTIC AMERICA

Prior to the Gorbachev period, the Soviet press was governed by one overriding criterion in its approach to the United States: it had to portray the superiority of socialism and the socialist system over capitalism.[3] This demonstrated to the Soviet population that their Communist rulers provided for them comparatively well, while justifying the Party's continued leadership in spite of its failure to bring about the promised utopia. Negative images of the West also served what can be called a negative-didactic function, that is, they taught Soviet citizens to be critical of Western values and practices, particularly those which might lead them to question the Soviet system.

A second but by no means unimportant role for the press was to demonstrate the inherent militaristic nature of American leaders and American society, particularly their rabid anti-Sovietism. This was designed to create fear amongst Soviet people and support for leaders and the Party which protected the Soviet Union from the external threat.

In part because of these requirements, coverage of the West, particularly the United States, was one of the most closely controlled areas of the Soviet press. In her work on *Novy Mir*, Spechler pointed out that in spite of the publication's special role in the 1950s and 1960s as a purveyor of 'permitted dissent', it was 'not at liberty to praise Western capitalism, democracy or social democracy or even Yugoslav self-management'.[4] Indeed, even neutrality on the subject exposed the journal to harsh criticism. For example, during the 'thaw' in the Khrushchev period, an article about a reporter's trip to the United States which appeared in *Novy Mir* resulted in strong attacks on the author and journal from *Izvestiya* and *Komsomol'skaya Pravda*, newspapers known at the time for their relative liberalism.[5] The *Izvestiya* writer criticized the author for the 'fifty-fifty method', claiming that the article could lead to 'declaring and confirming peaceful coexistence in the sphere of ideology'. He wondered how the author could 'fail to see the sharp social contradictions in American lifestyle and the war psychosis fanned by imperialist circles'. Concluding, he pointed out that 'The crux of the matter is not (the author's) factual errors, but the thoughtless and untrue generalizations and parallels which lead to bourgeois objectivism and sterile descriptive methods which distort reality.'[6]

If that was the situation in a 'liberal' period for the Soviet press, one could imagine the restrictions in a conservative period. Indeed, in the 1980s, with the war of ideas reaching a post-Stalin high, Shlapentokh claimed that the Soviet press was permeated with 'war propaganda,' which suggested that the leadership was conditioning the Soviet public for the real possibility of nuclear war for the first time since the Second World War.[7] Under such conditions, even vague neutrality was unacceptable.

In order to cover as many subjects as possible, yet give direction to the study of the Gorbachev period, three categories emblematic of press approaches will be addressed: *demonization*, *humanization* and *affirmative-didacticism*. Within these categories, a number of subjects will be addressed: culture and society, socio-economics, human rights, and politics.

DEMONIZATION

Demonization refers to the use of language, symbols and images which depict a group as aggressive, physically menacing and threatening to the values and norms of the demonizing group, which instil fear and create negative emotions, and which therefore legitimate any action, internal or external, to protect the demonizing group from the demonized.[8] From the start of the Gorbachev period, the Soviet press demonized American culture, society and its economic and political systems.

Press coverage of American culture and society was dominated by images of ignorance, militarism and hate. The American people were seen as war-mongering; many would be 'glad to see a war as early as today'.[9] Rambo was viewed as the archetypal hero of American mass culture. Americans flocked to movies which demonstrated 'pathological brutality' and 'glorified war' and listened to music which applauded nuclear weapons.[10] American literature was suited to market conditions, and thus, with few exceptions, was dominated by 'commercial-conformist' works which were indicative of 'the impoverished inner world of the individual in bourgeois society'.[11] Americans who saw such movies and read such literature were desensitized to the outside world. They knew little about the Soviet Union, especially compared with Soviet knowledge of America. Many thought that Hitler was Russian and did not know that America had been the first country to use the atomic bomb.[12] Violent social manifestations were spreading among the American masses, especially since the election of Ronald Reagan.[13] Naziism, a particularly sensitive subject to Soviets, was portrayed as rising, as was discrimination and racial hatred.[14]

America's depraved culture and society were depicted as products of the ruthless nature of the capitalist system and machinations of the ruling elite. Competition fostered by capitalism, unemployment and the division between rich and poor meant that in America 'violence and crime are inalienable attributes of life'.[15] On top of that, media-owning military corporations and an anti-Soviet administration cooperated to foment 'hate of the outside world', particularly the Soviet Union and its socialist allies.[16]

Although the Soviet leadership claimed that it harboured no ill will towards the American people, as opposed to the ruling elite, this was self-deluding, at least as far as propaganda images can be considered an expression of such sentiments.[17] Although the American people were seen as the unfortunate victims of capitalist society and bourgeois propaganda, they were also depicted as ignorant, violent and supportive of the militaristic policies of the ruling elite. Even Soviet writers who in 1988 and 1989 would be seen as leading beacons of perestroika and US/Soviet cooperation were, in 1985 and 1986, merciless in their criticism.[18]

The image of militarism and violence was not universal; countervailing messages, meaning competing communications which resulted in apparent contradictions, did show another side of America. In most cases, countervailing messages were produced by competing policy goals, such as the desire to depict America as a fundamentally militaristic society, yet to show at the same time the attractiveness of the Soviet Union for educated Americans. Thus, for example, there were frequent references to 'progressive circles' which, in spite of the evils of capitalism and the machinations of the ruling elite, resisted the temptations of capitalism and militarism and were actively opposed to the policies of American leaders. This well-educated group was portrayed as being particularly interested in the Soviet Union and supportive of Soviet peace initiatives.[19] Similarly, countervailing messages emerged over contending desires to portray American ignorance and yet to convey that the Soviet Union was an important world actor. Thus, for example, a *Pravda* claim that a 1986 Mikhail Gorbachev speech became 'the center of attention' in America and was covered 'in great detail (by) American radio and television networks', was contradicted two days later by an author who complained about the closed nature of American society, as demonstrated by the US government's sharp restrictions on the dissemination of Gorbachev's speech.[20] Countervailing messages did not undermine the dominant image of an ignorant, militaristic and uncultured society: they simply underline the crude approach to propaganda in the Soviet Union.

Like American culture, the US socio-economic system was demonized. Socio-economic system primarily refers to what the Soviet press called human rights, which consist of economic rights (rights to tangible items, such as clothes and shelter, and labour-related rights, particularly the right to work and to do so in safe conditions for fair wages) and social rights (rights which entail due process, like the right to a fair trial, and the right to live unencumbered by race, religious or gender discrimination). Socio-economics also includes business and business and managerial practices.

The American socio-economic system was continually portrayed as cruel, merciless and inhumane. As far as economic-oriented rights were concerned, the Reagan Administration was described as the 'the most anti-worker . . . in the post-war period'.[21] Homelessness and unemployment were continual foci of attention, found under captions such as: 'The Land of Violated Rights', 'Labour and Capital' and 'Behind the Facade of the Free World'. Pensioners could barely secure a living.[22]

Socially oriented rights were also addressed in a hyper-critical manner. There were frequent charges of government-led violence, racism and discrimination against women and minorities.[23] The Reagan Administration was portrayed as the most racist since the Second World War.[24] Its attitudes were even compared to those of the Ku Klux Klan and it was implied that the administration supported Klan activity.[25] The judicial system was portrayed as cruel and insensitive, especially regarding 'progressive forces' who were fighting for peace.[26] Criticism of unjust legal practices was frequently accompanied by revelations about American 'political prisoners'.[27] There were sometimes even articles about alleged American concentration camps.[28]

The general arguments were augmented by vignettes of the suffering of individual Americans. One interesting press campaign surrounded the plight of the supposed vagrant Joseph Mauri, who was seen as a victim of America's capitalist exploitation. Mauri was featured in dozens of articles in *Pravda*, *Izvestiya* and *Argumenty i Fakty*, and eventually visited the Soviet Union in September 1986.[29]

Even more attention was devoted to hunger-striking American doctor Charles Hyder whose plight served as proof of the ruling elite's willingness to commit the ultimate human-rights violation, to let a citizen die. His 100+-day hunger strike for nuclear disarmament, held opposite the White House in early 1987, was reported with a fervour which almost certainly reflected post-Reykjavik disappointment. In a short period, *Pravda* devoted no less than 25 major articles to Hyder, *Izvestiya* 21 and *Moscow News* four.[30] Ironically, a great deal of effort was put into a most implausible story. Many reporters asked retrospectively about Hyder were embarrassed and bitter about the press campaign and rather sceptical of Hyder's capacity to live for so long without food.[31] But at the time, the ideological war took precedence over veracity.

The sensitivity of Soviet journalists to Western accusations of human rights violations was clearly evident in the press. In keeping with the demands of the war of ideas, the Soviet press consistently rebuffed 'hypocritical' Western charges of human rights violations and counterattacked with mirror-image claims of American violations. In practically every issue *Argumenty i Fakty* rebutted claims of Soviet human rights violations raised by the Voice of America and United States Information Agency journal *America*, and launched counter accusations about human rights violations in the US.[32] This approach of rebuff and counterattack was well illustrated by a *Pravda* writer, who claimed that 'It is incomprehensible that the spiritual successors of negro-lynchers and organizers of genocide in regard to Indians would speak of "human rights", those who throw their poorest citizens out on the street even in the middle of winter and deny millions of Americans the right to work.'[33]

The attention devoted to countering Western claims is important for evaluating the overall portrayal of the American socio-economic system. While there were some manufactured stories in the Soviet press, most of the Soviet claims were factually based. Unemployment, homelessness and discrimination all existed. Moreover, it is almost certainly true that there were prisoners held in the US jails on the basis of fabricated or misinterpreted evidence. The problem with the Soviet approach was one of emphasis. The point is not that the Soviet press addressed these issues, but that it addressed them to the exclusion of other, more positive elements of American life. The image of America was thus gravely distorted. Such a conclusion is buttressed by Soviet journalists who complained later in the period that they were tired of writing exclusively about unemployment and homelessness.[34]

The vitriol directed at America's political system was even more poignant than that associated with culture and socio-economics. Through the middle of 1988, the American political system was largely shown in a uniformly negative manner. It was continually portrayed as undemocratic, controlled by a narrow class of elites.[35] The Reagan administration was singled out alternately as being part of, or led by, the most right-wing and militaristic fringe of this elite.[36] It was thus the object of never-ending vitriol. There were relatively few articles which discussed in any detail the mechanics of the system and how it functioned. Those which did gave rather unsavoury portraits of some of the more controversial and obviously less democratic elements of the system, such as political action committees and lobbies.[37]

There were some variations between reporters on the internal machinations of the elite. While in some cases, these were the product of subtleties in the interpretation of state-monopoly capitalism,[38] they were more often produced by countervailing messages. However, in spite of these differences, if one is talking about the overall portrayal of the US political system, the dominant image was that of a fundamentally undemocratic system. There may have been differences within the elite, but it was an elite which ruled. The public had little sway over policy.[39] Moreover, the American elite was singled out for its particularly cruel actions at home and abroad.[40] The attitude was summed up well in a statement by a *Pravda* commentator concerning the Iran–Contra affair, 'The actions of the present Washington administration ... have once again confirmed the truth that the notorious bourgeois democracy is nothing more than a cover which the ruling clique hides behind as it commits acts of tyranny and violence in domestic and foreign policy.'[41]

The depiction became even more harsh in the wake of the failed Reykjavik Summit when Gorbachev asserted that the military-industrial complex (MIC) dictated the Reagan administration's policies, preventing progress in negotiations.[42] All of the publications consulted supported the themes set out by the General Secretary, with *Argumenty i Fakty* devoting practically an entire double-issue to the MIC immediately after the Reykjavik failure.[43] Such images would continue to dominate until the emergence of humanization and affirmative-didacticism in the political sphere.

HUMANIZATION

Humanization emerged in response to the acceleration of internal reform in the Soviet Union and in the wake of the INF treaty and calls for a lessening of psychological tensions between the Superpowers. In the context of identity, humanization refers to the diminution of hostility and aggression associated with extreme cases of differential bonding. In the public sphere, it suggests the emergence of a discourse which is largely devoid of the hate language that can create enemy images and therefore legitimate violence against internal and external opponents. The practical implication for Soviet press coverage of the United States was a reduction of traditional critical and evaluative terms and a de-emphasis of once ubiquitous subjects such as militarism, violence, poverty and the violation of human rights. Articles increasingly appeared which were devoid of derogatory phraseology and which presented information that depicted the Soviet Union as being behind the United States in a number of important socio-economic categories, something unheard of even a few years earlier.[44]

In the cultural sphere, humanization began to emerge in the beginning of 1987. One of the first articles suggesting change was written by *Pravda*'s New York correspondent Vladimir Sukhoi in March 1987 about New York City's Rockefeller Center. In the article, Sukhoi was complimentary about the Center's appearance and described its history and the type of business being conducted in the complex. Most significantly, he made several references to the complex's residents, including Chase Manhattan Bank and NBC television, without evoking the evils of monopoly capitalism or the American mass media.[45] Sukhoi's article not only differed from those of other authors in the same period, who in describing similar phenomena were unequivocally hostile (for example, in that period *Pravda* editor Viktor Afanas'ev decried as 'human rights – American style' the New York City subway, where people are 'unceremoniously murdered, robbed and raped . . .'[46]), but it also differed from articles he had written a few months earlier which disparaged America's poverty, unemployment, homelessness and its citizens' lust for money.[47]

Although other articles taking de-ideologized approaches to American culture appeared at the time,[48] they were still relatively rare, and surrounded by criticism. However, following leadership calls for the end of the enemy image and the de-ideologization of interstate relations which occurred in the wake of the INF treaty, the press increasingly presented American culture without undercurrents of ideological criticism.

Emblematic of the humanization process was an article about the pop-star Madonna which appeared in *Pravda* in September 1987. The article, 'Kto eta devchonka?', a translation of her popular album 'Who's That Girl?', focused on Madonna's personality and her niche in American popular culture. Absent was meaningful criticism of the social context of the Madonna phenomenon and generalizations about Western culture. There was not even a reference to her self-proclaimed status as a 'material girl', a characterization which in the past would have begged criticism of Western bourgeois values.[49]

The less critical approach to American culture, particularly pop-culture, was witnessed increasingly from the middle of 1988 onwards. *Izvestiya* had non-critical biographies of American stars Michael Douglas, Ray Charles, Tom Cruise, Sylvester Stallone and Lawrence Kasden.[50] *Pravda* carried articles on Greta Garbo, Elvis, the Woodstock rock festival, the Academy Awards (or 'Oscars'), the renaissance of Broadway, Chicago Blues and life on the stock-car circuit.[51] *Argumenty i Fakty*, which began to present more facts than arguments, gave a very informative account of the participation of American super-stars in advertisements, ran a piece on America's Public Broadcasting System and had sensational accounts of the Playboy empire and the life of pornography star John Holmes.[52] It even ran a descriptive piece on the rights and obligations of soldiers serving in the American armed forces.[53]

The scope of change extended beyond popular culture, into accounts of American society and the American way of life. Whereas previously society, and the individuals and groups which constitute it, was regularly depicted as reflecting malevolent social forces engendered in the capitalist system, from the middle of 1987 onwards the ideological prism was often retracted. American citizens were increasingly presented in the multiple shades which constitute humanity, not as social puppets shaped by scientific laws.

This change was best captured by *Pravda*'s New York correspondent Viktor Linnik in an article exploring American leisure activities. That his approach was different from the past was made clear in his introduction when he implicitly criticized previous Soviet interpretations, stating, 'I have long thought that not all New Yorkers spend their time creating surplus values, going to protest demonstrations or electing presidents. Sometimes it is necessary to live for yourself.' The heart of the article described the life of New Yorkers. One pastime was going to restaurants, which Linnik described as fitting different budgets and not having queues (an important consideration for the *Pravda* reader accustomed to the difficulties of Soviet restaurants). Movies were another option which young Americans, like young Soviets, preferred. Other, more 'spiritual' activities enjoyed by New Yorkers included going to museums and exhibitions and visiting Broadway. The New York Public Library system was also singled out for its quality and accessibility.[54]

Linnik clearly intended to show a different, non-politicized side of America. Americans were presented as people, not objects of social forces. Moreover, the comparisons between average American and Soviet citizens, both explicit and implicit, were important, because they made Americans more life-like, more real.

A number of other articles in a similar vein appeared, all of which presented less ideologized views of Americans. There were further explorations of Americans' free time, including independent examinations of favourite pastimes, like exercise, bingo and attending flea markets.[55] A number of articles examined the experience of Americans in different geographic regions, like Alaska and small-town New England, and of social and religious groupings, like the Amish.[56] An article by a *Pravda* correspondent about Halloween formed a great contrast with an ideologically charged piece that the same author had written two years earlier about Thanksgiving.[57] An article on the city of Atlanta was interesting not only because it lacked criticism of racism and other ills traditionally found in Soviet press accounts of Southern US cities,[58] but because the city and its people were praised as 'enterprising, ambitious, businesslike and energetic'. Only Soviet trade representatives who ignored the city were criticized![59]

The shift in the war of ideas and a more sober view of America brought the Soviet reality into a more succinct comparison with its ideological adversary. The comparison was often not flattering. In 1987, for example, *Argumenty i Fakty*, a journal which was once the most committed to the 'war of ideas',[60] ran a series of articles which juxtaposed Soviet life expectancy with that of other countries. The figures were bleak; while the average life-span in the Soviet Union was only 69 (64 years for men and 73 years for women), the US average was 75 years (71 years for men and 78 years for women).[61] The subject was clearly delicate: life-expectancy figures for Western countries were presented only after a letter to the editor requested the information, a technique used to protect the newspaper from potential criticism. Moreover, the figures for the Soviet Union were printed in a different issue, meaning that readers had to compare issues in order to understand the gap.

Later in the perestroika period, however, the comparisons became more transparent and commonplace, particularly in reference to economic and socio-economic issues. Probably the most significant articles were written by Aleksandr Zaichenko of the Institute of US/Canada Studies. They appeared in *Moscow News* and *Argumenty i Fakty*.[62]

In the introduction to the *Moscow News* article, Zaichenko indicated his new approach to information, stressing, 'I think that the naked truth and honest comparisons (even if not favorable) are much more useful to the grand endeavor we have undertaken than the standard clichés which only eclipse the problems.'[63] He then illustrated the Soviet Union's low standard of living, primarily by comparing it to the United States. Not only did he speak of the Soviet Union's low industrial productivity, low wages and high cost of food and housing, but he also pointed out that by the mid-1970s state spending on social needs (including education, health care and social security) was lower as a share of national income than in the United States. Although he mentioned some problems related to income distribution in the United States, the overall image was that of a prosperous country versus a poor one. Even the editors acknowledged the significance of what was stated by adding a note at the end of the article stating that this was not 'the final word', but could 'serve to overcome dogmatic obstructions, which we must do if we are to come any nearer to the truth'.[64]

The article in *Argumenty i Fakty* was even more critical of Soviet reality. Based on Zaichenko's own formula of income, access to goods and consumption, he concluded that while in the US, 3 per cent of the population was rich, 17 per cent well-to-do, 60 per cent middle class and 20 per cent poor, in the Soviet Union 2.3 per cent was rich, 11.2 per cent middle class and 86.5 per cent poor.[65] Although the article was rebutted a few weeks later by someone using a different measure, the conclusion about the wealth of Soviet citizens remained bleak (the new figures placed the Soviet Union at 7.1 per cent upper class, 31.3 per cent middle class and 61.1 per cent lower class).[66]

The Zaichenko articles, and others focusing on everything from living standards to automobile production,[67] illustrate the collapse of the war of ideas. It is difficult to imagine that even the most militant cold warrior could present figures more gloomy than those of Zaichenko. If anything, the primary enemy for him and other authors appears to have been Soviet socialism. While the articles might have served to justify further reform, it is doubtful that even a reforming leadership could have desired the publication of such bleak figures. They left more a sense of doom than of hope.

Another critical area of humanization emerged in the press's approach to the most critical of issues: human rights violations. Although charges actually increased after the Reykjavik failure, from

Table 7.1   Major articles accusing United States of human rights violations[68]

Period	Average Articles per Year		Change vs. First Period	
	Pravda	*Izvestiya*	*Pravda*	*Izvestiya*
5/85–12/86[69]	52	44	–	–
1/87–8/87	70	60	+25%	+26%
9/87–5/88	22	10	–58%	–77%
7/88–7/90	14	07	–73%	–84%

the INF accord onwards the number of accusations decreased significantly. By the end of the period, accusations of human rights violations in *Pravda* and *Izvestiya* decreased respectively by 73 per cent and 84 per cent *vis-à-vis* the beginning of the Gorbachev period.

A few important phenomena not highlighted by Table 7.1 should be noted. Beyond the overall decrease in the number of articles containing accusations of human rights violations, the qualitative nature of accusations changed, becoming less hostile and cliché-ridden and more analytical.[70] Authors attempted to capture previously ignored nuances, such as racism between minority groups.[71] One author in *Moscow News* went further, lauding Western approaches to human rights while lambasting those of the Soviet Union. The author not only attacked as 'bankrupt' the traditional Soviet emphasis on economic as opposed to social rights, but also claimed that the West, particularly America, maintained a more just economic system. In the West, an individual was 'free to take care of himself', while in the Soviet Union, the state 'denied the people the right to provide for themselves, denied them the right to enterprise and hence the right to fend for themselves'.[72]

It is also worth noting that towards the end of the period, material criticizing American human rights violations tended to appear in the form of letters written from abroad or in articles extracted from foreign journals. This was especially the case in *Pravda*, where just under a quarter of the articles were of foreign origin.[73] Previously, articles and letters on such topics written by foreigners were rare, statistically insignificant. The use of foreigners to articulate once common criticisms reflects the perceived need to legitimate such accusations in the face of the dwindling credibility of Soviet authors, and perhaps fear on some editors' part of contradicting the general trend of de-ideologizing press coverage of the United States.

So great was the presumption against Soviet writers accusing America of human rights violations that in 1989, *Pravda* commentator Andrei Lyutyi felt the need to justify his article about the anniversary of the 'Wilmington Ten,' a racially charged case in North Carolina which began 18 years earlier. In writing about the case, Lyutyi admitted that he feared 'possible reproaches from readers' who would ask 'Why dawdle in the past?' or point to Soviet violations of human rights in the 'period of stagnation'. While Lyutyi justified his article, claiming that 'the violation of constitutional rights and the forgery of political processes did not disappear in the United States after (the Wilmington Ten)', the fact that he felt the need to defend himself is indicative of the radical nature of change.[74]

Humanization even found its way into coverage of the American political system. Two articles on lobbies, one written in June 1986, the other in October 1988, illustrate this development. The author of the 1986 article claimed that lobbyists 'go around essential laws and by hook or by crook attain privileges for their clients for which they have absolutely no right', and asserted that they constituted the fourth branch of government, 'the closest of all to the roots of real power – the monopolies'.[75] By 1988, however, a different direction was taken. The author criticized past approaches, claiming that it would be an 'over-simplification' to reduce the lobbying process to a means of 'supporting the interests of the military-industrial complex'. He then offered a more thoughtful interpretation, capturing many of the contradictory characteristics of the lobby system. For example, while corporate lobbyists were accorded significant power, they were not presented as being omnipotent. If anything, the author understated their influence. Moreover, he placed a great deal of stress on the role of newer lobbyists 'born from the social movements of the 1960s' who supported citizen-oriented issues. He also explained many of the practical functions of the lobby system and the safeguards designed to limit indiscretions such as bribery.[76] The article clearly reflected the move away from slogan-ridden material towards that which presented a more complex world and simultaneously a greater amount of information. The real mark on the political sphere, however, was in the sphere of affirmative-didacticism.

AFFIRMATIVE-DIDACTICISM

Affirmative-didacticism refers to the use of positive portrayals of political, social and economic phenomena so as to promote specific political outcomes. Understood in Gramscian terms, it entails the use of words and symbols to organize consent.[77] In the Soviet context, affirmative-didacticism entails the use of favorable images of the United States to promote the perestroika reform programme and its new vision of Soviet political, economic and social order. On one level, it refers to specific American practices and institutions which might be emulated in the Soviet Union. On another level, it refers to the use of positive images of the United States to reshape debate in the Soviet Union about the benefits of reform by demonstrating to the Soviet population the benefits of economic liberalization and political democratization associated with perestroika. In other words, it refers to both a teaching tool and the creation of incentives designed to produce popular support for reform.

The Soviet press always served a didactic function. However, as stated above, images of the West traditionally played what can be called a negative-didactic role, that is, they showed the Soviet population what they should reject, namely bourgeois-democracy and its malignant society and culture. During the Gorbachev period, however, everything was turned on its head. Instead of the United States representing what the Soviet Union should not be, the US increasingly served as a model for change.

The concept of affirmative-didacticism was not totally new. In previous periods, particularly during NEP and Khrushchev's general secretaryship, American managerial methods and technical approaches were held up as examples from which much could be learned. However, in evaluating the changes which began to appear in early 1987, three factors should be considered. First, the initial affirmative-didactic articles stood out because of the hyper-critical press coverage which surrounded them. In the first years of the Gorbachev period, *Pravda, Izvestiya, Moscow News, Argumenty i Fakty* and *Literaturnaya Rossiya*, simply did not have major affirmative-didactic articles. They might have contained occasional general-interest articles on scientific breakthroughs or a vague commentary on learning from Americans in the context of US/Soviet cultural exchanges, but even these materials appeared rarely. Such was the state of ideological competition that even specialty journals were extremely limited in their capacity to portray any aspect of the United States in a positive manner.[78] Second, with time, the context of affirmative-didacticism changed. While previously affirmative-didactic articles would contain or would be surrounded by ideologically couched criticism of the United States and claims of the impending 'crisis of capitalism', in the Gorbachev period, particularly after the re-evaluation of capitalism began in 1987, this was no longer the case. This gave affirmative-didacticism entirely new implications. It was not simply borrowing from a system on the verge of collapse, it was learning from a system which apparently had the capacity to survive and was thriving, certainly in comparison with socialism. Third, the scope of affirmative-didacticism in the Gorbachev era ultimately extended beyond that of earlier periods. Particularly towards the end of 1988 and in 1989 and 1990, affirmative-didactic articles appeared frequently and addressed issues which previously would have been deemed ideologically unacceptable. In the late Gorbachev period, America was not only a source of learning on subjects such as managerial techniques and scientific and technical methods, but it began to serve as a model for more fundamental concerns like political institutions and property relationships. That was exactly what Ideology Secretary Vadim Medvedev called for in October of 1988 when he said that the Soviet Union should not simply learn from the West's scientific and technical achievements, but from 'the many forms of the organization of public life'.[79]

The first affirmative-didactic articles which appeared in the popular press during the Gorbachev period focused primarily on economic issues related to production, management and service. The innovative nature of such articles, which began to appear in 1987, was underlined by the timid way in which they first appeared. For example, in one of the first affirmative-didactic articles found in *Pravda*, a US-based correspondent proposed that the Soviet Union produce a flexible ladder which he found in a store in New York. The climate was such that even such a seemingly harmless idea could not be put forward without some form of equivocation. The author was thus forced to make some reference to Soviet achievements, stating, 'After all, we probably have test models of such structures or even better ones. Our people have long had a knack for such inventions.' Nonetheless, he concluded that if this was not the case there would be 'nothing shameful in borrowing it'.[80]

Often, the earliest articles which addressed American successes did not suggest explicitly that the Soviet Union should borrow from

American experience. However, the message was still clear. One particularly interesting article, which appeared in July 1987, addressed the efficiency of the American Automobile Association (AAA) in assisting stranded motorists.[81] The innovation was that the suggestion to borrow from American experience came not from the reporter, but from a reader who wrote in a letter to the editor several weeks later: 'After becoming familiar with the material (about the AAA) the following suggestion came to me: what if we in the Soviet Union had a unified organization for repair services? I think that my suggestion would find resonance and support from all of the owners of auto-transport.'[82]

Letters did not appear by chance. Like articles, they served a purpose. *Pravda* received several hundred thousand letters-to-the-editor annually and those were augmented by others written by staff members who were responsible for 'organizing' letter-writing campaigns.[83] In this case the letter offered legitimacy to the growing movement within the popular press to demonstrate means of borrowing from the United States. In taking such an approach, the editors suggested that the demand to apply American experience to the Soviet Union originated from the Soviet people thus shielding themselves from critics who might have objected to borrowing from the ideological enemy.

As the Gorbachev period continued, the stream of affirmative-didactic articles grew. Most buttressed the broader goals of the leadership for 'radical economic reform' and, from June 1987, the 'socialist market'. They addressed issues like product design, management techniques, product guarantees, research and development, the use of modern technology in production, the advantages of express mail delivery networks and the benefits of American pension practices.[84] Some discussed more specific business and production issues, such as methods of selling and preserving books and the use of chemical additives in farming.[85]

Many also pertained to social and cultural issues of interest to the Soviet readership, such as treatment in abortion clinics and cleanliness and hygiene in restaurants.[86] Some addressed public and semi-public concerns, including the US national parks and forestry system, health-care, access to archival and public information, and support for the theatre.[87]

An article on New York's Metropolitan Opera by *Izvestiya*'s New York correspondent Alexander Shal'nev was particularly instructive about the nature of affirmative-didacticism. Shal'nev praised the performances and the company, describing it as 'one of the greatest in the world'. He discussed the various sources of income which sustained the Met while stressing that it is not dependent on government handouts. Most importantly, he compared the accessibility of the Met favourably with that of the Bolshoi, contrasting the Met's free 'Concerts in the Park', cheap tickets and orderly distribution system with the Bolshoi's culture for the privileged and its corrupt ticketing procedures which favoured foreigners with hard currency and the well-connected. Shal'nev ended succinctly: 'So, what is the conclusion?, asks the reader. The conclusion is simple: we have no monopoly on the concern of bringing art nearer to the people and we can learn from others in order that slogans get turned into deeds.'[88]

The article is interesting for three interrelated reasons. First, in criticizing the Soviet cultural establishment, Shal'nev used American experience and its apparent success to legitimate his argument. Without a counter-example, the criticism might have rung hollow. Second, Shal'nev did not simply describe the capitalist system, he painted it as being more just towards its population than the Soviet socialist system. Finally and most importantly, in relying on American experience to support his argument, Shal'nev created an image which was perhaps more flattering than real. For example, he implied that attending the Met was relatively inexpensive, costing between $35–$40 or roughly the cost of two hard-back books or six movie tickets. However, this misrepresented real costs to the Soviet reader because of the relatively inexpensive price of books and movies in the Soviet Union. Certainly forty dollars would have been a considerable price for most Americans to pay for a concert. Unfortunately, such intricacies might have taken away from Shal'nev's goal of using US experience to attack the Soviet establishment. This was indicative of both the symbolic power of the United States and the degree to which the image of the United States was changing.

The plethora of affirmative-didactic articles also addressed a wide variety of political subjects, such as professionalism and ethical standards for legislators, the role of local governments, civil service training, means of adjudication of complaints against the government and government officials, and the mobilization of state resources to respond to natural disasters, particularly earthquakes. There was even an article about the training academy of the oft-derided FBI.[89]

POLITICS OF AFFIRMATIVE-DIDACTICISM

A critical element of the affirmative-didactic phenomenon was the degree to which such articles were woven into the fabric of political debate about internal Soviet policies. Often, they played roles in propaganda or discussion campaigns, that is 'devices to illuminate goals of the leadership over a defined period, a period culminating in the adoption of a final draft of a document, such as a law or a resolution'.[90] In other words, they were used in a utilitarian fashion in order to support specific government policies. They would appear just before or just after a policy was announced, but always in support of the party/government line.

Many of the articles supported economic reform. For example, a 1988 article on the Archer Daniels Midland Corporation, a major American agro-industrial giant, offered implicit support for agricultural reform envisioned in the Law on Cooperatives, which had just been proposed and was being debated in the Supreme Soviet.[91] The author lauded the scope of managerial initiative, the 'astounding' range of maize and soya products, and a computerization process which assures 'a level of efficiency such that there is no waste of raw material'. He concluded by pointing out that the use of soya protein in animal feed helped America produce 20 per cent more meat per cow than in the Soviet Union.[92]

The article also fit in with many of the arguments put forward in the theses for the XIXth Party Conference which were published on the same day. Thesis Two highlighted the need for 'meeting the Soviet people's demand for foodstuffs' and stressed the need for 'better economic management'. Thesis Three addressed the need for 'scientific and technological progress'. Thesis Nine called for the 'self-motivated, creative participation by working people in the development of initiative and self-management.'[93]

A number of other articles addressed issues which were clearly pertinent to legislation promoting economic reform. *Pravda*'s Vladimir Sukhoi wrote a piece on New York's Hunts Point cooperative meat, fruit and vegetable market which fit in perfectly with newly published legislation on cooperatives.[94] He followed this with glowing articles about successful fish and cranberry cooperatives.[95] On the eve of a special Central Committee meeting on Agriculture, *Izvestiya* published an article written by a Soviet farmer which not only praised superior American agricultural methods, but also different forms of American ownership, particularly leasing.[96] An article on forms of ownership in the United States which highlighted the superiority and democratic nature of such ownership appeared in *Izvestiya* just prior to Supreme Soviet discussions on property.[97] In each case, the United States' system was presented as superior to that which existed in the Soviet Union and as a model which, if not to be adopted wholesale, had much which would be useful. No greater difference from previously dominant demonization could be imagined.

If economic methods and practices were the subject of most of the publicity campaigns featuring affirmative-didactic articles on the United States, articles addressing political issues were the most poignant. It was far easier to borrow a specific managerial or production method than to borrow from a political system which had always been portrayed as little more than a façade for repression. Indeed, the sensitivity to accusations that political reform might compromise core Communist values was such that when the reform process began in 1987, a *Pravda* editorial stated clearly, 'What is happening today is no convergence, but a widening of the chasm between socialist democracy and the dictatorship of monopoly capitalism, which adroitly conceals its character behind a vocabulary of democracy.'[98] However, as the political reform process accelerated after Gorbachev's speech at the XIXth Party Conference in which he called for the 'fundamental reform of the political system',[99] the directed use of the United States as a means of legitimating reform became a prominent theme in the Soviet press.

Perhaps the most vivid example of the use of affirmative-didacticism to promote political reform occurred in late 1988, when the decision was made to create a new legislative body, the Congress of People's Deputies, which would in turn elect a reified Supreme Soviet. The decision was followed by two articles which focused on the concept of checks and balances and the system of separation of powers.

Traditionally the Soviet popular press had dismissed the concept of separation of powers, treating it as a part of the artifice behind which the ruling classes exercised unlimited control over the American polity.[100] However, in November 1988 the concept of checks and balances gained currency in the Soviet Union when Mikhail Gorbachev made his first public reference in support of such a system not long after the old Supreme Soviet approved the programme for political reform.[101] His endorsement, however, did not appear in a vacuum.[102] The ground had been prepared in part through affirmative-didacticism.

Until 1988, the popular press only mentioned the concept of separation of powers in passing.[103] However, just prior to Gorbachev's comments the two articles on separation of powers appeared.

The first appeared in October 1988. Stanislav Kondrashov, *Izvestiya's* experienced political commentator, addressed the issue in an interview which appeared in *Moscow News* under the title 'A Long Look at America, Them and Us: Changing Images in a Changing World.' In speaking of the need to prevent the recurrence of a Stalin-style dictatorship, Kondrashov referred to the separation of powers, stating, 'In implementing our political reform, it would be advisable to take a better look at the division of control and the separation of powers in American democracy, at the relationship between the President, the Congress and the Supreme Court.' He also justified affirmative-didacticism and called for the further use of American experience as a basis for Soviet reform, because 'Authoritarian, bureaucratic socialism dreads American democracy like the devil dreads incense. The democratic, creative socialism which we have started to build finds much which is of use in America's democratic experience.'[104]

The second reference to the American approach to checks and balances appeared in *Pravda* in November 1988, in a long article entitled 'A Little about the Art of Preserving the Republic'. The article was entirely devoted to an exploration of the American system of checks and balances and focused on its contribution to the stability of the American political system. It must be noted that unlike Kondrashov, the author, New York correspondent Victor Linnik, was openly hostile towards what he perceived to be the callous nature of American democracy. However, like Kondrashov, he commended the role of the principle of checks and balances in preventing dictatorship. He also justified borrowing from American experience:

> Many of the constitutional methods and practices, having served in the American case for the affirmation of the domination of the bourgeoisie, could serve for the affirmation of other classes replacing the bourgeoisie. Why not? Mutual enrichment of mankind today comes not only from the transfer of technology and the exchange of cultural values. Values of political experience also mean more than a little.[105]

The difference in the way in which the two authors used the American example is instructive. While Linnik was still critical of the American political system, Kondrashov (as others who would later write on the separation of powers) was not, avoiding any systemic criticism of American democracy. Indeed, the image of America which he portrayed was that of a reasonable country, with strong values and traditions based in an essentially sound democratic political structure.[106] The differences between authors are indicative of the impact of shifting policies on the press. The press was supposed to develop new approaches to capitalism, show a less hostile and more humanized view of the West and support decisions made in the Soviet Union. This still left a tremendous range for legitimate controversy. Even those reporters who were willing to follow loyally the government line had a wide range of interpretations to choose from, because the sphere of legitimate controversy had become so wide.

A number of other articles on the US also appeared to support government policies. Two articles on the institution of the American presidency appeared just prior to the Supreme Soviet's vote on the creation of an executive presidency, one on the day of the vote itself.[107] Stanislav Kondrashov wrote a long article on the superiority of the American multi-party system over the Soviet system soon after Gorbachev announced the need for the Communist Party to compete for power.[108] A long article on the American Supreme Court also appeared in the wake of broad discussion on the need for judicial reform.[109]

However, the Soviet leadership, or at least those journalists who supported its policies, did not only use affirmative-didacticism in support of reform. Such was the growing impotence of Marxism-Leninism that American experience was used to legitimate critical government decisions about internal affairs. The clearest case of this was in articles about the American system of federalism.

Until the post-June 1988 period, the concept of American federalism, and the procedural implications of state and local rights, was never really addressed in the Soviet press. It was indirectly referred to when state and local officials complained about the Reagan administration, or when a locality declared itself a nuclear-free zone, but such articles did not entail real analysis.

The relative silence on the issue was shattered in 1989 and 1990 when no fewer than four articles appeared in *Izvestiya* and *Pravda* which addressed in detail aspects of American federalism. The first two articles appeared in February 1989, not long after Lithuania and Moldavia had taken significant steps towards asserting their independence by initiating restrictive language laws. The others appeared when separatist tension heated up.[110] A common denominator of the articles is that they all stressed the ultimate superiority of the central government over state and local governments. They also implicitly suggested that if individual states could not leave America's union, then it was legitimate for Soviet central authorities to demand the same of their republics.

The more comprehensive of the first two articles was written by *Izvestiya* journalist Leonid Koryavin.[111] The subjects which Koryavin chose to omit, as much as those he included, were revealing of his intent. He repeatedly stressed that while states maintained rights in certain spheres, these rights were circumscribed by a number of federal prerogatives. The president, for example, had the authority to ensure that states fulfilled their constitutional obligations, including the honouring of federal legislation and the defence of the rights of citizens. He pointed out, moreover, that the federal government possessed a variety of levers which it could use to compel the states to comply with its wishes, 'from direct "intervention" . . . to the distribution of finances'.[112]

Federal prerogatives were further highlighted in discussions of America's 'nationalities problem', which referred to the Spanish-speaking population, and in terms of issues related to the protection of minority rights. In the latter context, he underlined the federal government's role as 'mediator, coordinator, and if necessary, peacemaker'. He also pointed out that the federal government could use military intervention to ensure the rights of citizens, noting that Presidents Eisenhower and Kennedy sent in the army after 'serious disturbances in the implementation process of desegregation'.[113]

As important as Koryavin's description of America's nationalities problem was his discussion of the integrity of the union. While noting that the needs of states varied, he underlined that, 'What is most important is that not one of the American states has made it an aim to break the historical chain forming the interconnections of the entire system.' This last sentence is crucial for understanding the article because it is patently untrue. Anyone with a rudimentary knowledge of American history knows that the American civil war was largely fought over the rights of states to secede from the union. Moreover, there are contemporary secessionist movements, albeit small ones, in states such as Texas, Alaska and California. Koryavin was a correspondent in the United States and a specialist commentator on American political issues. He would almost certainly have known the federalist component of the American civil war. His failure to address this was almost certainly intentional: to mention federalism and the potential of civil war would have undermined the Soviet government's position *vis-à-vis* the republics and suggested an unacceptable outcome. At the same time he justified the use of force to resolve centre-periphery conflicts. Although he stressed that negotiation was the norm in America, implying that the same should be true in the Soviet Union, he also prepared the way for more drastic actions if such measures did not work.

As if to underline this, a reworking of Koryavin's article appeared a year later, in March 1990, two weeks after Lithuania's declaration of independence when paratroops had already situated themselves in Vilnius and conflict appeared likely. Citing American constitutional and legal sources, he pointed out that in extraordinary situations, including 'uprisings and mass disorders', the president 'is authorized to resort to the use of military force'. He later expanded on this, claiming that the president could also call in the army or national guard in cases of 'illegal interference' in the functioning of state authority and the execution of laws and when 'illegal associations' are created and activated or when they 'inflame revolt'. In such instances, 'military force can be used to those limits, "which the president deems necessary" for the re-establishment of law and order'.[114]

JOURNALISTS' VALUES

The leadership, however, was not the only entity to benefit from the proliferation of affirmative-didacticism. The widening sphere of legitimate controversy and the general endorsement of affirmative-didacticism meant that journalists did not only have to promote leadership interests, but could use their positions to lobby for their own concerns. This could entail minor issues of a personal nature, such as availability of tickets to the Bolshoi[115] or a perceived over-reliance on government handouts by the cultural establishment.[116]

Perhaps the most interesting cases centred on journalists' corporate interests. The best example of this was a piece on the relationship between the American media and the Congress which appeared in

Pravda just prior to the opening of the Congress of People's Deputies. The article outlined the interaction between legislators and the press, while underlining journalists' independence. Particular attention was devoted to press access to the affairs of Congress, from the floors of the House and Senate to committee rooms. The author concluded that the information received by the American public, the ultimate test of the press in its relationship with Congress, was 'sufficiently full'.[117] In defending the rights of journalists to attend proceedings of the Congress of People's Deputies, the reporter, if not contradicting the leadership, at least supported practices which defended journalists' corporate interests in an area in which the leadership had not clearly demonstrated a commitment. In doing so he demonstrated how an expanded sphere of legitimate controversy allowed journalists, and even publications, to use the press and images of the United States to promote increasingly diverse goals.

DISCUSSION AND CONCLUSIONS

The transformation in Soviet press coverage of domestic America in the period from March 1985 to July 1990 is astounding. At the beginning of the period, almost every aspect of American culture and society and its socio-economic and political systems was continually criticized in harsh terms. Ideological warfare against capitalism's leading power, the United States, was the primary concern of reporters and editors. There was practically no legitimate controversy concerning the United States, only consensus that the United States should be demonized. However, the Gorbachev period saw the emergence of a more humanized vision of the United States and the use of affirmative-didacticism to promote and legitimate reform. The result was that the United States, its culture, economy and even its political system emerged as more legitimate, humane, productive and democratic than the Soviet Union.

While there was still isolated criticism, sometimes employing old formulas, such criticism was relatively rare. Moreover, the criticism was generally neither as harsh nor as broad as in the past. Specific aspects of American culture and society were portrayed negatively, but rarely its fundaments. For example, the release of a Rambo film in 1988 was interpreted as an attempt by some right-wingers to undermine US/Soviet relations, not as a sign of the bankruptcy of American mass culture or the militarism of American society.[118] So strong was the tendency towards positive portrayals that writers who retained the old approaches, or even modifications thereof, were tangibly on the defensive. It was a great irony that in 1990 when *Pravda* political correspondent Thomas Kolisnichenko wanted to criticize the influence of the military-industrial complex on the Bush administration he felt it necessary to justify himself, stating parenthetically: 'To those readers who consider this formulation to have come from a propagandist's cliché, I remind you that this definition was not thought up by Soviet journalists, but by the president of the USA, Eisenhower.'[119] Kolisnichenko's accusation would have been the norm three years earlier, but in the context of 1990 it was the exception.[120]

Some writers went so far as to publicly rebuke others for conveying overly positive images of the United States. For example, in writing on US/Soviet cultural exchanges and the general Soviet approach to America, *Pravda*'s Pavel Bogomolov was critical of the excessive deprecation of Soviet achievements as well as the over-glorification of America. He spoke of the 'gold-leafed euphoria' concerning America and concluded that 'This is not surprising, given that on the screens and in publications a totally problem-free "shining" image of America and its culture is portrayed'. While he was not calling for a return to the old-style confrontation, he hoped for a 'move away from the extremes'.[121]

Despite such calls for greater balance, the communicative value of American experience proved too great, and the voices calling for restraint were, in early 1990, drowned out. Indeed, the emergence of affirmative-didacticism, when combined with minimal criticism, particularly from a class-oriented perspective, created an image of the United States which was perhaps more positive than accurate.[122]

The changes in the print media's depiction of the United States did not happen in a vacuum. The changing images of the United States correspond with progress in US/Soviet relations and the process of domestic Soviet reform. Humanization became a dominant theme of press coverage of the US after the INF agreement which was agreed to in the summer of 1987 and signed in the spring of 1988. Affirmative-didactic articles about economic concerns appeared in 1987, after the June plenum devoted to economic reform, when Gorbachev began to advocate a 'socialist market', as opposed to market influences in a planned economy. Then, in the middle of

1988, when the leadership turned its attention to political reform, the American political system was used to promote the agenda of the Soviet leadership. The last anti-American campaign, in the form of charges of violations of human rights, occurred in the spring of 1988, just prior to the Moscow Summit, when all publications examined united in a brief campaign which appeared to anticipate criticisms of US President Ronald Reagan.[123] Within two years, however, everything had changed. As *Pravda's* Viktor Linnik indicated in late 1989, 'The general thesis is there. The general direction is there. You write not to criticize, but to try to relate the American experience to our reality. This is the general line these days.'[124]

This is not to say that the Soviet leadership dictated press content throughout the Gorbachev period. An examination of leadership speeches and articles, particularly in 1987 and 1988, demonstrates four primary policy positions concerning domestic America: first, capitalism should be reappraised; second, there should not be an enemy image of America; third, ideological confrontation should be minimized; and fourth, American experience should be used to aid the Soviet Union in its reform process. Together these meant that the more barbaric criticism of the past was unacceptable and new, more reasoned analyses were required. However, there was no clear direction on where the capitalist system stood in the Soviet mind-frame. Gorbachev and his allies did not seem to support wholesale transference of the American system or American values, but it was never exactly clear where they drew the line.[125] Some reporters, therefore, fulfilled their duty to support government policies and retained a somewhat critical view of the American system. Their criticism, however, was muted not only by the 'general line', but because reporters were cognizant of their audience's displeasure with old clichés. Others took the opposite route and assiduously avoided all criticism of the United States, promoting a reform strategy which probably exceeded that of the government. Some also chose to use the freedom of the new government 'line' to promote their own corporate interests.

The breadth of legitimate controversy also allowed publications to take more distinctive editorial lines. For example, by 1990, in keeping with its pro-market line, *Moscow News* avoided practically any form of criticism of the United States. There were dissenting voices, like those of *Literaturnaya Rossiya*[126] whose foreign editor claimed that his journal opposed the movement towards a Western market and felt that others exaggerated America's achievements and ignored its failures because they wanted a similar system. At the same time he indicated that *Literaturnaya Rossiya* did not seek to project the degree of hostility towards America as it had in the past. Indeed, as was the case with other publications, *Literaturnaya Rossiya* used the United States in an affirmative-didactic manner. This process demonstrates how, in the wake of waning ideological censorship and less-defined consensus, the press was gaining independence from government control.

The overall impact of Party policies to use the United States as a model for change, combined with journalists' desires to please their readership and emerging pro-American editorial lines in publications like *Moscow News*, meant that by the end of the period, ideas of consensus and deviance were nearly inverted. Within a wide sphere of legitimate controversy, positive accounts of American society and culture, its socio-economic and political systems were much closer to the ring of consensus than were critical approaches, particularly those applying a class-perspective. The reliance on positive images of the United States to legitimate political and economic decisions also underscores the bankruptcy of Soviet ideology. The multiple references to the former capitalist enemy suggested that Marxism-Leninism was rotten to the core and had to be replaced, not reformed.

8 The Russian Press and Images of the United States

This chapter examines changes in the Russian press (the Soviet press's most direct descendant) and Russian images of the United States five years after the fall of the Soviet Union. The goal of the chapter is to outline implications of the transition towards a free press system for the print media and analyze how these changes, and particularly Russia's search for a new identity, have influenced the press's depiction of the United States. It will be argued that in spite of the difficult challenge posed by the transition to a free press system, Russian press content is pluralistic and demonstrates great diversity both in its approach to the United States and in the news values underlying editorial approaches. The Russian press, for all of its financial difficulties, has the capacity to express competing interpretations of Russia's present and advocate for alternative visions of her future.

PRESS STRUCTURE

Five years after the demise of the Soviet Union, the Russian press reflects many of the promises, contradictions and disappointments of other national presses which have experienced the transition from authoritarian to free press systems.[1]

The legal and institutional bases for press freedom in Russia were strengthened greatly by the Russia Press Law of 1991. This law amplifies many of the guarantees of the Soviet Press Law of 1990, prohibits censorship, institutionalizes basic provisions for freedom of information and creates barriers to the arbitrary closing of publications, while permitting the establishment of independent newspapers in Russia for the first time since 1917.[2] Freedom of expression is reinforced by the 1993 Russian Constitution, which guarantees 'the right to freely seek, obtain, transmit, produce and disseminate information by any legal method'. Together with other laws, these

137

have helped the press to continue its movement away from the ideological and discursive limits of post-totalitarian communism while insulating it from potentially constrictive new post-communist ideologies.

However, as in other countries which experienced transitions to so-called free press systems, the result for the press is by no means a well-balanced marketplace of ideas. The Russian press, having thrown off many of the shackles of authoritarianism, has been ensnared by new types of constraints.[3]

The paradox of the transformation is that while the press served as a leading force for political and economic reform in the Soviet Union and Russia, it was also one of the first sectors to bear the full brunt of the impact of the market. Several factors coalesced to undermine the print media. Since 1992, the press has experienced dramatic increases in the cost of publishing, with steep rises in the price of paper and printing and the cost of distribution.[4] At the same time, changes in the overall economic environment mean that the population generally has less disposable income (and more attractive ways to spend what income they have) and less free time to read. Interest in the press has also been curbed by general news fatigue: after years of reading once-secret 'revelations' about the horrors of Soviet realities, the population tired. Now interests have splintered leaving no clear prescriptions for the press.[5]

The overall result has been a significant decline in circulation for Russian print-media, particularly of the Moscow-based national dailies, the descendants of all-Union papers.[6] In the *glasnost'* era, Russians often subscribed to six or seven publications, and most subscribed to at least one national (all-Union) and one regional publication. The post-*glasnost'* period has witnessed not only a decline in overall subscriptions, but a proportional shift towards less expensive regional and local publications, which tend to contain less international news than their national counterparts.[7] The overall circulation of all-Union/national dailies declined from 110 million in 1991 to 95 million in 1992 to just below 45 million in 1993 and then to less than 10 million in the first part of 1996. In the period from 1991 to 1995, *Pravda*'s circulation fell from 2.6 million to under 200,000; the weekly *Argumenty i Fakty* dropped from an astonishing 24.5 million to 4.2 million; and *Izvestiya* fell from 4.7 million to just over 800,000, and then to 600,000 in 1996. The conservative daily *Sovetskaya Rossiya* fell from 750,000 in 1993 to 272,000 in 1996.[8]

The difficult financial conditions have also left the press exposed on the political front. Publications are often dependent on the state for support. This occurs either through direct subsidies (most of which are distributed through the State Committee on the Press, which is part of the executive branch and whose chair is nominated by the President),[9] tax relief or through access to distribution networks and printing plants (over 80 per cent of which are owned by the state).[10] While it is clear that such issues affect local and regional media more than the Moscow-based press, they still raise concerns about the relative autonomy of the press *vis-à-vis* the government.[11] With economic conditions promising to worsen, the scope for potential government interference may grow.[12]

Beyond the potential of continuing government interference, the transition to a free press system has created other potentially greater dangers for the press. Financial realities have meant that publications, which began the transition effectively as autonomous players because of declining government authority and the nature of the Soviet and Russian press laws,[13] have increasingly been bought up by wealthy investors. In the words of the founder and editor-in-chief of *Nezavisimaya Gazeta* Vitaly Tretyakov, 'To survive [today] Russian newspapers need to find a sponsor.'[14] The form which this sponsorship has taken in Russia has been increasingly through the purchase of shares by Russia's leading corporate and banking elite. A number of concerns have been raised by the massive investment in print and broadcast media by Russia's leading financial powers and those who head them (listed in parentheses), including the huge energy monopoly Gazprom (Rem Vyakhirev), the oil giant LUKOIL (Vagit Alekperov), the MOST banking group (Vladimir Gusinsky), the LogoVAZ company (Boris Berezovsky), Bank Menatep (Mikhail Khodorkovsky) and Unexsimbank (Vladimir Potanin).[15]

These investments do not come for free. As in the case of all free press systems, private ownership is in no way a guarantee of press freedom. The owners' interests may simply replace those of the state in guiding editorial content.[16] Most analysts assume that because media organs tend to be money-losing the goal of the investors is to create favourable coverage for the parent company and, more importantly, to increase the company's political influence.[17] Nowhere was the impact of the new media/business elite highlighted more than in the 1996 presidential elections when nearly all major private media supported and helped ensure the election of President Boris Yeltsin over his Communist rival Gennady Zyuganov.[18] The media's devotion was paid back in a number of ways after the election. The MOST group, for example, was permitted to extend its NTV network to the whole country, to extend its daytime programming and to launch a satellite news network NTV+. Sometimes the pay-back was more in the political sphere, as in the cases of Potanin of Unexsimbank and Berezovsky of LogoVAZ who were respectively named first deputy prime minister and deputy secretary of the Security Council.

Even those organs which have escaped the grasp of Russia's new politically connected entrepreneurs face difficulties. The Soviet Union's most celebrated newspaper, *Pravda,* has faced a long string of crises. Once the backbone of the Soviet press, its publication was suspended no less than five times from 1991 to 1996. In two instances, the continuing political struggles in Russia were the major sources of difficulties, the newspaper having been forcibly closed after the attempted *putsch* of 1991 and the conflict between President Yeltsin and the Duma in 1993.[19] In other cases, the paper's closure was related to the economic hardships befalling many publications in Russia. With its circulation plummeting from over 11,000,000 in the mid-1980s to less than 200,000 by the summer of 1996, even the Greek investors whose financial backing had saved *Pravda* had had enough, explaining: 'The editors and reporters drink too much (and) they publish nothing that is worth reading.'[20] It is likely that the 1996 Presidential elections strongly affected the timing of their decision: when Communist Gennady Zyuganov failed to displace Boris Yeltsin, the investment appeared to be heading toward little long-term pay-off. Although at the moment of writing *Pravda* is limping on, its welfare remains in doubt for the foreseeable future.

The transition has raised other difficulties for the new Russian press. Publications which defined themselves against the Soviet regime have had a difficult time finding a new editorial voice when prescriptions are not as clear, the readership is more fickle, and economic pressures immense.[21] The need for advertising (*Izvestiya,* for example, obtains 90 per cent of its revenue through ads) has also created editorial pressures to ensure that sponsors are not alienated and have meant that advertisements fill space once devoted to news.

For journalists, the market culture has also crept into day-to-day work, and some now appear willing to provide positive press coverage for a fee.[22] Such practices, which are endemic in media systems experiencing the impact of the market for the first time, have done little to help the reputation of journalists or the press as a whole, and have contributed to the decline in the public's respect of journalism as a profession.[23] Journalists also raised questions when, as a corporate collective body, they overwhelmingly and uncritically supported Boris Yeltsin in the 1996 presidential campaign. In supporting Yeltsin, they often perceived themselves to be acting in favour of the preservation of freedom of expression and other democratic freedoms. However, their actions indicate that they still view themselves as political actors who are not bound by journalistic standards of objectivity.[24]

The situation reflects the precariousness of the transition. On the one hand, the 'complex web of interdependencies' between the government and emerging business/media conglomerates leaves the press susceptible to direct and indirect influences on editorial content, especially in the context of the difficult economic environment.[25] This was certainly the case with the presidential election. On the other hand, there is little doubt that the publications, especially the Moscow-based dailies, enjoy significantly more editorial freedom than they had during most of the Soviet period. There are no indications that the government determines and vets press coverage on a daily basis as it did in the past. Although dangers of government intervention persist, the press enjoys a large degree of relative autonomy *vis-à-vis* the government on a daily basis. Moreover, there is no evidence that the different media groups which are emerging are so united or well organized that they are significantly limiting the pluralism of the print media on a regular basis. They may have formed a relatively cohesive block (together with allies in the government and anti-Communist journalists) for the presidential election when the stakes were high, but day in and day out they do not approach the efficacy of the Communist Party apparatus. Indeed, a study of contemporary press content outlined below reveals that the Russian press continues to exercise its right to articulate openly competing views.

PRESS CONTENT: CONTINUITY AND CHANGE IN IMAGES OF THE UNITED STATES

Russian press coverage of the United States in 1996 reflects both a continuation of trends seen in the *glasnost'* period and changes which are the product of the new environment in which the press operates.

In order to examine the evolution of the Russian press, the content of *Pravda*, *Izvestiya*, *Sovetskaya Rossiya*, *Moskovskie Novosti*, *Argumenty i Fakty*, *Segodnya* and *Nezavisimaya Gazeta* was examined in February, July and August 1996. As representatives of the Moscow-based press, they are the most important opinion leaders and agenda-setters for other Russian print media, in spite of their declines in circulation outlined above.[26] The survey of content was designed to allow for the press to reflect potential influences of the 1995 parliamentary elections, which brought a Communist Party plurality, and the 1996 presidential elections, which saw another victory by Boris Yeltsin.

RUSSIAN IDENTITY, THE UNITED STATES AND THE PRESS

The depiction of the United States in the Russian press is integrally interlinked with the transformation in Russia from a Soviet to a Russian identity. In the Soviet period, especially in the mid-1980s, there was a near obsession with the United States, the Soviet Union's most important inter-subjective 'other' which helped constitute its self-identity. The result, as we have seen in previous chapters, is that the Soviet press directed a steady and robust stream of vitriol against its military and ideological enemy. It used 'war propaganda' to suggest that the United States posed an imminent military threat, asserted that the United States government, controlled by a military-industrial complex, regularly committed massive violations of human rights, militarized American culture, and perpetuated poverty and homelessness across America. The obsession with the United States was continually manifested in public discourse through a united party leadership which ensured a largely uniphonous press.

In the *glasnost'* period, with the emergence of new political thinking, there was a reorientation of Soviet ideology and thus of the Soviet press's approach towards the United States. In terms of foreign affairs, the military threat posed by the United States was for the most part downplayed and the United States was depicted as much as a partner as an enemy. In evaluating domestic America, changes brought by new political thinking encouraged the press to re-evaluate more positively America's economy, society and culture. Equally as important, images of the United States were often utilized to express ideas which could not be communicated effectively through the Soviet Union's ideologically restrictive discourse: America's enduring democracy and its effective methods of government and production were exemplified as justification for Soviet political and economic reforms. If anything, images of domestic America became excessively positive, as journalists swung radically to follow what was perceived as the latest official line and to please readers who were tired and sceptical after years of anti-American vitriol.

The collapse of the Soviet Union and the emergence of an independent Russia has resulted in the process of a search for a new identity.[27] While expressions of Russian national identity were permitted in the Soviet period, particularly as the mobilizing power of Marxism-Leninism waned,[28] they were always closely guarded and never allowed to develop to the point where it might threaten the regime and the dominant ideology. Although it is not the place here to get into a detailed discussion about Russian national identity in the post-Soviet era, a few key conclusions should be touched upon with particular reference to Russian foreign policy and perceptions of the United States.

First, no distinct identity has emerged to capture leaders, policy-makers or the public.[29] Russia lacks the clarity of the Cold War, the certitude of Marxism-Leninism and the univocacy of a single party articulating the country's interests and foreign policy priorities. It also lacks political leadership from a head of state who seems incapable of articulating a clear policy. Moreover, with reified political institutions, it has a more diffuse decision-making process which allows for multiple perspectives. This is particularly the case in the foreign policy sphere.[30]

Second, Russian nationalism is reasserting itself across the political spectrum. In the late Soviet period and just after the fall of the Union, the dominant vision articulated by Russia's 'Democrats' and the Yeltsin leadership was clearly pro-Western and pro-market. In the political context of the time, this transformed into a pro-American stance. These attitudes largely reflected the ideology of opposition against the *ancien régime*, in which Russian independence was defined against Soviet power.[31] This distinct pro-Western orientation, often associated with former Foreign Minister Andrei Kozyrev, would not continue. Particularly from 1993 onwards, a more confident and obviously self-interested Russia began to emerge. National self-assertion could only be expected as Russia and the Russian people attempted to restore self-esteem in the wake of the perceived humiliation associated with the break-up of the Soviet Union, the difficulties of Russians outside the homeland and the dark revelations about the Soviet past.[32] Under such conditions, a continuation of the distinctly pro-Western policy could only be associated with subservience and weakness.

Here we are not simply speaking of fervent nationalism, most notably represented by Vladimir Zhirinovsky's Liberal Democratic Party, but of the desire to recapture esteem and confidence which emerged across the Russian political spectrum. Russia's political outlook is divided into various points along the traditional Westernizer/Slavophile continuum, but it seems clear that since the romantic period of Western orientation, in which the agenda was set by 'democratic, internationalist, market-oriented, pro-Western, learn-from-America intellectuals',[33] a more sober view has developed. The Russian leadership, and even the strongest 'Westernizers,' have been able to dis-articulate the desire for democratization and a market economy from an unquestioningly pro-Western and pro-American foreign policy, and have adopted a more self-interested and critical approach. This has meant an end both to the ideologically driven Cold-War animosity and the equally fervent anti-Communist pro-Western ideology represented by Kozyrev and Democratic Russia in the early post-Soviet period.[34]

Third, the process of transformation from a Soviet to Russian identity has meant that the United States is no longer the primary referent point, no longer the inter-subjective 'other' at the core of Russian/Soviet identity. This is a product not simply of the elimination of Marxism-Leninism as Russia's guiding ideology, but also of a general reorientation of Russia's view of the world around it. As Russia searches to define itself, its interests in the territory of the former Soviet Union and in Europe have grown.[35] As the analysis of press content will demonstrate, the remnants of differential bonds remain, and the United States still plays a legitimating function for political argumentation. However, the turn away from a distinctly pro-Western foreign policy and the dis-articulation of America from Europe, particularly after 1992, has meant that its role is clearly diminished from that which it played in the Gorbachev and immediate post-Gorbachev period.

PRESS CONTENT

The change in Russian psychological approaches to the United States found its clearest reflection in the significant decline in press coverage of America in 1996 compared to the *glasnost'* period. With the absence of Marxism-Leninism's fundamental antipathy towards capitalism and debates on the future nature of Soviet socialism, there is no need for the Soviet press's successor to focus continually on the world's leading capitalist power. News values have changed and, continuing a trend from the very end of the *glasnost'* period, the media now looks more within than outside. International press coverage, which was regularly allocated one to two pages of dense print in all-Union publications in the Soviet period, has now lost space to domestic news and advertisements. While Russian–American relations are still given significant, albeit reduced, coverage, there is far less space for the exploration of domestic American issues. They are simply no longer news as was once the case.

DOMESTIC ISSUES: SOCIO-ECONOMICS, CULTURE AND POLITICS

In terms of domestic issues, the change in news values has not simply meant a decline in coverage of the United States, but that articles which do address American issues tend to contain an explicit Russian angle. Continuing from the late *glasnost'* period, American issues are often used to communicate political ideas about contemporary Russia. However, the method and purpose of communication appear to have changed. In the *glasnost'* period, images of the United States were often used in lieu of a discourse which could effectively articulate arguments concerning political and economic alternatives for the Soviet Union. Images of the United States would often serve as a substitute for argumentation because the Soviet lexicon was so laden with specific ideological meanings that reformist ideas could not be communicated without external referent points. How could, for example, the Soviet leadership sell the long-derided 'bourgeois' concept of a separation of powers without demonstrating its efficacy elsewhere? Images of the long-time ideological adversary thus became one of the primary means of communicating reformist ideas. In contemporary Russia, however, the situation is different. The passing of time since the collapse of the Soviet

Union and the explicit differentiation by many Russian leaders of Russian as opposed to Soviet experience have meant that the ideological constraints of the Soviet period have dissipated. The Russian press can refer to its own, albeit troubled, experience with democracy and economic reform. It can also refer to the experience of others. But isolated from the constraints of Soviet ideology, such references are not inherently so value-laden. Articles on the United States are now often used as a platform for explicit rather than symbolic debate about contemporary Russia, or as a means of criticizing specific political leaders – something unheard of in the *glasnost'* era. Moreover, the discourse has advanced to a level where more balanced and analytic approaches to the United States are possible. Where one stands on the United States is no longer in and of itself a defining indicator of one's position on Russia's future, as it was for editors and journalists in 1989 and 1990. In other words, while articles on the United States' domestic situation can serve as a platform for explicit debate about Russian political alternatives, the image of the United States is no longer so constricted by such potent symbolic imagery: it does not have to be so black and white. Thus conservative newspapers are more likely to recognize US economic achievements and more liberal ones are more likely to criticize American political and social shortcomings because to do so is not to sacrifice important positions in the internal debate about the future of reforms.

The use of the United States as a platform for debate is well illustrated by an article which appeared in *Pravda* in February 1996. The author, after citing a speech by US Senator Edward Kennedy on the disastrous consequences for society of the economic vulnerability felt by millions of Americans, quickly shifts his focus to Russia, criticizing its ever widening socio-economic polarization and pointing out its relatively low level of economic development and weak social safety net. The author then uses Kennedy's comments to launch into an explicit attack on the Russian government, citing its abysmal failure to protect Russian society from the perils of the market. He also derides the government's post-election claims that it would increase social protection, asserting that 'only elections which threaten to throw VIPs out of their comfortable offices make them sympathize with the population suffering from reforms'. He concludes by asserting that the 'market chaos' experienced by Russia only helps 'New Russians' raise their bets at casinos, leaving society as a whole languishing.[36]

It is not simply the more 'conservative' publications which used the United States as a platform to make political points. For example, *Moskovskie Novosti*, known for its more liberal views, contained a piece about the Oliver Stone movie *Nixon* which was a not so subtle attack on Russian presidential corruption. In the article, the author asserts that Russians are likely to be surprised by the crimes for which the former US president was forced to resign: 'Is that all?' he thought Russians would ask, noting that given the regular improprieties surrounding the Russian presidency, most Russians would consider Nixon's transgressions insignificant.[37] In other cases, liberal and conservative journalists use coverage of American themes as a platform to criticize many leading politicians, including Boris Yeltsin, Viktor Chernomyrdin and Anatolii Chubais, as well as then-presidential contenders Gregory Yavlinsky, Vladimir Zhirinovsky and Gennady Zyuganov.[38]

In all of the publications examined, coverage of American socio-economic and political affairs is neither constantly critical nor laudatory. For example, an article in *Izvestiya* on the experience of Russian reporters and athletes at the 1996 Atlanta Olympics mentions America's social disparities and the persistence of racism, but it also notes its material wealth and the leading role the US played in organizing an Olympic boycott against apartheid-era South Africa.[39] Some Russian angle is usually found in articles on Americans and America's society and economy. Emblematic of this change is an article which *Izvestiya* ran on a homeless American. However, the article, which is the only reference to homelessness in the sample period, contains a twist: the homeless American is living in Moscow and the article cites his complaints about the rising cost of living in Russia.[40] In a similar vein, *Argumenty i Fakty* has contained articles on how Russians have fallen victim to American financial scam-artists and on US/Russian cooperation to halt the Russian mafia in the United States. It also had a piece in which a young Russian recounts his semi-successful experience of working illegally in the United States.[41] *Nezavisimaya Gazeta*, with a somewhat more critical approach to the United States, ran one article reminiscent of the affirmative-didacticism of the Gorbachev period. The author explores the inner-workings of American security services, then proposes that Russia could learn from and emulate American experience.[42] *Segodnya*, which has adopted a dispassionate editorial approach reminiscent of American-style objectivity, contained a piece explaining how a strict new immigration bill affects Russian immigrants living in the US[43] and ran numerous fact-filled articles on the presidential election.[44] *Moskovskie Novosti* had an article on the 'black racism' espoused by Louis Farakhan (a subject which never would have been discussed ten years earlier) that contains warnings to the people of the European republics of the former Soviet Union about the rapid population growth of Central Asians.[45] *Sovetskaya Rossiya* had an article soberly analyzing the US presidential contest which credits President Clinton with maintaining relatively high rates of economic growth and low rates of unemployment while at the same time preserving high levels of social security. The same article, however, notes that President Clinton could not help his 'friend Boris' (Yeltsin) because Congress did not want to increase aid expenditures and American conservatives have increased isolationism with the fall of the Soviet Union.[46]

One trend to note is the use of articles on the United States as a platform to promote Russian national values. Thus, for example, in an interview in *Pravda*, Alexander Shakhmatov, a returned émigré who spent several years in Australia, asserts that the United States has succeeded as an economic, scientific and cultural power largely because of Russian contributions:

> To a considerable extent, the United States became rich at the expense of Russia, using our minds and talents. Very few Russians understand the extent to which we have contributed to American culture, science and technology! Even Hollywood during its best years borrowed from Stanislavsky and Mikhail Chekhov's acting school.[47]

While nationalist declarations became very heated in articles on foreign policy, in the domestic sphere they were relatively benign. Even more progressive publications contain articles with a nationalist focus. Thus, for example, *Moskovskie Novosti* ran a piece which criticizes the United States Information Agency's efforts to create a Russian version of the popular American children's show *Sesame Street*. The author notes that for the same money, numerous children's programmes of Russian origin could be supported.[48] The article acknowledges concerns almost certainly held by many Russians while at the same time avoiding the tones of former Soviet attacks on USIA and the 'foreign voices' it used to beam to Russia. The article also represents a significant change from the late 1980s when *Moskovskie Novosti* seemed to offer exclusive praise for all things American. In other words, the author was able to write an interesting piece which was unfettered by ideological orthodoxy.

The above analysis is not meant to suggest that all articles on the United States have a Russian angle. Publications regularly contain pieces on American movies and music stars, reflecting the Americanization of international popular culture more than any pro- or anti-American orientation.[49] In its bi-weekly insert, *Finansovye Izvestiya*, *Izvestiya* contains regular articles, mostly taken directly from the insert's co-sponsor, the *Financial Times* of London, which provide information about the latest financial and commercial activities in the United States and in American foreign trade.[50] *Moskovskie Novosti* runs the occasional piece on American life. One focuses on economic gains experienced by American women over the past two decades.[51]

The point, however, is not that the Russian press requires a Russian angle to cover the United States; rather, it is that the Russian press has broken away from the Soviet-era obsession with the United States. Its news values are no longer determined by a Manichaean battle of communism versus capitalism, but by the interests of Russia and Russian readers.

PRESS COVERAGE: FOREIGN AFFAIRS

The Russian press's portrayal of US foreign policy reflects Russia's search for a new identity. Russia's attempt to follow its national interests, rather than the immutable ideological prescriptions of Marxism-Leninism,[52] means that for all publications there is far less space devoted to US foreign policy than in the Soviet period. Drastically reduced is detailed coverage of American activities in the developing world and what used to be called 'hot spots' around the globe, subjects which saturated the Soviet press and reflected the Cold War's global zero-sum game. Those articles which do appear contain a more obvious Russian angle. However, the determination of what constitutes Russian interests and specifically how those interests are reflected *vis-à-vis* the United States is manifested in very different ways.

Three primary but overlapping approaches to the United States can be identified which generally reflect different views of Russian identity.[53]

The first grouping, which can be termed *patriots*, are nationalists and xenophobes who see the United States as naturally being inimical to Russian interests. Patriots blame the United States for the unwanted collapse of the Soviet Union and believe that the US seeks to undermine Russia and take advantage of its weakness, both in the 'near abroad' and in traditional areas of Russian interest. Occasionally revealing tinges of Marxism in their critique of the West, particularly with reference to activities of Western multinational corporations, patriots also remain most locked into differential bonds which characterized US/Soviet relations during the Cold War.

A second grouping, and on the opposite end of the political spectrum from the patriots, is composed of what can be termed *Westernizers*. Westernizers are liberal, Western-oriented thinkers who maintain a positive, if not somewhat idealized, view of the United States. They continue to view the United States in a positive light, both because the US represents Western civilization to which Russia naturally belongs and because the US is largely seen as sharing the same interests as Russia and therefore becomes a natural partner in the international sphere. While the purest, rose-tinted view of the Westernizers has dissipated since the early post-Soviet period,[54] the US can still be important because it continues to play a leading symbolic role in the debate over the future of Russian democracy and market economy.

Between patriots and Westernizers lies the largest grouping, the *realists*. Realists are democratically oriented, 'pragmatic nationalists', who see the United States and the West as important partners for Russia, but who feel that the partnership should be 'based on mutual benefit, on a balance of interests, rather than on terms that favour the West'.[55] Often alienated by American behaviour which they perceive as arrogant and demeaning, and disappointed by failed promises of American assistance, they are circumspect in their approach to the US. As a matter of policy, they also look more toward the states of Eurasia for Russia's key national priorities. In the words of Kozyrev, this position manifests itself as both a 'semi-confrontation with, and semi-integration toward the West'.[56] Since 1993, the Yeltsin/Kozyrev and Yeltsin/Primakov foreign policy has increasingly moved towards the realist position, with Russia particularly asserting its authority within post-Soviet space. The realist view contains many variations along a continuum between patriots and Westernizers. For our purposes, the term 'right' realists will be used for those who are more suspicious of the United States, while the 'left' realists suggests those who display more confidence in the US as a potential partner.

As we will demonstrate below, these three approaches to the United States can be associated with general editorial lines of publications. However, it is important to note that editorial practices and writing styles mean that each publication may offer multiple approaches. It is a sign of strength of the post-Soviet press that not only is a many-layered pluralism of views expressed within the print media but that editors of individual publications are often willing to explore different sides of the same issue.

The patriotic line is most clearly articulated by *Sovetskaya Rossiya* and *Pravda*. *Sovetskaya Rossiya* is more extreme, with continual references to American attempts to undermine Russia. Perhaps the best example of this is an article by a dismissed Russian general whose primary thesis is that the United States is in the process of winning the 'third world war'. Using extremely provocative language, he suggests that Western machinations were largely responsible for the collapse of 'the socialist system and her once powerful economic and military potential', that in achieving the 'domination' of Europe, the US accomplished something 'about which Hitler only dreamed', and that Western organizations have the capacity to dictate the 'programmatic formulation of Russian foreign and domestic politics'.[57] Other articles in *Sovetskaya Rossiya* touch on similar themes, accusing the US of reducing Russia to a 'semi-colonial state',[58] charging the US with stealing Russian scientific trade secrets and asserting that the United States instigated the break-up of the Soviet Union to gain access to cheap raw materials and that it is trying to replicate its success in Russia.[59]

Often the attacks are laced with criticism of President Boris Yeltsin and other 'democrats'.[60] The general attitude is summed up well in a poem submitted by a reader:

To Bill Clinton and Bush
Borya Yeltsin sold his soul.
But for his soul
I don't give a damn
'cause now he's selling
his motherland![61]

Interestingly, the remnants of the strong differential bonds associated with the Cold War are manifested in the sometimes schizophrenic way in which *Sovetskaya Rossiya* uses articles on the United States to criticize the Yeltsin administration. At times the desire to attack the Yeltsin administration even exceeds that of criticizing the

West, and authors paint interaction with the West as beneficial, or at least tolerable, in order to attack their domestic opponents. Thus one author notes ironically that in spite of previous ideological and political differences, Western businessmen preferred dealing with the Soviet Union than with 'today's chaotic and criminalized Russia'.[62] Similarly, two articles written after a flaring up of the American conflict with Cuba note the relative restraint of the Clinton administration, while directing more venom at the Russian government for its failure to defend Cuba at the UN Security Council.[63]

Pravda echoes many of the patriotic tendencies of *Sovetskaya Rossiya*. Although its journalists normally avoid the more militant patriotic approaches of *Sovetskaya Rossiya*, they do reveal a strong nationalist voice, and often use articles on Russian–American relations as a platform for attacking the government and such figures as Boris Yeltsin, Andrei Kozyrev and Anatolii Chubais. For example, an author writing on the proposed START II treaty claims that America 'does not see limits to its imperial pretensions', and asserts that the treaty, 'prepared by Kozyrev and his team in great haste, corresponds more to Washington's long-term aspiration to disband our nuclear potential than to the national and state interests of Russia to preserve security'.[64] Another article, entitled 'Global Games: What will Russia be – A Great Power or a Market for Raw Materials?', asserts that American goals are 'the neutralization of Russia's strategic-nuclear potential; the disintegration of the Commonwealth of Independent States; the prohibition of Russian leadership in post-Soviet space; and 'incremental investment in the economies of Russia and other independent states to the degree which would make them dependent on the US'.[65] It should be noted that *Pravda*'s authors consistently refer to Russian national interests rather than to Marxism-Leninism. As the author of the article 'Russian Interests: Above all Others', writes, 'Russia is a great power. She had and continues to have tall ambitions and vitally important state and national interests. These interests should be placed at the front of political priorities. They should exceed all others.'[66] Moreover, while *Sovetskaya Rossiya* was regularly hostile, *Pravda* did not always seek to find the worst in American intentions, and its stress on Russian national interests often resulted in right-realist approaches. For example, a Russian student who spent time in the US claims in a long article:

> It is thought that to a great extent Americans are responsible for our poverty: that Americans are insidious and aggressive. But

the simplicity and democratic nature of Americans is much closer to us than anything found in 'stiff Europeans'. Russia's present anti-Americanism, in my opinion, either comes from poor information about true intentions of Americans or from a lack of will to understand them.[67]

On the other end of the spectrum lies *Segodnya*. Although it tends to offer articles which reflect American-style objectivity and thus contain minimal editorial comment, it has positioned itself in the Westernizing camp, or at least on the Westernizing side of the realist spectrum, through its choice of subject-matter, its omission of criticism and its editorializing. On the one hand, it often ignores, downplays or denies the potential threat posed to Russia by developments which are incendiary for the patriotic press, like NATO expansion,[68] the threat of the US to pull out of the Anti-Ballistic Missile Treaty,[69] and US relations with other countries of the former Soviet Union.[70] On the other hand, it runs articles applauding US assistance (referring to a financing deal offered by US Ex-Im Bank),[71] and even criticizes the Yeltsin administration and the Russian Defence Ministry for taking 'provocative' actions which might endanger relations with the US.[72] A piece on NATO expansion made very clear the Westernizing orientation of *Segodnya*: '(The presidential leadership) understands very well that namely through relations with the West, and only through them, can Russia count on a productive partnership. Many times the president has had the opportunity to convince himself of this, but nonetheless he finds it necessary to at times wheel out the same tired tune of NATO's military threat.'[73]

The other publications consulted approach US foreign policy from a right to left realist continuum. *Nezavisimaya Gazeta* tends to fall towards the patriotic side of the realist camp. Articles regularly criticize 'Westernizers,' 'Atlanticists' and the 'pro-American lobby' in Moscow (which includes Burbulis, Gaidar, Kozyrev, Starovoytova and Yavlinsky) whose pro-Western policies and market reforms are seen as running counter to Russia's 'sovereign development' and her 'national-state interests'.[74] Others criticize US arrogance and messianism, actions taken against Russian interests in the Newly Independent States,[75] America's failure to abide by the ABM treaty[76] and American hypocrisy in supporting Boris Yeltsin after his blatantly anti-democratic activities.[77] As one author explains: 'We ask for respect as equals, and they say to us that they will respect us only when we become obedient and fall in love with Gaidar and

Chubais. In recent years, the 'active assistance of the US administration of democratic reforms in Russia' has been marked by
violations of the moral principles and values of Western democracy.'[78]

At the same time, *Nezavisimaya Gazeta* does not contain as sustained or fierce attacks on the United States as the more patriotic
publications. The US might be hypocritical in its actions *vis-à-vis*
Russia, but that does not mean that it is implacably hostile towards Russia, nor that it is responsible for the fall of Communism
or the break-up of the Soviet Union, as the patriots would have
it.[79] Moreover, the picture presented by no means precludes serious
co-operation with the United States. As one author puts it, 'The
fact that our Russian foreign policy will be becoming more "pro-
Russian," meaning pragmatic and based on clearly defined national
interests, does not imply that it has to be anti-American or anti-
Western.'[80]

Izvestiya presents a picture which situates it on the 'Westernizing' side of the realist perspective. While avoiding the explicit
pro-Western outlook of *Segodnya*, *Izvestiya*, through omission of
criticism and selected areas of coverage, offers a view which is fairly
sympathetic to Western values and to the potential to deal with
the US as a legitimate partner. For example, it refrains from the
biting interpretations found in the patriotic press over issues like
US activity in the Commonwealth of Independent States,[81] NATO
expansion[82] and foreign assistance.[83] It does not discuss American
machinations against the Soviet Union and instead stresses relative American disinterest in Russia. US priorities of 'democratic
development' in Russia are not attacked, nor is the US approach
characterized as interference in Russia's internal affairs.[84] The many
articles in *Finansovye Izvestiya*, which address various export deals,
also implicitly support a Westernizing approach by legitimating trade
agreements with the US.[85] Perhaps what is most notable about
Izvestiya, other than this Westernizing tendency, is the relative absence of detailed analysis of US relations. Coverage is often
dispassionate, and the volume has declined significantly over previous years, with the publication focusing more on Russia and losing
a significant amount of editorial space to advertisements which
Izvestiya needs in order to survive.

Moskovskie Novosti takes a similar if not even more dispassionate line towards US foreign policy. While it does not devote
considerable space to US foreign policy issues, the articles which it
does run offer relatively balanced, if marginally critical, accounts,

of such issues as the START II Treaty[86] and NATO expansion,[87] mixed in with realistic analysis of Russia's limited military potential.[88] *Moskovskie Novosti* does, however, reveal some of its editorial leaning by using discussions of US relations with Russia and the 'globalization of the economy' as a means of attacking Communist leader Gennady Zyuganov.[89] Indeed, one article suggests that freezing the process of NATO expansion is the best way of preserving democracy in Russia and the best protection against Russian imperialism.[90] It also applauds the efforts of Hungarian/American Philanthropist George Soros in setting up Internet centres in Russia, something which would never appear in the patriotic press, because, as *Moskovskie Novosti* itself points out, the 'patriotic press' views Soros's actions in Russia as a front for CIA activities.[91]

COMMISSION ON ECONOMIC, SCIENTIFIC AND TECHNICAL CO-OPERATION

The different approaches towards US foreign policy manifested in the Russian press are exhibited in the varying approaches to the sixth session of the so-called Gore–Chernomyrdin Commission which took place on 29 and 30 January 1996.

Of the patriotic and right-realist publications, *Sovetskaya Rossiya* not only dismissed ecological agreements as 'openly propagandistic', but unyieldingly attacked the financial agreements, claiming that they created a 'lord' and 'vassal' relationship between the United States and Russia,[92] and that 'the current ruling regime in Russia is selling off the greatest achievements of Soviet science and technology for a pittance' while America denies Russia access to its markets.[93] *Pravda* noted the stagnation (*zastoi*) in US/Russian relations, but was more interested in underlining that little was going to come of lasting utility with the Russian presidential elections on the horizon.[94] *Nezavisimaya Gazeta* focused on the relatively weak position of Russia *vis-à-vis* the United States and Russia's accommodation of American businesses while criticizing as 'unjustifiable' American trade practices which exclude Russian access to the American market. The undercurrent addressed by *Nezavisimaya Gazeta* was that Russia was in a 'weak' position *vis-à-vis* the United States because of the upcoming presidential elections and the concomitant need for IMF stand-by loans. While refraining from suggesting that the United States was seeking to undermine Russia, the authors who addressed the issue clearly pointed out the political nature of the discussions, alluding to Clinton's attempt to offer 'moral support to his "friend" Boris', and were sceptical of the overall impact of the meeting.[95]

Moskovskie Novosti, on the other hand, celebrated the success of the meetings, including achievements in cooperation against organized crime and contributions to support the conversion of the Russian defence industry. It was particularly supportive of the achievements in the ecological sphere. Although the article cited a lack of progress in the access of Russian uranium to the US market, the entire session was positively evaluated, concluding with a long statement by Prime Minister Chernomyrdin who triumphantly exclaimed that 'During the course of the commission's work, and also in conversations with President Bill Clinton and Vice-President Gore, I repeatedly underlined that the movement of Russia along the path of reform is not coming to a halt and will not be diverted from the path we have been taking for the last four years. President Boris Yeltsin, as the guarantor of the continuation of the course of reform, and the government will do everything possible to make sure it continues.'[96] *Segodnya* demonstrated a combination of objectivity and a pro-Western stance, noting successes in ecological and space issues and unresolved issues in the energy sphere. It acknowledged the impact of the meetings on Russia's access to IMF loans, which it supported, while noting that the loans were contingent upon the Russian government moving forward with reforms.[97] *Izvestiya*'s coverage was neither as supportive of the endeavour, nor as critical of American aims. While acknowledging that many agreements had been reached during previous Gore–Chernomyrdin Commission meetings, it was also noted that 'there are far more unresolved problems than real achievements' for the Commission.[98] One author noted that it was 'unfortunate' that with the exception of firearms, Russian goods were not competitive on the American market.[99] Most importantly, *Izvestiya*'s Washington-based correspondent, Vladimir Nadein, questioned the *raison d'être* of the talks which, in his mind, were boring for participants. Instead, he suggested that 'The end of global confrontation has removed the reins of the economy from the hands of government. Business should be conducted by businessmen. They are far more successful at it than governments.' He felt that Russian business should work with American businessmen to learn from America and borrow from American experience. He also cited a number of recent cooperative efforts between Russian and American businessmen. Finally he stressed that it is better that businessmen learn from American experience, than government bureaucrats, because they are more effective and because they 'contribute their own money, not that of taxpayers'.[100]

CONCLUSION

The post-Soviet Russian press is marked by a pluralism of opinions in its coverage of the United States. While the volume of press coverage has declined, journalists and editors can freely express competing views about the United States. The press can freely criticize the policies of the President and his advisors, and it can cogently and in detail explain the advantages and disadvantages of American society, and approaches to Russian–American relations. It can also choose not to, and pick a clearly defined nationalistic perspective. Although the economy is difficult, the press still trumpets competing perspectives. The fear of financial 'oligarchs' re-creating a uniphonous press has thus far proved unfounded, at least as far as the print media are concerned.

The search for a post-Soviet Russian identity has meant an important and, I would argue, healthy evolution in the meaning of the United States for Russia. The United States is usually no longer 'the' enemy, nor 'the' model. That is not to say that the symbol of the United States has lost all meaning: differential bonds clearly remain, and the United States is still a powerful symbol for patriots and Westernizers alike. The important point is that in most cases, the US is not used as a symbol which serves as a substitute for debate, however ferocious. The press has the opportunity to address critical issues facing Russia in whatever way it chooses. What that future is remains unclear, as do clear definitions of Russian national interests. However, by breaking the cycle of enmity created by Marxism-Leninism, and moving away from symbolic extremes, the press permits the debate over interests to take place in the open. That is surely why so many have fought for a free press.

Conclusion

The Soviet press was supposed to be a key tool in the Communist Party's efforts to transform humanity. However, when the press failed in this transformative role, the Party offered it a more conservative function. The primary task of the press was to perpetuate the Party's rule. It was to do this by contributing to the imposition of a limited discourse on society, by generating fear of an outside threat and by demonstrating the superiority of the Soviet life-style *vis-à-vis* that of the Soviet Union's ideological opponents.

These final two demands fell particularly harshly on the United States, at least as far as media images were concerned, because the US was viewed as both the chief military and ideological threat to the Soviet Union. The result was that prior to and into the early stages of the Gorbachev period, the Soviet press demonized the United States. There was an overwhelming consensus of negativism. Most press content was cliché-ridden and predictable in its anti-American content. Some was striking in its belligerence, comparing the United States to Nazi Germany and US leaders to members of the Ku Klux Klan. There was little substantive debate about the United States and its domestic and foreign policy, and the coverage was monotonous, lacking depth. Although the Soviet press as a whole demonstrated diversity, albeit diversity sanctioned by the regime, foreign press coverage, particularly that of the United States, was one of the most strictly controlled subjects. Even publications which occasionally demonstrated 'sanctioned diversity' or 'permitted dissent' were cautious when dealing with the Soviet Union's chief enemy. The result was an extremely narrow sphere of legitimate controversy, consisting primarily of minor debates about the theoretical implications of capitalism. Even those were found predominantly on the pages of specialized journals, rarely in the popular press, which has been the focus of this study.

The changes which occurred in the Soviet press's portrayal of the United States during the Gorbachev period were dramatic. Political cartoons, perhaps the clearest expressions of the battle of ideas, showed the most obvious signs of change. By 1989, there were hardly any cartoons directed against the United States and some were even pro-American and anti-Soviet.

In the foreign policy and military spheres, the changes were significant, but uneven. The use of key ideological terms declined drastically as did the most ideologized and mechanistic explanations of US foreign policy. The most cruel images of the United States, which portrayed the government and the American people as creators of the AIDS virus and mutilators of Latin American children, disappeared. So did the overarching emphasis on bi-polarity. The United States was still seen as the most important foreign actor, but it was no longer viewed as the force behind all that was wrong with the world. US allies were viewed less frequently as victims of American arrogance, and developing countries with whom the United States was in conflict were not always portrayed as innocent victims. At times there even emerged what some called a 'friend' image, which portrayed the United States as a stable long-term partner. However, the overall tone of press coverage of US foreign and military policy remained suspicious. The United States was still seen as overly anxious to use aggression abroad and it was still viewed as the chief threat to the Soviet Union. At the end of the period, the most brutal images might have largely disappeared and been considered deviant, but caution and suspicion of US foreign and military policies tended to outweigh any friend image.

The greatest and most significant changes emerged in the images of domestic America. By humanizing the United States and holding it up as a model for change in the Soviet Union through affirmative-didactic articles, the press radically altered its image. Here, press coverage was practically inverted. What was once consensus, the inferiority of American culture, society, economy and political system, almost became deviant. Reporters who used old-style criticism of the United States felt the need to justify themselves to their readers. If anything, the image of the United States at the end of the period was overly flattering.

But why did changes occur as they did? The answer lies in the vagaries of the liberalization process, in a combination of change from above and change from below.

CHANGE FROM ABOVE

The initial and most important changes in the period under consideration were products of both deliberate Party policies to change press content and the organizational structure of the press which produced an inherent bias in support of the Party line. At times the Party ordered changes in press coverage and required specific items to appear. However, this was frequently unnecessary, because the Party's supervision of personnel appointments and its pre- and post-publication controls meant that journalists had a predisposition to support its policies. Journalists understood what to write through formal and informal processes, ranging from meetings in the departments of the Central Committee to reading the speeches of Party leaders. For the *mezhdunarodniki*, this predisposition remained in 1987, when the first key changes began to emerge in press coverage of the United States.

The relationship between changing policies and changing press coverage of the United States was demonstrated throughout the empirical analysis. In terms of foreign and military press coverage, the most brutal images of the United States, including those associated with the AIDS and baby parts campaigns, decreased drastically after the Soviet government made such assurances to US representatives in late 1987. Soon after Gorbachev called into question the inherent link between imperialism and militarism in November 1987, the use of those words to describe the United States declined sharply. When Georgi Arbatov challenged the West to join the Soviet Union in eliminating the enemy image, Soviet political cartoons, one of the strongest conveyors of that image, dwindled.

In terms of domestic press coverage, initial changes in the image of the United States coincided with the Party's push for substantial economic reform in 1987. It was at this time that the first affirmative-didactic articles appeared, focusing on economic and social issues. It was also not long after that the press started to show the Soviet Union as being materially behind the United States in some key areas, demonstrating to the population the need to support economic reforms. Then, when political reform moved onto the Party agenda in late 1988, the press followed with corresponding affirmative-didactic articles on the American political system. The overall tone of the press was put well by *Pravda*'s Linnik who said in late 1989 that learning from Western experience was the 'general direction', it was the 'line.'

The changes in domestic and foreign images of the United States, and, indeed, the leadership's evaluation of capitalism, were closely linked with progress in US/Soviet relations. In early 1987, after the Reykjavik Summit failure, conflicting policies emerged. On the one hand, criticism grew more powerful, with the emergence of the Hyder and baby parts campaigns, the acceleration of the AIDS campaign and the growing number of charges of American human rights violations. On the other hand, this was the period when the first affirmative-didactic and 'de-ideologized' articles appeared, and when Aleksandr Bovin spoke of a 'general policy of improving the international psychological atmosphere' to pave the way for international accords. It seems that the Soviet leadership was preparing for a new approach to press coverage of the United States, but was not willing to institute the policy in full force until tangible achievements had been achieved in US/Soviet relations. When the first affirmative-didactic articles about ladders and auto clubs appeared, they were introduced timidly. The campaign surrounding the telebridges, which occurred in March and April 1987, was a way of justifying the new approach. However, it was only after the INF agreement, and then the Senate approval of the treaty, that the policy would be felt in full. The delay was most likely caused by differences of opinion in the leadership. Certainly there were differences over approaches to the West, as demonstrated by the public dispute over foreign policy in the summer of 1988 between Aleksandr Yakovlev, Eduard Shevardnadze and Igor Ligachev.

This is not to say that all changes in the press were attributable to deliberate leadership policies. If we are to ask why Soviet press coverage of the United States took its ultimate form, then we must also look at developments taking place within journalism itself and within the broad realm of identity.

CHANGE FROM BELOW

At the beginning of the Gorbachev period, the Soviet press was subordinated to and identified with the Communist Party. Its task was to promote the line of the Party's leaders in the language of the dominant ideology.

The Gorbachev period, however, gave journalists opportunities for greater self-expression. The press liberalization engendered in the policy of *glasnost'*, for all of its limitations, allowed a greater degree of autonomy for the media; the depth and breadth of coverage expanded significantly as did the sphere of legitimate controversy. The goals of *glasnost'* might have been instrumental, but the process itself brought about significant changes in the press.

The scope of press liberalization in the Soviet Union, however, did not stop with *glasnost'*. Pressure built for freedom of the press, a very different concept. What occurred was a revolution in the idea of journalism in the Soviet Union. Journalists stopped playing the role of Party publicists and started to look to their audience and their own convictions for guidance. They used their forum to present ideas which were different from those advocated by the leadership. They also searched for ways to communicate ideas which would have been impossible a few years earlier. They were aided by vague leadership policies, by divisions within the Party itself, by the breakdown of some of the Party's mechanisms of control and by support from the population. Many journalists, probably the majority, were timid and waited for instructions. However, others individually and collectively pressed for greater freedom by slowly, almost mechanically, pushing the boundaries of the acceptable.

In the sphere of press coverage of the United States, the new role of journalism had a tremendous impact, contributing to what some identified as an overly positive view of the United States. The commitment to the readership meant that many journalists were afraid to criticize the United States, lest they receive massive criticism from their readership. An *Izvestiya* reporter spoke of criticism being 'taboo' because of readership reaction and a *Pravda* reporter indicated that he portrayed the United States in a positive manner, because he did not want his readers to 'hate him'. Indeed, those reporters who did choose to criticize the United States in late 1989 and early 1990 approached their topic apprehensively, almost apologetically. The tables had been turned; journalists who wanted to criticize the US proceeded with a sense of caution similar to those who first presented affirmative-didactic articles.

The desire of journalists to assert independent opinions also affected press coverage of the United States. The United States represented for many the most powerful symbol of liberal democracy and a market economy. As such, it became an important weapon in the new ideological war, the new war of ideas about the Soviet Union's political and economic future. In this battle, the symbol of the United States became an acid test for where people stood on reform. As *Moscow News'* foreign affairs editor said in explaining his publication's approach to the United States:

> With the polarization between democrats and conservatives or reactionaries in the Soviet Union, if we were to show how awful life is in the United States, if we attempted to show how bad life is under capitalism, it would signify support for reactionaries in

the Soviet Union. That is, a newspaper like *Sovetskaya Rossiya* continues to show ulcers of capitalism – to a lesser extent, but it continues. The subtext of this is that in today's terms it would mean that the market is bad, and that the totalitarian system of management from above is good.[1]

For people like Volovets, it did not matter so much if the overall image of the United States produced in his publication was distorted, because to have done otherwise would have meant compromising *Moscow News'* stand on the future of reform in the Soviet Union.

This approach is indicative of how journalists were able to take advantage of the policy of *glasnost'* and vague Party prescriptions, turning them into distinct editorial lines. As far as coverage of the United States was concerned, the leadership might have wanted to use the press to show the need for reform, but there was no hint that it wanted published claims that 86.5 per cent of its population was living in poverty while only 20 per cent did in the West. It was one thing to criticize, another to denigrate. It might also have wanted to borrow from American experience, but there was no indication that it supported the scope of change found in *Moscow News*, nor that it supported the abandonment of a distinctly socialist society, as the editorial line of *Moscow News* suggested. This was not what the leadership had in mind when it introduced the policy of *glasnost'*, and it would appear from his speeches in meetings with media personnel that Gorbachev never reconciled himself to the media's assertion of independence.

This process, of course, worked both ways. Journalists at *Sovetskaya Rossiya* and *Literaturnaya Rossiya* were able to use vague Party guidelines to the opposite ends, to show their rejection of Western values and a Western-style market economy. Again the United States was a key symbol in the battle, although it should be noted that the images rarely reached the extent of demonization which had existed a few years earlier. Indeed, in every publication consulted, images of the United States were used in affirmative-didactic ways, regardless of emerging positions on the market economy.

SOVIET/RUSSIAN IDENTITY AND THE SYMBOL OF THE UNITED STATES

The Gorbachev leadership and those committed to reform faced an acute problem: with alienation and apathy rife, how could they convince people to support reform? How could they sell ideas, like pluralism, the separation of powers and limited private ownership when these concepts had all been previously denigrated and viewed as unnecessary in a country led by a political Party which is guided by a scientific ideology?

The answer could not lie exclusively in the language of the traditional ideology because it was limited in its capacity to communicate ideas so antithetical to its core. Instead, it was necessary to find points of reference outside the parameters of official discourse. The United States, the ideological enemy, served as an ideal symbol and tool. For better or worse, the United States had long been an integral part of Soviet identity and played an important unifying role as the common enemy of the multi-ethnic, supranational Soviet state. As the measuring point of Soviet progress, it was also the object of envy and jealousy, at least amongst the Soviet elite who were more familiar with its material wealth.

The leadership and others committed to reform recognized the powerful communicative powers of the symbol of the United States, and images of the United States were used to legitimate and support reforms ranging from the promotion of cooperatives to the creation of a system of checks and balances. So powerful was the symbol of the United States and so tarnished was the official discourse that American experience was even used to legitimate armed intervention in independence-minded republics: by late 1989 arguments for 'proletarian internationalism' simply rang hollow.[2] Indeed, the use of the symbol of the United States began to take on a logic of its own. As *Izvestiya*'s Shal'nev said, 'When you want to make a point and you want to make sure your point is going through, you just have to make a reference to the experience in the United States of America.'[3] It did not matter if the image was accurate; people needed a means for communicating ideas and the symbol of the United States supported their arguments. The same logic even applied to those who opposed the direction of reform: Marxism-Leninism was so devoid of meaning that even nationalists chose to use images of the United States to support their view of change.

There were alternative symbols to the United States which were used as a means of communicating ideas. For those more committed to socialism, there was Lenin and the NEP period. However, the Soviet past had been so discredited that such references were largely ineffective. Some turned to countries with a more social-democratic nature, like Sweden and Canada. Others looked to the authoritarian Asian Tigers and Chile. Nonetheless, the US image was dominant; it was so ingrained in the Soviet mindset that no other reference point could compete in the transition from socialism.[4]

Towards the end of the period under consideration, and after the new press law was introduced, there were fewer references to the United States than there had been in 1988, 1989 and early 1990. However, that was because the symbol had already gone a long way towards undermining the restrictions imposed on Soviet society by Newspeak. It helped give words, like pluralism and freedom of the press, new meaning. It legitimated calls for a multi-party system. In short, it helped make substantive debate over the future of the Soviet Union possible.

THE COLLAPSE OF THE POST-TOTALITARIAN PRESS SYSTEM

The post-totalitarian press system which existed in the Soviet Union at the beginning of the Gorbachev period was essentially a conservative press couched in the discourse of a transformative ideology. It spoke of building a new man and creating a new society. But perhaps its most outstanding feature was its capacity to define the enemies of the new society. This, more than any of its positive attributes, helped to legitimate the rule of the ageing gerontocracy overseeing the slow demise of the Soviet system.

The changes which occurred in the Gorbachev period in terms of press coverage of the United States demonstrate the difficulties of limiting liberalization in a post-totalitarian context. In order to build support for reform, the press had to be granted some level of autonomy and allowed a means to communicate outside the boundaries of the traditional discourse. However, once the discourse was undermined and new points of reference had been created, once people could acknowledge in public that the propaganda of Soviet success was not true, that the Soviet Union was behind the West, in short, that the emperor had no clothes, the chances of limiting liberalization decreased rapidly. The government either had to allow changes to proceed beyond its original intentions, or go back to old repressive methods.

The regime chose not to go back. By the end of the Gorbachev period, especially after the adoption of the new press law, the press moved beyond post-totalitarianism. Gorbachev himself recognized the new free press elements and stopped using the term *glasnost'*.[5] But he and others could not entirely reconcile themselves to press freedom. He threatened revocation of the press law and indirect restraints on the press proliferated, the most important being limits on paper.

In this period, however, the Soviet press enjoyed tremendous freedom. It was not yet overpowered by market forces and was not under government control. It existed in a society in which there was little consensus. It had also found a means of expressing ideas which it previously could not have expressed. It became a marketplace of ideas and a check on government. What started as a controlled liberalization became something more akin to freedom of the press.

POST-SOVIET PERIOD

The collapse of the Soviet system and the emergence of an independent market-orientated Russia had a tremendous impact on print media. The primary threat to press freedom shifted from the party to the market. While a multiplicity of views can be openly articulated, the transition has resulted in the concentration of media in the hands of the few, a dwindling number of subscribers, particularly for national dailies, a reduction in international press coverage and the growth of sensationalism.

As far as press coverage of the United States is concerned, a more healthy evolution has taken place. While differential bonds remain, the United States is no longer 'the' model. Russia may still face internal upheaval, and no doubt some will blame the US for Russia's problems, but most debate, and certainly the most serious, focuses on internal issues. Russian journalists have the capacity to examine issues facing Russia on their own terms, not through external symbols. While the future of the Russian press remains cloudy, the boundaries, be it for coverage of the United States or other issues, remain open.

Notes

INTRODUCTION

1. Quoted in Fred Siebert, Theodore Peterson and Wilbour Schramm, *Four Theories of the Press* (Urbana: University of Illinois) 1963, p. 32.
2. Peter Kerenz, *The Birth of the Propaganda State: Soviet Methods of Mass Mobilization 1917–1929* (Cambridge: Cambridge University Press) 1985, p. 4.
3. B.A. Grushin and L.A. Onikov, *Massovaya Informatsiya v Sovetskom Promyshlennom Gorode* (Moscow: Izdatel'stvo Politicheskoi Literatury) 1980, p. 306 ff; Stephen White, 'Propagating Communist Values in the USSR', Problems of Communism, vol. xxxiv, no. 6, November/December 1985, pp. 1–17; Stephen White, *Political Culture and Soviet Politics* (London: Macmillan) 1979, pp. 113–42.
4. Moshe Lewin, *The Gorbachev Phenomenon* (Berkeley: University of California Press) 1991, p. 55.
5. Howard F. Stein, 'Psychological Complementarity in Soviet–American Relations', *Political Psychology*, vol. 6, no. 2, 1985, p. 255.
6. Vladimir Shlapentokh, 'Moscow's War Propaganda and Soviet Public Opinion', *Problems of Communism*, vol. xxxiii, no. 5, September/October 1984, pp. 88–94; Grushin and Onikov, *Massovaya Informatsiya*, 1980, p. 306 ff.
7. Thomas F. Remington, *The Truth of Authority: Ideology and Communication in the Soviet Union* (Pittsburgh: University of Pittsburgh Press) 1988, pp. 84–6; Michael Voslensky, *Nomenklatura: The Soviet Ruling Class* (New York: Doubleday) 1984, p. 296; Alexander Zinoviev, *The Reality of Communism* (London: Viktor Gollancz) 1984, p. 218; Jeffery Goldfarb, *Beyond Glasnost: The Post-Totalitarian Mind* (Chicago: University of Chicago Press) 1991, p. 110.
8. Goldfarb, *Beyond Glasnost*, 1991, p. x.
9. Shlapentokh, 'War Propaganda, 1984, p. 92.
10. See Antony Buzek, *How the Communist Press Works* (London: Praeger) 1964; John C. Clews, *Communist Propaganda Techniques* (London: Methuen) 1964; Lilita Dzirkalis, Thane Gustafson and Ross Johnson, *The Media and Inter Elite Communication in the USSR* (Santa Monica: Rand Corporation) 1982; Alex Inkeles, *Public Opinion in Soviet Russia* (Cambridge: Harvard University Press) 1950; Theodore E. Kruglak, *The Two Faces of Tass* (Minneapolis: University of Minnesota Press) 1962; Siebert, Peterson and Schramm, *Four Theories*, 1963.
11. Angus Roxburgh, *Pravda: Inside the Soviet News Machine* (New York: George Braziller) 1987. Ellen Mickiewicz, *Split Signals: Television and Politics in the Soviet Union* (Oxford: Oxford University Press) 1988; Remington, *Authority*, 1988; Françoise Thom, 'The Gorbachev Phenomenon', in Françoise Thom and David Regan (eds), *Glasnost, Gorbachev*

and Lenin (London: Policy Research Publications) 1988; Martin Ebon, *The Soviet Propaganda Machine* (New York: McGraw Hill) 1987; Iain Elliot, 'How Open is Glasnost', *Survey: Journal of East–West Studies*, vol. 30, no. 3, October 1988, pp. 1–22; Natalie Gross, 'Glasnost', Roots and Practice', *Problems of Communism*, November/December 1987, vol. xxxvi, no. 6, pp. 69–80.

12. Stephen P. Gilbert, *Soviet Images of America* (London: Macdonald and Jane's) 1977; Franklyn J. Griffiths, *Images, Politics and Learning in Soviet Behavior Toward the United States*, Ph.D. dissertation (New York: Columbia University) 1972; Neil Malcolm, *Soviet Political Scientists and American Politics* (London: Macmillan) 1984; Richard M. Mills, *As Moscow Sees Us: American Politics and Society in the Soviet Mindset* (Oxford: Oxford University Press) 1990; Morton Schwartz, *Soviet Perceptions of the United States* (Berkeley: University of California Press) 1978.

13. The image of the United States in the popular press was far more 'black and white' than in specialty journals because it was designed for a mass audience, not a specialist elite. As Malcolm writes, 'It is clear that with the exception of the post-Second World War decade Soviet academic authors have always been allowed a sizeable degree of license to depart from the "newspaper" version of State Monopoly Capitalism.' Malcolm, *Political Scientists*, 1984, p. 23.

14. Roxburgh, *Pravda*, 1987, p. 10.

15. The English language *Moscow News* was chosen instead of the Russian language *Moskovskie Novosti* both because the former is more accessible and because it was specifically directed at an English-speaking foreign audience, particularly the United States. However, the two editions are essentially the same. For most important articles, the *Moskovskie Novosti* edition was consulted to confirm that the material appeared and that the translation was accurate. There were only a few cases of notable differences.

1 PRESS SYSTEMS

1. Voslensky, *Nomenklatura*, 1983, p. 296.

2. Siebert, Schramm and Peterson conclude that the press, in principle, 'takes on the form and coloration of the social and political structures within which it operates', and it 'especially reflects the system of control whereby the relations of individuals and institutions are adjusted'. Siebert, Peterson and Schramm, *Four Theories*, 1964, p. 1.

3. Much of the work on media systems is done either by journalists or experts in the study of communications. Because of this, authors have missed much valuable research in the field of politics which could help to clarify important distinctions between systems.

4. According to Schramm, totalitarian media systems include state ownership, censorship, a utilitarian function in the construction of socialism and a devotion to Marxist-Leninism. Siebert, Schramm and Peterson, *Four Theories*, 1963, p. 121 ff. According to Friedrich, totalitarian systems

contain six elements: '(1) a totalist ideology; (2) a single party committed to this ideology and usually led by one man, the dictator; (3) a fully developed secret police; and three kinds of monopoly or, more precisely, monopolistic control: namely that of (a) mass communications; (b) operational weapons; (c) all organizations, including economic ones, thus involving a centrally-planned economy.' Carl J. Friedrich, 'The Evolving Theory and Practice of Totalitarian Regimes', in Carl J. Friedrich, Michael Curtis and Benjamin R. Barber, *Totalitarianism in Perspective: Three Views* (New York: Praeger Publishers) 1969, p. 126.

5. See Juan J. Linz, 'Totalitarian and Authoritarian Regimes', in Fred Greenstein and Nelson W. Polsby (eds), *Macropolitical Theory* (Reading: Addison-Wesley) 1975.

6. According to Linz, authoritarian political systems are 'political systems with limited, not responsible, political pluralism, without an elaborate and guiding ideology, but with distinctive mentalities, without extensive nor intensive political mobilization, except at some points in their development, and in which a leader or occasionally a small group exercises power within formally ill defined limits but actually quite predictable ones'. Linz, 'Totalitarian and Authoritarian Regimes', 1975, p. 264. See also, Negrine, *Media in Britain*, 1989, p. 26. See also Siebert, Schramm and Peterson, *Four Theories*, 1963, p. 10; McQuail, *Communication*, 1983, p. 84; Jean Seaton and Ben Pimlott, 'The Role of the Media in the Portuguese Revolution', in Smith (ed.), *Newspapers and Democracy*, 1980, p. 175. See also Warren K. Agee and Nelson Traquina, *A Frustrated Fourth Estate: Portugal's Post-Revolutionary Mass Media*, Journalism Monographs, no. 87, February 1984, p. 10 and Francisco Pinto Balsemao, 'Democracy and Authoritarianism and the Role of Media in Portugal, 1974–1975', in Maxwell (ed.), *The Press and the Rebirth of Iberian Democracy*, 1983, p. 117; Habte, 'Third World', 1983, p. 106. See also Dennis L. Wilcox, 'Black African States', in Curry and Dassin (eds), *Press Control*, 1982, p. 212; William A. Rugh, *The Arab Press: News Media and Political Process in the Arab World* (Syracuse: Syracuse University Press) 1987; Munir K. Nassar, 'The Middle East Press: Tool of Politics', in Curry and Dassin (eds), *Press Control*, 1982, pp. 187–208.

7. Most works in political science concentrate on negative control, which would symbolically be represented as *A controls B with regard to B's not doing x*. Here, I focus equally on positive control, or *A controls B with regard to B's doing x*. This is of crucial importance because positive control by the government over the press is a key distinguishing feature of totalitarian press systems.

In applying the concepts of negative and positive control to the press, it can be said that negative control implies that: 1) the press has a powerful predisposition against publishing material which the government opposes; and 2) should the press seek to publish such material, the government can either (a) convince it not to publish the material, or (b) prevent it from publishing the material. Positive control implies that: 1) the press has a powerful predisposition towards publishing material desired by the government; and 2) should the press be inclined not to publish material which the government desires, the government can either (a) convince it to publish the material, or (b) force it to publish the material. Much of this is borrowed from Felix Oppenheim, 'Power and Causation', in Brian Barry (ed.), *Power and Political Theory: Some European Perspectives* (London: John Wiley) 1976, p. 114. See also Robert A. Dahl, *Dilemmas of Pluralist Democracy: Autonomy vs. Control* (New Haven: Yale University Press) 1982, p. 17; Steven Lukes, *Power: A Radical View* (London: Macmillan) 1990, p. 40.

8. Remington, *Authority*, 1988, p. 4 ff.
9. Carl J. Friedrich and Zbigniew K. Brzezinski, *Totalitarian Dictatorship and Autocracy* (Cambridge: Harvard University Press), p. 10; Friedrich, 'Totalitarian Regimes', 1969, p. 144.
10. I will accept Friedrich and Brzezinski's definition of ideology as an 'action related system of ideas'. Friedrich, 'Totalitarian Regimes', p. 138. I am sympathetic to Schull's definition of ideology as 'a form of discourse or a political language – a body of linguistic propositions expressed as speech acts and united by the conventions governing them', because it is particularly appropriate to Soviet-style systems. The arguments put forward about the role of ideology in distinguishing totalitarian press systems would fit this definition. Indeed, many of the arguments below about the impact of language on a political system are similar to Schull's. However, the concept of ideology as discourse has not been sufficiently developed. Schull does not devote enough attention to the ideational sources of the particular linguistic propositions and therefore what distinguishes different types of ideologies. See Joseph Schull, 'What is Ideology? Theoretical Problems and Lessons from Soviet-Type Societies', *Political Studies*, vol. xl, 1992, p. 729.
11. Goldfarb explains: 'Life really is different in an old-fashioned tyranny than in a totalitarian order. Though traditional autocracies may sometimes be more unpleasant and brutal, human ontology is not undergoing a conscious, politically enforced, systematic redefinition.' Goldfarb, *Beyond Glasnost*, 1991, p. 4; Hannah Arendt, *The Origins of Totalitarianism* (New York: Meridian Books), 1958, p. 470 ff.
12. John Wesley Young, *Totalitarian Language* (Charlottesville: University Press of Virginia) 1991, p. 31.
13. On the importance of the goals of the party, see T.H. Rigby, 'Introduction: Political Legitimacy, Weber and Communist Mono-Organizational Systems', in T.H. Rigby and Ferenc Fehér (eds), *Political Legitimation in Communist States* (London: Macmillan) 1982, pp. 1–26.
14. Goldfarb, *Beyond Glasnost*, 1991, p. 48.
15. George Schopflin, *Censorship and Political Communication in Eastern Europe* (New York: St Martin's Press) 1983, p. 5; Young, *Totalitarian Language*, 1991, p. 31.
16. A good example of the difficulties with taking on the dominant ideology was the attempt of Lysenko's opponents to undermine his influence. Criticism had to be made more on ideological than scientific grounds. Goldfarb, *Beyond Glasnost*, 1991, p. 44. Schull associates such difficul-

ties with Gorbachev, asserting that he 'did not jettison (Soviet) ideology quick enough, but tried to reform it from within a language that is impervious to reform'. Joseph Schull, 'The Self-Destruction of Ideology', The Harriman Institute Forum, vol. 4, no. 7, July 1991, p. 2.

17. Goldfarb, *Beyond Glasnost*, 1991, pp. 110, 55; Young, *Totalitarian Language*, 1991, p. 31.
18. Siebert, Peterson and Schramm, *Four Theories*, p. 4 ff.
19. In speaking of what he views as an absence of ideology in most authoritarian regimes, or at least of the comparative weakness of authoritarian versus totalitarian ideologies, Linz writes, 'The student of an authoritarian regime would be hard pressed to identify explicit references to ideas guiding the regime in legal theorizing and judicial decisions in nonpolitical cases, in art criticism and scientific arguments, and would only find limited evidence of their use in education.' Linz, 'Totalitarian and Authoritarian Regimes', 1975, pp. 267–8.
20. Linz, 'Totalitarian and Authoritarian Regimes', 1975, p. 265.
21. Linz, 'Totalitarian and Authoritarian Regimes', 1975, p. 191.
22. Linz, 'Totalitarian and Authoritarian Regimes', 1975, p. 229. For different examples of writing about the post-Stalin Soviet political system, see Brown, 'Political Power', 1984, p. 56; Grzegorz Ekiert, 'Democratic Processes in East Central Europe: A Theoretical Reconsideration', *British Journal of Political Science*, vol. 21, pt. 3, 1991, p. 293; Paul Cocks, 'The Rationalization of Party Control', in Chalmers Johnson (ed.), *Change in Communist Systems* (Stanford: Stanford University Press) 1970, pp. 153–90; Richard Lowenthal, 'Development vs. Utopia in Communist Policy', in Johnson (ed.), *Change in Communist Systems*, 1970, pp. 33–116; Gabriel Almond and Laura Roselle, 'Model Fitting in Communism Studies', in Thomas Remington (ed.), *Politics and the Soviet System* (London: Macmillan) 1989, p. 172 ff; Allen Kassoff, 'The Administered Society: Totalitarianism without Terror', *World Policy Journal*, vol. 16, July 1964, pp. 558–75.
23. Lowenthal, 'Development vs. Utopia', 1970, p. 51; Jeremy A. Azrael, 'Varieties of De-Stalinization', in Johnson (ed.), *Change in Communist Systems*, 1970, p. 138.
24. Linz describes the life of the totalitarian regime in two phases. The first is a 'highly ideological' phase, followed by a second phase where there is a 'more instrumental attitude towards ideology'. In describing this process moving towards post-totalitarianism, he says, 'The more remote the ideological initial thrust and commitment becomes and the more scholastic the use of the ideology, the more the system will either turn to personal power or, once the staff in a Weberian process proceeds to the routinization of charisma and its institutionalization in the party, toward a process of de-ideologization.' Linz, 'Totalitarian and Authoritarian Regimes', 1975, p. 229; Goldfarb, *Beyond Glasnost*, 1991, p. xv.
25. Diane R. Spechler, *Permitted Dissent in the USSR* (New York: Praeger) 1982; The Rand study indicated that while there was some leadership control of debate, 'central directives on coverage notwithstanding, each journal or newspaper has a certain latitude to take a position that

reflects the public it is addressed to or the official function it serves . . . Different media do diverge from one another in details of their coverage, but the Central Committee remains unconcerned so long as the diversity remains within accepted bounds . . .'. Dzirkalis, Gustafson and Johnson, *Elite Communication*, 1982, p. 66.

26. Spechler, *Dissent*, 1982; Goldfarb, *Beyond Glasnost*, 1991, p. 57 ff.
27. Goldfarb, *Beyond Glasnost*, 1991, p. 57 ff; Jerry F. Hough and Merle Fainsod, *How the Soviet Union is Governed* (Cambridge: Harvard University Press) 1979, p. 294 ff.
28. Spechler, *Dissent*, 1982, p. 255.
29. Schull, 'The Self-Destruction of Ideology', 1991.
30. Voslensky, *Nomenklatura*, 1984, p. 296.
31. Adam Przeworski, *Democracy and the Market* (Cambridge: Cambridge University Press) 1991, p. 54; Remington, *Authority*, 1988, p. 84; Glazov, *The Russian Mind*, 1985, p. 11; Voslensky, *Nomenklatura*, 1984, p. 296.
32. This model is taken from Daniel Hallin's analysis of the Western media regarding the Vietnam war. The significance of the three spheres has been altered in order to take into account totalitarian and authoritarian media systems. Daniel C. Hallin, *The Uncensored War* (Berkeley: University of California Press) 1989, p. 117 ff.

2 SOVIET COMMUNICATIONS POLICY

1. K. Chernenko, *Pravda*, 12 December 1984, p. 1.
2. Quoted in Siebert, Peterson and Schramm, *Four Theories*, 1954, p. 112.
3. T.D. Orlova, *Vvedenie v Zhurnalistiku: Organizatsiya Raboty Redaktsii Gazety* (Minsk: Universitetskoe) 1989, p. 100; Alexander Pumpyansky, 'Are We Really So Tired of the Truth?', *New Times*, no. 14, 8–14 May 1990, p. 34.
4. The idea of social engineering was more a product of Stalin than Lenin. It was originally believed that a change in environment brought about by the worldwide revolution would be sufficient to change people. However, in keeping with the grand campaigns of the Stalin years, the stress moved to the active creation of a new social being, with the press playing a key role. Benn, *Persuasion*, 1991, p. 57 ff; Kerenz, *Birth of the Propaganda State*, 1985, pp. 5–6; Robert Conquest, *The Politics of Ideas of the USSR* (London: Bodley Head), 1967, pp. 8–9.
5. Siebert, Peterson and Schramm, *Four Theories*, 1964, p. 132.
6. It is, of course, difficult to know exactly what people thought. However, it would seem unlikely that all people in the Soviet leadership had actually given up the hope of a revolutionary transformation brought by socialism. Certainly most leaders still referred to 'moulding' a new man in their speeches. Even Gorbachev was dogged in his refusal to abandon socialism.
7. P.I. Agzamov, *Zhurnalistskoe Issledovanie Aktivnosti i Lichnosti* (Kazan: Kazanskaya Universiteta), 1989, p. 59 ff; M.F. Nenashev, *Gazeta, Chitatel', Vremya* (Moscow: Mysl') 1986, p. 17 ff; V.K. Fedin, *Sotsialisticheskoe Sorevnovanie i Gazeta* (Moscow: Mysl') 1986, p. 71 ff.

8. Remington, *Authority*, 1988, pp. 84–6; Voslensky, *Nomenklatura*, 1984, p. 296; Zinoviev, *Reality of Communism*, 1984, p. 218.
9. Schopflin, *Political Communication*, 1983, p. 5.
10. Although the Party's overt mode of legitimation remained its unique ability to lead the transition to communism, what Rigby calls 'goal-rational authority,' the Soviet Communist Party, like its fraternal parties in Eastern Europe, also legitimated its rule in covert ways. Markus points out that in Eastern Europe, these covert means of legitimation were particularly felt when speech became ritualized. More broadly, she wrote, 'Generally speaking, the system of covert legitimation is far from being, or even attempting to be, coherent. In this sense it "adapts" itself to "commonsense" which is never a systematic world view. At least in some of its elements, it attempts to introduce a kind of traditional legitimation for basically modern, i.e. dynamic societies, for a type of society which was originally created in the name of a radically different future and which – in its overt ideology – retains the emphasis on the future and on the rational character of the chosen alternative. At the same time, it radically changes the evaluation of this alternative itself, by transforming the overt thesis which refers to the given social reality as the best alternative, into negative proof that any other alternative is non-existent and even impossible ... Such a change in basic perspective means at the same time a shift in the emphasis of legitimation from the evaluation of the regime on its own merits to the acknowledgment of its effectiveness as compared usually with the historical past of the country concerned or where possible with its least successful neighbors.' I would suggest that in the case of the Soviet Union, especially as it approached 70 years of communism, the reference point tended to be the West. Maria Markus, 'Overt and Covert Modes of Legitimation in East European Societies', in Rigby and Fehér (eds), *Political Legitimation*, 1982, pp. 82–94; Rigby, 'Political Legitimacy', 1982, p. 12; Agnes Heller, 'Phases of Legitimation in Soviet-type Societies', in Rigby and Fehér (eds), *Political Legitimation*, 1982, pp. 56–7.
11. Although many people were aware that the Soviet Union was materially behind the West, the Party still used two arguments to assert the superiority of socialism. First, it was catching up with the West and would soon leave it behind. Second, superior social conditions made for a more equitable and just society and thus a better overall standard of living.
12. Markus, 'Overt and Covert Modes of Legitimation', 1982, p. 89.
13. V.M. Gorokhov, *Osnovy Zhurnalistskogo Masterstvo* (Moscow: Vysshaya Shkola) 1989, p. 15; Orlova, *Vvedenie v Zhurnalistiku*, 1989, p. 89; Brian McNair, *Glasnost, Perestroika and the Soviet Media* (London: Routledge) 1991, p. 20.
14. Remington, *Authority*, 1988, p. 170.
15. N.N. Lipovchenko, quoted by McNair, *Glasnost*, 1991, p. 21. See N.N. Lipovchenko, *Ocherk, Teorii, Zhurnalistiki*, 1985.
16. McNair, *Glasnost*, 1991, p. 20.
17. Siebert, Peterson and Schramm, *Four Theories*, 1963, p. 140; Hale,

Captive Press, 1964, p. 76 ff. Curry may be correct in stating that, 'state ownership does not necessarily taint and restrict information, nor does private ownership guarantee its freedom'. However, the scope of control necessary for a totalitarian (or post-totalitarian) press system would almost unquestionably necessitate state ownership. Indeed, it is difficult to imagine the totalitarian (or post-totalitarian) system existing in a country with private press ownership, assuming ownership was more than a façade. Curry, 'Media Management and Media Systems', 1982, p. 261.

18. 'The general guidance of the press, including those who worked in international journalism, occurred in the Propaganda Department of the Central Committee of the CPSU. The primary means through which this guidance occurred was through the selection of editors-in-chief and political cadres, that is, without the approval of this department of the Central Committee of the Communist Party, no editor-in-chief of a newspaper could be named. This frequently applied to members of the editorial board, and the heads of the departments, if it is a big newspaper.' Sergei Volovets, Foreign Editor, *Moscow News* (Moscow, May 1990).

19. Volovets (Moscow: May 1990).

20. Thomas F. Remington, 'Politics and Professionalism in Soviet Journalism', *Slavic Review*, vol. 44, no. 3, Fall 1985, p. 492 ff.

21. Remington, 'Politics and Professionalism', 1985, p. 494; Remington, *Authority*, pp. 138–9; Ellen Mickiewicz, 'The Functions of Communications Officials in the USSR: A Biographical Study', *Slavic Review*, vol. 43, no. 4, Winter 1984, pp. 650–51.

22. Remington, *Authority*, 1988, pp. 115 ff.

23. Remington, 'Politics and Professionalism', 1985, p. 498.

24. Sergei Grigoriev, formerly of the Ideology Department of the CPSU, author interview (Middletown: April 1992); Viktor Linnik, Foreign Correspondent, *Pravda*, author interview (New York: December 1989).

25. Grigoriev (Middletown: April 1992).

26. Remington, *Authority*, 1988, p. 104.

27. The Rand Survey said of the Propaganda Department: 'It is the dominating department *vis-à-vis* the media. Other departments participate in deciding what information the media will present in their own areas of competence, but our respondents maintained that the Propaganda Department usually retains the final say.' Dzirkalis, Gustafson and Johnson, *Elite Communication*, 1982, p. 13. Many of the reporters whom I interviewed indicated that in the spring of 1990, the Ideology Department continued to play the leading role.

28. Viktor Gribachev, Foreign Editor, *Zhurnalist*, author interview (Moscow: May 1990).

29. Grigoriev (Middletown: April 1992).

30. Linnik (New York, December 1989). Before becoming a reporter at *Pravda*, Linnik served in the International Information Department.

31. Grigoriev (Middletown: April 1992). The Rand report said that the International Department received 'evaluations of international developments prepared in "brain centers" associated with different Polit-

buro members and utilizes these together with other information, to prepare media directives. Both TASS and Novosti receive(d) specific department directives on how to handle particular events and Novosti is told what to promote in the foreign media.' Dzirkalis, Gustafson and Johnson, *Elite Communication*, 1982, pp. 20–21.

32. Grigoriev (Middletown: April 1992).
33. Grigoriev (Middletown: April 1992).
34. Volovets (Moscow: May 1990). Gribachev (Moscow: May 1990).
35. *Pravda*'s Linnik mentioned that his editor, Afanas'ev, was frequently telephoned by Politburo members who gave orders for the publication of specific materials. Author interview (New York: December 1989).
36. Alexei Pankin, Deputy Editor, *Mezhdunarodnaya Zhizn'*, author interview (Moscow: June 1989); Alexander Sychev, Senior Correspondent, *Izvestiya*, author interview (Moscow: June 1990).
37. The Rand study claimed that their respondents 'dismissed as a mere formality *Glavlit*'s subordination to the Council of Ministers,' stating that 'in practice, the Central Committee Propaganda Department and the KGB supervise *Glavlit*', with the Propaganda Department providing 'ideological and political guidelines'. Dzirkalis, Gustafson and Johnson, *Elite Communication*, 1982, p. 38; Mickiewicz, 'Functions of Communications,' 1984, p. 642.
38. *New York Times*, 18 July 1989.
39. Gribachev (Moscow: May 1990). For example, Varje Sootak, editor-in-chief of *Universatatus Tartuensis*, said that a simple sketch of Mikhail Gorbachev was ruled unacceptable by the Estonian Glavlit, because it was considered disrespectful. Author interview (Tartu: March 1990).
40. Yuri Sigov, Staff Correspondent, *Argumenty i Fakty*, author interview (Moscow: June 1990). For example, Gribachev at *Zhurnalist* said that 'There was rather serious ideological control. For example, take Havel. After 1968 he was considered a dissident and we never wrote about him, because every editor knew that if he attempted to, say, print a discussion with Havel, there could have been repression of the publication or the editor.' Author interview (Moscow: May 1990).
41. Several writers and editors indicated this. See also Dzirkalis, Gustafson and Johnson, *Elite Communication*, 1982, p. 37 ff.
42. Ernest J. Simmons, 'The Writers', in H. Gordon Skilling and Franklyn Griffiths (eds), *Interest Groups in Soviet Politics* (Princeton: Princeton University Press) 1971, pp. 253–89.
43. While different authors might list variations of the six principles, the differences were rarely substantial. The six were listed in Bogdanov and Viazemskii, which was the most detailed account consulted. N.G. Bogdanov and V.A. Vyazemskii, *Spravochnik Zhurnalista* (Moscow: Lenizdat) 1971, pp. 20–39. For more recent accounts, see E.P. Prokhorov, 'Sistema printsipov sotsialisticheskoi zhurnalistiki', *Vestnik Moskovskogo Universiteta no. 10: Zhurnalistika*, no. 2, 3, March–April, May–June 1988, pp. 7–18, 13–22; Orlova, *Vvedenie v Zhurnalistiku*, 1989, p. 73 ff; See also McNair, *Glasnost*, 1991, p. 17 ff.
44. This imbalance was in part a product of the role of the Party which, although bearing in mind the mood and views of the masses, was

never to find itself in a position of following them (*khvostizm* or tail-ending), for that would be counterproductive. Buzek, *Communist Press*, 1964, p. 13.

45. A. Avraamov, 'Bez osobykh tseremonii', *Zhurnalist'*, March 1988, p. 64. See also Robert English and Jonathan Halperin, *The Other Side: How Soviets and Americans Perceive Each Other* (Oxford: Transaction Books) 1987, p. 53.

46. Remington, 'Socialist Pluralism', 1989, p. 273.

47. Dzirkalis, Gustafson and Johnson, *Elite Communication*, 1982, p. vii; Remington, *Authority*, 1988, p. 149; Remington, 'Socialist Pluralism', 1989, pp. 281–2, n. 31.

48. Quoted by Paul Lendvai, 'What is Newsworthy and What is Not in the Communist World', in Martin and Chaudhary (eds), *Comparative Media Systems*, 1983, p. 69.

49. '[P]roviding objective information was not among the functions of the press. This presupposed a different role and different relations between the press, the reading public and the authorities.' Pumpyansky, 'Tired of the Truth?', 1990, p. 34.

50. A Soviet book on information and the press, in commenting on a *Komsomol'skaya Pravda* article on whales, said: 'Journalists, especially in the information department, must always think about the purpose of the material being published. Why is it being printed? What does it give to the reader? What does it teach? What example does it inspire? A paragraph which serves no social, educative or didactic function is a sop which must have no place in the Soviet press.' P. Gurevich, quoted by Benn, *Persuasion*, 1989, p. 72.

51. Roxburgh, *Pravda*, 1987, p. 85; Ellen Mickiewicz, 'Policy Issues in the Soviet Media System', in Erik P. Hoffmann (ed.), *The Soviet Union in the 1980s* (Vermont: Capital City Press) 1984, p. 115; Nenashev, *Gazeta, Chitatel', Vremya*, 1986, p. 1.

52. Roxburgh, *Pravda*, 1987, p. 48.

53. Spechler, *Dissent*, 1982; Dzirkalis, Gustafson and Johnson, *Elite Communication*, 1982, p. 66.

54. Goldfarb, *Beyond Glasnost*, 1991, p. 44. In speaking generally about the social sciences, Evgeny Arbamatsumov noted, 'Given the atmosphere of ostentation and social apologetics, this was an intellectually fruitless, but paying occupation. This is why many young and some mature scientists took the line of least resistance, adjusting themselves to the situation. If they dared to pose a burning question, they tended to mask it with verbosity, seeking safety behind platitudes and commonplace statements.' Quoted by Archie Brown, 'Perestroika and the Political System', in Pravda and Hasegawa (eds), *Perestroika*, 1990, p. 58.

55. Benn, *Persuasion*, 1989, p. 72.

56. As Mickiewicz states, 'Actually, the hypodermic effects theory is a broadcaster's dream, the total actualization of his effort, but like most dreams, wishful thinking.' Mickiewicz, *Split Signals*, 1988, p. 181. See also Jack M. McLeod and Lee B. Becker, 'Testing the Validity of Gratification Measures Through Political Effects Analysis', in Jay G.

Blumer and Elihu Katz (eds), *The Uses of Mass Communications: Current Perspectives on Gratifications Research* (Beverly Hills: Sage), 1974, p. 137.

57. Benn, *Persuasion*, 1989, p. 53. Alfred Meyer said, for example, that 'Soviet citizenship training has succeeded and the basic tenets of the ideology have been internalized'. Samuel Huntington said that the Soviet Union was probably 'the most successful case [which exists] of planned political culture change'. Quoted by White, *Political Culture*, 1979, p. 114.

58. Peter Vihalmm, Sociology Department, Tartu University, author interview (Tartu: March 1990); Stephen White, 'Propagating Communist Values in the USSR', *Problems of Communism*, vol. xxxiv, no. 6, November/December 1985, p. 3.

59. Mickiewicz, *Split Signals*, 1988, p. 182.

60. Grushin and Onikov, *Massovaya Informatsiya*, 1980, p. 242 ff; White, 'Propagating Communist Values', 1985, pp. 1–17.

61. Mickiewicz, for example, spoke of the words which were 'totally meaningless' to the population cited in the Taganrog study. However, she never addresses the other data from the same study which point to success in building inimical views of the West and positive views of the Soviet Union. *Split Signals*, 1988, p. 182. For some thoughtful analysis on the impact of Soviet propaganda, see White, *Political Culture*, 1979, pp. 141–2.

62. Mickiewicz, *Split Signals*, 1988, p. 182.

63. Grushin and Onikov, Massovaya Informatsiya, 1980, p. 312 ff; Shlapentokh, 'Two Levels of Public Opinion', 1985, p. 450.

64. Shlapentokh, 'War Propaganda', 1984, p. 89.

65. Benn, *Persuasion*, 1989, p. 188.

66. Mickiewicz, 'Soviet Media', 1984, p. 118.

67. Shlapentokh, 'War Propaganda', 1984, p. 88.

68. Mickiewicz, *Split Signals*, 1988, p. 196. See also Mickiewicz, 'Soviet Media', 1984, p. 115; Shlapentokh, 'War Propaganda', 1984, p. 89. White pointed out that the same was true for political education classes and other forms of agitation. White, *Political Culture*, 1979, p. 125.

69. Roxburgh, *Pravda*, 1987, p. 94; White, *Political Culture*, 1979, p. 138.

70. Roxburgh, *Pravda*, 1987, p. 94; Shlapentokh, 'War Propaganda', 1984, p. 89.

71. Dzirkalis, Gustafson and Johnson, *Elite Communication*, 1982, p. 23.

72. Gayle Durham Hollander, 'Political Communication and Dissent in the Soviet Union', in Rudolf L. Tokes (ed.), *Dissent in the USSR* (Baltimore: Johns Hopkins Press) 1975, pp. 266–7.

73. Benn, *Persuasion*, 1989, pp. 297–8, citing Nadezhda Nazarova, *Formirovanie Kommunisticheskoi Ubezhdyennosti Molodezhi* (Kiev) 1981. Western estimates show similar results. One indicated that in a given week approximately 20% of the Soviet population was exposed to at least one of the four leading Western broadcasters – Radio Liberty, Voice of America, the BBC and Deutsche Welle. See also Mickiewicz, 'Soviet Media', 1984, p. 115; Roxburgh, *Pravda*, 1987, p. 94.

74. Lewin, *Gorbachev Phenomenon*, 1991, p. 47 ff.

75. Benn, *Persuasion*, 1989, p. 154.

76. David Binder, *New York Times*, 1 June 1987. See also Maurry Lissann, *Broadcasting to the Soviet Union* (New York: Praeger) 1975.

77. The United States Information Agency estimates that the Soviet Union in the past has employed 15,000 technicians and spent up to $500 million dollars jamming Western broadcasts. USIA News Release, 30 April 1987. See also Roxburgh, *Pravda*, 1987, p. 94.

78. Ellen Mickiewicz, 'The Functions of Communications', 1984, p. 649. There was particularly growing concern because of the West's advantages in communications technologies. Mickiewicz, 'Soviet Media', 1984, p. 115.

79. White claimed that in 1940, perhaps only 2% of the Soviet population were able to listen to foreign radios, by 1950 it was 8% and by the 1970s it was 50%. Stephen White, *Gorbachev in Power* (Cambridge: Cambridge University Press), 1990, p. 58

80. Concern became even more pronounced as the United States threatened to broadcast satellite television in the early 1980s. See Viktor Yasmann, 'Glasnost versus Freedom of Information: Political and Ideological Aspects', *Radio Liberty Report on the USSR*, vol. 1, no. 29, 21 July 1989, p. 4; Sergei Drozhin, 'Potok nesvobodnoi informatsii', *Zhurnalist'*, September 1988, pp. 55–7.

81. Peter J. Humphreys, 'The International Political Economy of the Communications Revolution: The Case for a Neo-Pluralist Approach', *Government and Opposition*, vol. 25, no. 4, 1990, p. 515; Viktor Yasmann, 'Freedom of Information', 1989, pp. 1–6; Marshall Goldman, *Gorbachev's Challenge* (New York: W.W. Norton) p. 86 ff; Robert Levgold, 'The Revolution in Soviet Foreign Policy', *Foreign Affairs*, vol. 68, no. 1, 1989, pp. 82–98.

82. *Pravda*, 6 May 1979, pp. 1–2.

83. *Pravda*, 28 November 1978, p. 2. The commission was almost certainly influenced by the findings of the above-cited Taganrog study which highlighted the failures of the press. The Taganrog study was conducted between 1967 and 1974, although it was not published as a book until 1980. Benn, *Persuasion*, 1989, p. 154.

84. Note the banal statement of Brezhnev at the XXVth Party Congress in 1976 that: 'In the period under review, the questions of raising the ideological level of the mass information and propaganda media and improving their coordination and operational efficiency held an important place in the Central Committee's activity. As a result, the media's influence in the development of the economy, science and culture and on all social life grew still more.' *CDSP*, vol. xxviii, no. 8, 1976, p. 27.

85. *Pravda*, 6 May 1979, p. 1.

86. Yakovlev, *CDSP*, vol. xxxiii, no. 34, pp. 1–3. (This was not the future Politburo member.)

87. *Pravda*, 6 May 1979, p. 1.

88. The policy of détente may have reinforced the Brezhnev leadership's tendency towards domestic conservatism in order to compensate for

the external compromise with the ideological enemy. As Alex Pravda stated, 'the disquieting influences involved in the détente policy probably reinforced the natural inclination of a conservative and cautious regime to maintain tough controls over political developments, particularly dissidence.' A. Pravda, 'Introduction: Linkages between Soviet Domestic and Foreign Policy under Gorbachev', in Hasegawa and Pravda (eds), *Perestroika*, 1990, p. 2.

89. The full text read, 'In essence, what is involved here is the restructuring – yes, this was not a slip of the tongue, I meant restructuring – of many sectors and spheres of ideological work. Its content must be made more topical, and its forms should meet the present-day needs and requirements of the Soviet people.' L.I. Brezhnev, *XXVI S"ezd Kommunisticheskoi Partii Sovetskogo Soyuza* (Moscow), 1981, p. 94.

90. Certainly Chernenko showed continuity in articulating similar notions after he became General Secretary later that year. On Chernenko, see Remington, 'Strategy of Glasnost'', 1989, p. 59.

91. Referring to specific press organs, Chernenko stated, 'Persistently and persuasively conveying the truth about our foreign policy to the masses, winning public opinion over to the side of this policy and exposing the plans of imperialist circles are extremely important tasks for TASS, the Novosti Press Agency, the State Committee for Television and Radio and other agencies engaged in foreign policy propaganda. The CPSU Central Committee International Information Department must coordinate all this work as much as possible.' *Pravda*, 15 June 1983, pp. 1–3. See *CDSP*, vol. xxxv, no. 24, pp. 2–10.

92. Chernenko indicated: 'We must switch from appraising the state of ideological processes to actually forecasting them, from random studies of public opinion to systematic polls and perhaps we must set about organizing a center for the study of public opinion.' *Pravda*, 15 June 1983, pp. 1–3.

93. *Pravda*, 16 June 1983, p. 1.

94. See Jonathan Steele and Eric Abraham, *Andropov in Power* (Oxford: Martin Robertson) 1983, especially p. 165 ff.

95. White, 'Propagating Communist Values', 1979, pp. 1–15. *Izvestiya*'s Alexander Bovin said of the resolution, 'People might have thought that it was necessary to say a couple of words about the situation, but later they did not do anything or they did very little.' Author interview (Moscow: May 1990). *Izvestiya* editor G. Deinchenko concurred, stating bluntly, 'nothing ever changed'. Author interview (Moscow: April 1990).

96. Yakovlev, *CDSP*, vol. xxxiii, no. 34, 1981, p. 3.

97. *Pravda*'s editor, Viktor Afanas'ev demonstrated the conservatism of the leadership when he wrote: 'Unfortunately, we journalists sometimes relish . . . shortcomings; we unload them without discrimination onto the pages of our publications and onto the airwaves. And we often do not reflect that all of this is "bread" for our opponents, for the denigration of Soviet reality.' Quoted in Benn, *Persuasion*, 1989, p. 79.

98. Alexander Krivapolev, Foreign Correspondent, *Izvestiya*, author interview (London: March 1990); Krainov (Moscow: April 1990).
99. Thomas Remington, 'Gorbachev and the Strategy of Glasnost', in Remington (ed.), *Politics and the Soviet System* (London: Macmillan) 1989, pp. 62–70.
100. Remington indicated that ideological policy began to change between January and the spring of 1985 when 'a number of articles signalled that the media were under pressure to fight secretiveness in public life, to develop greater trust between officials and citizens, to fight phenomena such as complacency, report padding, waste and mismanagement, and concealment of deficiencies'. He attributed this to Gorbachev's position of responsibility for ideology as Chernenko became increasingly incapacitated. Remington, 'Strategy of Glasnost', 1989, p. 59; See also Archie Brown, 'Gorbachev – New Man in the Kremlin', *Problems of Communism*, vol. xxiv, no. 3, May/June 1985, pp. 8–9.
101. Perhaps because of the radical nature of the speech for the time, it was not covered in full in *Pravda* or *Izvestiya*. Brown, 'New Man in the Kremlin', 1985, p. 19. See Gorbachev, 'Zhivoe tvorchestvo naroda', 1984 in Gorbachev, *Izbrannye Rechi i Stat'i*, vol. 2 (Moscow: Izdatel'stvo Politicheskoi Literatury) 1987, pp. 75–107.
102. Remington pointed out that Gorbachev's stress on economics in the 1984 speech 'reflected an unstated rejection of the Chernenko line, which had stressed the inculcation of Marxist-Leninist consciousness as the main objective of ideological work'. Remington, 'Strategy of Glasnost'', 1989, p. 59.
103. Gorbachev, 'Zhivoe tvorchestvo naroda', 1984, p. 99.
104. For example, Gorbachev stated, 'In terms of its intensity, contents and methods, the "psychological warfare" that imperialism is currently waging constitutes a special variety of aggression that flouts the sovereignty of countries.' Gorbachev, 'Zhivoe tvorchestvo naroda', 1984, p. 99 ff.
105. Gorbachev, quoted in Remington, *Authority*, 1988, p. 21.
106. Benn quite accurately concluded that Soviet propaganda and censorship as a whole were 'more effective in a negative than a positive sense' doing 'far more than the Communist Party needed in order to remain in power, but far less than it needed in order to win the hearts and the minds'. Benn, *Persuasion*, 1989, p. 221.

3 *GLASNOST'* VS FREEDOM OF THE PRESS

1. Przeworski, *Democracy and the Market*, 1991, pp. 57–8. Perhaps more applicable for the press in the Soviet case is the policy of *glasnost'*, which is more like *apertura* and *odnowa*, meaning a social and political opening, rather than *perestroika*, which refers first to economic restructuring. For the case in Czechoslovakia, see Dusan Havlicek, 'The Mass Media and their Impact on Czechoslovak Politics in 1968', V.V. Kusin (ed.), *The Czechoslovak Reform Movement: 1968* (London:

International Research Documents) 1973, p. 246; for Poland, see Madeleine Korbel Albright, *Poland: The Role of the Press in Political Change* (New York: Praeger) 1983, p. 26.

2. Samuel Huntington, *Democracy's Third Wave* (Norman: University of Oklahoma Press) 1991, p. 9; Przeworski, *Democracy and Market*, 1991, p. 57. Andrzej Korobonski, 'Liberalization Processes', in Carmelo Mesa Logo and Carl Beck (eds), *Comparative Socialist Systems: Essays on Politics and Economics* (Pittsburgh: University of Pittsburgh) 1975, pp. 192–214.

3. Ekiert, 'Democratic Processes in East Central Europe', 1991, p. 293, n. 22. I see no reason to distinguish between humanization and liberalization.

4. For a more thorough study of sources of liberalization, see Alfred Stepan, 'Paths toward Redemocratization: Theoretical and Comparative Considerations', in Guillermo O'Donnell, Phillippe C. Schmitter and Laurence Whitehead (eds), *The Breakdown of Democratic Regimes* (London: Johns Hopkins Press), 1986, pp. 64–84; Huntington, *Third Wave*, 1991.

5. Strictly speaking, the adoption of guarantees of freedom of the press could be considered democratization, which for the study of mass media would be associated with the emergence of a free press system. Unfortunately, the term democratization poses some problems, whether it is applied to regimes or media systems. It combines a process (democratization) with specific outcomes (democracy/free press model). This makes it an inappropriate description of incomplete or unfolding processes, because it is deterministic, implying particular conclusions. It is best applied historically, after definitive results of liberalization have been attained. For the processes described in this chapter, liberalization is a more apt term. On the role of press in democracy, see Dahl, *Polyarchy*, 1971, p. 20; Juan J. Linz, 'The Breakdown of Democratic Regimes', in Linz and Alfred Stepan (eds), *The Breakdown of Democratic Regimes* (Baltimore: Johns Hopkins) 1978, p. 5; Huntington, *Third Wave*, 1991, p. 7.

6. Dzirkalis, Gustafson and Johnson, *Elite Communication*, 1982, p. vii; Remington, 'Socialist Pluralism', 1989, p. 281.

7. Remington, *Authority*, 1988, p. 149.

8. Mikhail Gorbachev, *Krasnaya Zvezda*, 14 February 1987, p. 1.

9. James P. Scanlan, 'Reforms and Civil Society in the USSR', *Problems of Communism*, vol. xxxvii, no. 2, March/April 1988, p. 47; Martinez Soler, 'Press Freedom', 1980, p. 157; Kaplan, *Winter into Spring*, 1977, p. 54, 67.

10. Kaplan, *Winter into Spring*, 1977, p. 53.

11. Martinez Soler, 'Press Freedom', 1980, p. 157; Theodore Friedgut, 'The Democratic Movement and Perspectives', in Rudolf L. Tokes (ed.), *Dissent in the USSR* (Baltimore: Johns Hopkins) 1975, p. 130; Timothy Garton Ash, *Polish Revolution: Solidarity 1980–1982* (London: Jonathan Cape) 1983, p. 20.

12. Mickiewicz, 'Soviet Media', 1984, p. 115; Friedgut, 'Democratic Movement', 1975, p. 130.

13. Yasmann, 'Freedom of Information', 1989, pp. 1–6. Aleksandr Yakovlev, in recognizing the importance of communications in the changing world, said in 1986, 'Today's world is becoming smaller in the communications sense, even more interconnected. To think that it is possible in this world to create some sort of niche or cloister cut off from external influences and to sit it out there in timid resignation is not only to indulge in illusions, but also to doom ourselves to defeat...'. Quoted by Yasmann, p. 2.

14. See Maury Lisann, *Broadcasting to the Soviet Union* (New York: Praeger) 1975.

15. Kaplan, *Winter into Spring*, 1977, p. 54.

16. Albert Vlasov, 'To Raise the Quality of Information on International Issues', *International Affairs* (Moscow), no. 11, November 1988, p. 19. The change in the press was sufficiently successful that the Gorbachev regime decided to stop jamming many foreign broadcasts in 1987 and 1988.

17. Gitelman, 'Power and Authority', 1970, p. 241.

18. According to Remington, only 15% of journalists indicated that Party officials had discussed readers' interests with them. Remington, *Authority*, 1988, p. 169.

19. White, *Political Culture*, 1979, p. 140; Nassar, 'The Middle East Press', 1982, p. 196.

20. Kaplan, *Winter into Spring*, 1977, pp. 53, 67; Gitelman, 'Power and Authority', 1970, p. 247; Gross, 'Glasnost'', 1987, p. 73.

21. Mikhail Gorbachev, *Perestroika* (London: Collins) 1987, p. 102.

22. Beginning with his 1984 speech, he spoke of the need for 'participation of an ever larger mass of working people in management – in the elaboration, discussion, adoption and the implementation of social and economic decisions,' and greater mass involvement in 'socialist self-government', partly through greater activity of the soviets. Gorbachev, 'Zhivoe tvorchestvo naroda', 1984, pp. 82 ff.

23. Gorbachev, 'Zhivoe tvorchestvo naroda', 1984, p. 95. *Izvestiya* editor Ivan Laptev was even more succinct about the role of the press in reactivating society: 'By telling the people the truth, by revealing to them what had been hidden, by giving them the opportunity, not only to have their own opinion but also to voice it, the Party and the mass news media have tremendously increased this "national strength of the people's mood", interest and activeness.' *CDSP*, vol. xl, no. 32, 1988, pp. 12–13.

24. *Pravda*, 6 May 1979, p. 1.

25. Pumpyansky claimed that the reader was treated as 'an imbecile who doesn't know what is good for him and therefore has to be agitated, propagandized and collectively organized'. Pumpyansky, 'Tired of Truth', 1990, p. 34.

26. For a good description of the changes, see Walter Laqueur, *The Long Road to Freedom: Russia and Glasnost* (New York: Charles Scribner's Sons) 1989. For examples of some highly critical articles, see Vitaly Korotich and Cathy Porter (eds), *The Best of Ogonyok* (London: Heinemann) 1990.

27. 'Glasnost must now help introduce democratic attitudes and economic methods of management. It is especially important to search for and support everything that is new – new experience and new achievements.' Gorbachev, *SWB*, SU/0048/B/6, 14 January 1988. See also Jane Leftwich Curry, 'Media Control in Eastern Europe: Holding the Tide on Opposition', in Curry and Dassin (eds), *Press Control*, 1982, p. 118; Huntington, *Third Wave*, 1991, p. 65.

28. See Chapter 7.

29. 'It must be admitted that the administrative-command methods of the past implanted in propaganda illusions and goals which in effect reduced the human factor to naught and spawned arrogance and illusory abstract slogans . . .'. Vlasov, 'To Raise the Quality of Information', 1988, p. 19.

30. For a good analysis on the problems of secrecy in the Soviet Union see V. Rubanov, 'Ot kulta sekretnosti' – k informatsionnoi kulture', *Kommunist*, no. 13, September 1988, pp. 24–36. As Remington wrote, 'In the early 1980s, matters reached the point that only the lowliest and weakest agencies and territorial organizations' bodies were unable to fend off routine criticism'. Remington, 'Socialist Pluralism', 1989, p. 275.

31. Jadwiga Stanizskis, *Poland's Self-Limiting Revolution* (Princeton: Princeton University Press) 1984, p. 162; Curry, 'Media Control', 1982, p. 118.

32. Kaplan, *Winter into Spring*, 1987, p. 3. Havlicek, 'Mass Media Impact', 1973, p. 243.

33. Gorbachev, *Perestroika*, 1988, pp. 78–9. A *Pravda* editorial claimed that *glasnost'* is supposed to encourage 'involvement of the working people in the daily discussion and solution of matters concerning the work of organs of people's rule . . .', 'Glasnost' v rabote', *Pravda*, 27 March 1985, p. 1.

34. Gorbachev quoted by Yasmann, '*Glasnost'* versus Freedom of Information', 1989, p. 2.

35. Quoted in Gross, '*Glasnost*", 1987, p. 72.

36. Mikhail Gorbachev in *Krasnaya Zvezda*, 18 February 1987.

37. Gorbachev, *SWB*, SU/8621/B1–8, 16 July 1987.

38. Gorbachev, *SWB*, SU/0149/C1, 13 May 1988.

39. Gorbachev, *SWB*, SU/0242/B1-B7, 3 April 1989.

40. Gorbachev in a speech to *Pravda* editors, *Pravda*, 25 October 1989, p. 3. He also claimed that 'The press is a public matter. It should serve society. And since today society is moving along the path of restructuring and renewal, this means that our press should serve this cause too.' This occurred after a stormy meeting with media executives. See *Moscow News*, 22 October 1989, p. 4 for a summary of that meeting.

41. Vitaly Ganyushkin, 'At Close Range, with Gusto . . .'. *New Times*, no. 9, 27 February 1990, pp. 28–9.

42. V. Lashin, 'From Glasnost to Freedom of Speech', *Moscow News*, no. 15, 9 April 1989, p. 2.

43. Remington, *Authority*, 1988, p. 5.

44. The Rand study was prescient when it warned that diversity in the press, though initiated from above, could 'take on some additional life of its own, creating complications for political controllers ...'. Dzirkalis, Gustafson and Johnson, *Elite Communication*, 1982, p. 12.
45. As Bill Keller said, 'By purging one editor, threatening another and rebuking Soviet journalists in general for a lack of team spirit, Mr. Gorbachev has reminded the world that he sees glasnost, his policy of openness, not as a right but as a tool – and a tool that, just now, is not working the way he wants.' *International Herald Tribune*, 24 October 1989, p. 6.
46. Huntington, *Third Wave*, 1991, p. 137; Przeworski, *Democracy and the Market*, 1991, p. 56; Kaufman, 'Liberalization and Democratization in South America', 1986, p. 93.
47. I use the term to refer to any form of momentum which expands liberalization. This is different from Huntington, who uses it to describe the impact of changes in neighbouring countries on regimes, more or less like a reverse domino effect which Kissinger once spoke of. Samuel Huntington, 'Democracy's Third Wave', *Journal of Democracy*, vol. 2, no. 2, spring 1991, p. 6.
48. Kaplan, *Winter into Spring*, 1977, p. 50; Havlicek, 'Mass Media Impact', 1973, p. 249; Albright, *Poland*, 1983, p. 45; Goldfarb, *Beyond Glasnost*, 1991, p. 88 ff. The press also plays an important role in agitating for liberalization of regimes. See Przeworski, *Democracy and the Market*, 1991, p. 58; Kaufman, 'Liberalization and Democratization in Latin America', 1986, p. 95; Ekiert, 'Democratic Processes in East Central Europe', 1991, p. 304.
49. N. Andreev, Political Observer, *Novoe Vremya*, author interview (Moscow: April 1990).
50. V. Sukhoi (New York: September 1988).
51. The Congress of Peoples' Deputies contained 60 journalists, or 3 per cent of the total number of representatives. This was far greater than the 6 in the old Supreme Soviet, which accounted for 0.5 per cent. Viktor Danilenko, 'Electoral Reform', in Robert T. Huber and Donald Kelly (eds), *Perestroika Era Politics* (London: M.E. Sharp) 1991, p. 46.
52. Havlicek, 'Mass Media Impact', 1973, p. 249; Kaplan, *Winter into Spring*, 1977, p. 4. As we will see below, it is arguable that *Moscow News* and other publications began to form their own proto-interest groups.
53. S. Zavorotny, Literary Editor, *Komsomol'skaya Pravda*, author interview (Oxford: November 1990).
54. As one *Izvestiya* foreign correspondent explained, his understanding of what was permissible frequently came from 'what was in the newspapers, what happened in the articles. It was the spirit of the stories. And we saw that after these stories, if the journalist was still abroad, it would be possible for us to write like him, or be even more radical.' Alexander Sychev, Senior Correspondent, *Izvestiya*, author interview (Moscow: May 1990). The same case was true in Eastern Europe. See Curry, 'Media Control', 1982, p. 118.

55. Zavorotny (Oxford: November 1990); Alexander Shal'nev, Foreign Correspondent, *Izvestiya*, author interview (New York: March 1991).
56. While previously the editor was viewed by reporters and sub-editors as a braking mechanism, in the Gorbachev period writers looked at the editor as a potential defender who could shield his staff from repercussions. As one *Izvestiya* editor said, 'The editor-in-chief is needed for support, like a wall which protects, giving security.' Deinchenko (Moscow: April 1990).
57. Curry, 'Media Control in Eastern Europe', 1982, p. 119; *Maxwell, Press and Iberian Democracy*, p. 21; Albright, *Poland*, 1983, p. 45; Kaplan, *Winter into Spring*, 1977, p. 50. For an account of the implementation of the press law in the Soviet Union, see Thomas F. Remington, 'Parliamentary Government in the USSR', in Robert T. Huber and Donald Kelly (eds), *Perestroika Era Politics* (London: M.E. Sharp) 1991, pp. 186–94.
58. Kaplan, *Winter into Spring*, 1977, p. 76. In the Soviet Union, for example, see L. Koryavin, 'Prezident i pressa', *Izvestiya*, 11 August 1989, p. 5; Melor Sturua, 'Skazat' po pravde', *Zhurnalist*, December 1988, p. 59. *Moscow News* used comments by Westerners as a means of justifying further press freedom. See 'The Press and Politics: Soviet and American Students Discuss the Media vis-à-vis the Government Today', *Moscow News*, 15 May 1988, p. 8.
59. Fedor Burlatsky, 'Dva vzglyada na mezhdunarodnuyu zhurnalistiku', *Sovetskaya Kultura*, 21 May 1987, p. 6; Stanislav Kondrashov, 'Tochnyi obraz mira', *Kommunist*, no. 14, September 1987, pp. 51–9; A. Kuvshinnikov, 'Davaite sporit' – v gazete, a ne za chashkoi kofe', *Zhurnalist*, March 1988, pp. 14–17; A. Bovin, 'Let's Break Through the Ice on Foreign Policy', *Moscow News*, no. 24, 12 June 1988, p. 4; A. Medvedenko, 'Pravo myslit', obyazannost' myslit', *Zhurnalist*, November 1988, pp. 32–3; Alexei Pankin, 'Glasnost in Foreign Policy: The Ultimate Goal and Intermediate Stages', *International Affairs* (Moscow), November 1988, pp. 104–7; Sturua, 'Skazat' po pravde', December 1988, p. 59. Perhaps the most detailed account of the difficulties of being a foreign journalist were highlighted in a *Pravda* roundtable discussion which gathered *mezhdunarodniki* from six publications and central television. See 'Rupor ili zerkalo?', *Pravda*, 2 March 1990, p. 6.
60. One *Izvestiya* reporter said of self-censorship, 'For sixty years in the Soviet Union journalists were under strict control and right now we are free like birds, but don't know how to fly.' A. Sychev (Moscow: May 1990); See also Curry, 'Media Control', 1982, p. 110.
61. V. Ovchinnikov, 'Don't Rush Aside', *Moscow News*, no. 1, 1 January 1989, p. 10. For a response, see M. Sturua, 'Don't Shilly-Shally, Get Cracking with Perestroika', *Moscow News*, no. 3, 15 January 1989, p. 4.
62. 'From my point of view objectivity is not only a term for East bloc countries or the West, it is a reality. It doesn't depend on what type of journalist you are, socialist or capitalist.... If you are quite a truthful man, you will be objective in your articles.... Nowadays there are more possibilities for objectivity in our country. That is

why more and more publications, more newspapers bring truth to their readers and that is the essence of objectivity.' V. Sukhoi (New York: September 1988).

63. The European approach means that the editorial position of the publications should be visible on every page, not simply those marked as opinion. Such an approach makes sense given the traditional Soviet stress on advocacy. Ben Bradlee, editor of *Washington Post, International Herald Tribune*, 17 July 1990.

64. One editor of a more liberal publication asked me to gather material on the social lives of embassy personnel, a certain sign of changes of the time. The same movement towards sensationalism happened in the liberalizations in Portugal and Spain. See Martinez Soler, 'Press Freedom', 1980, pp. 153–73 and Balsemao, 'Media in Portugal', 1983, pp. 117–26.

65. Shal'nev (New York: March 1991).

66. See V. Korotich, 'Vremya otkrovennosti', *Literaturnaya Rossiya*, 19 September 1986, p. 2.

67. Gitelman, 'Power and Authority', 1970, p. 241.

68. As Curry points out in the Eastern European cases, the publication of controversial articles 'opened a Pandora's box', and 'encouraged further public questioning of the party and its policies'. Curry, 'Media Control in Eastern Europe', 1982, p. 118.

69. Kaplan, *Winter into Spring*, 1977, p. 50.

70. Curry, 'Media Control in Eastern Europe', 1982, p. 118; Stanizskis, *Poland's Self-Limiting Revolution*, 1984, p. 162.

71. D. Makarov, Editor for Socialist Countries, *Argumenty i Fakty*, author interview (Moscow: May 1990); Y. Sigov (Moscow: June 1990). Vladislav Starkov said of the attempt, 'They offered me others job (*sic*) with high pay, a special car, and access to special food and shops. But I said that if I accepted I would lose the trust of the journalists and my family.' Rupert Cornwell, *The Independent*, 25 October 1989, p. 12.

72. One old *Pravda* writer, in speaking of international affairs, said, 'At present an international journalist will win enormous popularity by saying as much bad about us as he can and as much possible good about them'. V. Ovchinnikov, 'Don't Rush Aside', *Moscow News*, no. 1, 1 January 1989, p. 10.

73. Shal'nev (New York: May 1991).

74. Dzirkalis, Gustafson and Johnson, *Elite Communication*, 1982, p. 37.

75. A. Kuprianov, Foreign Correspondent, *Komsomol'skaya Pravda*, author interview (Oxford: November 1990); Zavorotny (Oxford: November 1990).

76. Indeed, some journalists who covered the United States indicated that by 1990 they were not always sure of the political line.

77. Paul Landy, 'Mass Media: Ignorance is Strength', in Robert Delaney (ed.). This is Communist Hungary (Chicago: Henry Regnery) 1958, pp. 85–117; Curry, 'Media Control in Eastern Europe', 1982, p. 122; Curry, 'Media Management and Political Systems', 1982, p. 267.

78. George W. Breslauer, *Khrushchev and Brezhnev as Leaders: Building*

Authority in Soviet Politics (London: George Allen and Unwin) 1982,
p. 11; Stepan, *Rethinking Military Politics* (Princeton: Princeton University Press) 1988, p. 37 ff.
79. Archie Brown said, 'No Soviet leader in his first year of office has presided over such sweeping changes in the composition of the highest party and state organs as Mikhail Gorbachev.' Brown, 'Change in the Soviet Union', p. 1048. See also Jerry Hough, 'Understanding Gorbachev: The Importance of Politics', in Ed A. Hewitt and Victor H. Winston (eds), *Milestones in Glasnost and Perestroyka: Politics and People* (Washington: Brookings Institution) 1991, pp. 470–72; Iain Elliot, 'The Consolidation of Gorbachev's Political Power', in David A. Dyker (ed.), *The Soviet Union under Gorbachev* (London: Croom Helm) 1987, pp. 21–57. These press exposés served notice to other opponents and potential challengers that they were subject to public exposure (and to possible subsequent legal proceedings) for their past transgressions. This unquestionably made Gorbachev's personnel changes in the following months and years easier to justify and helped pave the way for the extension of his personal power throughout the government structure.
80. Nina Andreeva, 'Ne mogu postupat'sya printsipami', *Sovetskaya Rossiya*, 13 March 1988, p. 3.
81. Although it is doubtful that Ligachev had a hand in writing the letter, there is a strong chance that he was aware of its contents prior to publication. Moreover, on the day after its publication, he gathered editors of several newspapers to the Kremlin and, according to *Izvestiya* editor Ivan Laptev, said: 'I read an excellent article yesterday in *Sovetskaya Rossiya*, a wonderful example of Party political writing. I hope that you have all read it. I would ask you, comrade editors, to be guided by the ideas of this article in your work.' Angus Roxburgh, *The Second Russian Revolution* (London: BBC Books) 1991, p. 84 ff; White, *Gorbachev in Power*, 1990, p. 197.
82. Marie Mendras, 'Soviet Foreign Policy: In Search of Critical Thinking', in Hasegawa and Pravda (eds), *Perestroika*, 1990, pp. 213–15.
83. S. Pankratov, Staff Correspondent, *Trud*, author interview (Moscow: April 1990).
84. Pankratov (Moscow: April 1990).
85. Albright, *Poland*, 1983, p. 81. For example, many people interviewed claimed that the Soviet publication *Moscow News* received special protection from Politburo member and Gorbachev confidant Aleksandr Yakovlev. Even if this was not the case (and no one at *Moscow News* would confirm this) the very perception of the guardian relationship no doubt contributed to *Moscow News'* freedom to challenge the limits of government control. See editor Yegor Yakovlev, 'Flagship Glasnost' in Stephen F. Cohen and Katrina Vanden Heuvel, *Voices of Glasnost* (New York: W.W. Norton), pp. 207–8.
86. The latter replaced the Propaganda Department in late 1988. The International Information Department ceased to exist in 1986 and was folded into the other two.
87. 'The old forms are obviously giving way. The ideological department

of the CPSU Central Committee for unknown reasons did not publicly express its attitude to Burlatsky's candidacy, so Burlatsky paid a visit to the department only after the appointment.' Ivan Podshivalov, 'Elected by Colleagues', *Moscow News*, no. 16, 16 May 1990, p. 14.

88. Volovets (Moscow: May 1990).
89. Pankin (Moscow: May 1990).
90. On the television show *Vzglyad* in June 1990, the editor-in-chief of *Krasnaya Zvezda* indicated that his last order was a year earlier. Soviet television, 9 June 1990.
91. Krainov (Moscow: April 1990); V. Gribachev (Moscow, May 1990).
92. Volovets (Moscow: May 1990). A similar view was put forth by *Izvestiya*'s Krainov (Moscow: April 1990).
93. Makarov of *Argumenty i Fakty* and Volovets of *Moscow News* both indicated that as of spring 1990 they no longer sought approval of articles. Author interviews (Moscow: May 1990).
94. These included *Izvestiya*'s Bovin, *Moscow News*' Volovets and *Zhurnalist*'s Gribachev. It should be noted, however, that there were still forms of ideological censorship at least through the middle of 1989. See Julia Wishnevsky, 'A Rare Insight into Soviet Censorship', *Radio Liberty Research Bulletin*, 7 September 1990, pp. 5–7. See also interview with Director of *Glavlit* Vladimir Alekseyevich Boldyrev, *CDSP*, vol. xl, no. 44, pp. 1–4.
95. Volovets (Moscow: May 1990).
96. Volovets (May 1990). The Rand report indicated that the editors of *Pravda* and *Izvestiya* could bypass *Glavlit* if they chose. Presumably they would have had to face the consequences for a gross violation of protocol. Dzirkalis, Gustafson and Johnson, *Elite Communication*, 1982.
97. With the new press law, Glavlit offices were still located in most publications, but Glavlit representatives only served in an advisory role, helping to determine, if asked, whether an article revealed state secrets. Michael Dobbs, 'Glavlit is Dead but Advice is for Hire,' *International Herald Tribune*, 2 August 1990, pp. 1–2.
98. Kavel Vilgats, a reporter with Tartu's *Edassi*, indicated in early 1990 that his newspaper had already ignored Glavlit for a few years. Author interview (Tartu: March 1990).
99. Sigov (Moscow: June 1990).
100. A.S. Kapto, Head of the Ideology Department, 'Siloi primera, siloi ubezhdeniya', *Pravda*, 20 February 1989, p. 2. Although Kapto indicated that the new media subdepartment did not mirror the former section of the Propaganda Department, it is certain that it fulfilled at least part of the former's tasks.
101. A.S. Kapto, *Pravda*, 20 February 1989, p. 2.
102. Volovets (Moscow, May 1990). Even in 1990, *Ogonek*'s editor Vitaly Korotich said, 'It is interesting, but in this country we still have censorship. We still have censorship, and from time to time the censor arrests one or two articles in my magazine. Also, I still have internal censorship.' *The Nation*, 30 July/6 August 1990, p. 1.
103. Grigoriev (Middletown: April 1992). Viktor Gribachev said that

although the situation became much freer by the middle of 1990, there were 'still attempts to influence the press, to try and hide things . . . there are expressions of dissatisfaction with various publications'. Author interview (Moscow, May 1990).

104. Aleksandr Bovin indicated that that was still the practice at *Izvestiya* in May 1990. Author interview (Moscow: May 1990). Melor Sturua stated: 'While you (the Foreign Ministry) no longer initial our commentaries, it's done elsewhere. It would be perfectly quixotic to put the Central Committee with its echelons in charge of foreign political activity outside the equation.' Quoted by Alexei Pankin, 'Diplomacy and International Journalism', *International Affairs* (Moscow), no. 6, June 1989, p. 96.

105. Makarov (Moscow: May 1990).

106. Although some journalists at *Pravda* and *Izvestiya* claimed that they were free to print what they wanted in 1990, they also admitted that they were more restricted than those at other newspapers, like *Moscow News*, which always seemed to be cited as the counter-example. In keeping with such analysis, the Foreign Editor of *Moscow News*, Volovets, was emphatic that the reverse was true, that is, that newspapers like *Moscow News* possessed greater freedom than press organs with formal ties to the Party and state, especially the larger ones. *Izvestiya*'s Deinchenko and TASS's Fedyashin cited *Moscow News* as a counter example. Bovin, who wrote for both *Izvestiya* and *Moscow News*, claimed that he had more latitude to move away from the government line when he wrote for *Moscow News*. The editor of *Moscow News*, Yegor Yakovlev, concurred. Fedyashin, interview with author (Washington: September 1989); Deinchenko, interview author (Moscow: May 1990); Bovin, interview author (Moscow: May 1990); Yakovlev, 'Flagship of Glasnost', 1989, p. 205.

107. Volovets (Moscow: May 1990). In some cases, the official sponsors attempted to assert their own control over the publications. For the battle over *Literaturnaya Gazeta*, see Ivan Podshivalov, 'Elected by colleagues', *Moscow News*, no. 16, 16 May 1990, p. 14.

108. Deinchenko (Moscow: April 1990).

109. Gorbachev, *CDSP*, vol. xxxviii, no. 8, pp. 36–7.

110. Gorbachev, quoted by Eduard Shevardnadze, *The Future Belongs to Freedom* (London: Sinclair Stevenson) 1991, p. 173.

111. Remington, *Authority*, 1988, p. 118.

112. For example, the TASS article in *Izvestiya* cited 20,000 US nuclear mishaps since 1979 (*Izvestiya*, 5 May 1986, p. 4). Another TASS article in *Pravda* referred to an accident at a Nevada nuclear test site (*Pravda*, 4 May 1986, p. 5). There were other articles by *Izvestiya* and *Pravda* correspondents. See, for example, A. Shelkov, 'Nedelikatniye sosedi', *Pravda*, 10 May 1986, p. 1; V. Gan, 'Razglyad faktami', *Pravda*, 19 May 1986, p. 5.

113. See, for example, G. Vasil'ev, 'Na urovne neandertaltsev', *Pravda*, 6 May 1986, p. 5; T. Kolisnichenko, 'Udar kolokola', *Pravda*, 18 May 1986, p. 4; S. Beglov, 'Poisoned Cloud of Anti-Sovietism,' *Moscow News*, no. 18, 11 May 1986, pp. 1–3; N. Zyatykov, 'Vokrug Chernobyla:

chernaya propaganda i deistvitelnost'', *Argumenty i Fakty*, no. 20, 13–19 May 1986, pp. 1–3.

114. Linnik (New York: December 1989); Mickiewicz, *Split Signals*, 1988, p. 68 ff.

115. Dmitiri Lyubosvetov, *Pravda*, 19 May 1986, p. 3. Cited from Mickiewicz, *Split Signals*, 1988, p. 68.

116. Mickiewicz points to the letter as a key signal of change (*Split Signals*, 1988, p. 68). It is difficult to draw conclusions, because she studies television and the article was directed towards television. Of the reporters and editors interviewed, not a single one mentioned this article when asked about initial indications of change.

117. For a more complete discussion of telebridges and the expansion of the Soviet media's exposure of Western ideas to the Soviet audience, see Mickiewicz, *Split Signals*, 1988, p. 34 ff.

118. P. Donahue and V. Pozner, 'Dialog o dialoge', *Izvestiya*, 7 February 1987, p. 7.

119. G.N. Bochevarov, 'Uchit' nenavisti?', *Izvestiya*, 14 March 1987, p. 7.

120. A. Bovin, 'Net, uchat vzaimoponimaniyu', *Izvestiya*, 14 March 1987, p. 7.

121. In an interview held later, Bovin seemed to support this interpretation when he referred to a 'positive article' which he had written 'about the television spacebridge programs featuring Phil Donahue and Vladimir Pozner'. Alexander Bovin, 'Semi-Glasnost', in Cohen and Vanden Heuvel (eds), *Voices of Glasnost* (New York: W.W. Norton) 1989, p. 272.

122. Other articles justifying the telebridges include S. Kondrashov, 'Na ostrove v lagune', *Izvestiya*, 4 April 1987, p. 6; D. Kosyrev, 'Dvoinoi glasnosti ne byvaet', *Pravda*, 21 April 1987, p. 5; V. Ovchinnikov, *Moscow News*, no. 6, 8 February 1987, p. 6; Y.N. Zasurskii, 'Otvetstvennost' zhurnalistov', *Argumenty i Fakty*, no. 13, 4–10 April, 1987, p. 5. *Argumenty i Fakty* also offered a round-table discussion in which the telebridges were mentioned. See no. 5, 7–13 February 1987, p. 8. A similar call for new approaches to the West was heard in Kondrashov's critical review of the television interview conducted by Soviet journalists of British Prime Minister Thatcher. Kondrashov called for the international journalists to catch up with their domestic counterparts in the jettisoning of stereotypes. S. Kondrashov, 'Net khuda bez dobra', *Izvestiya*, 11 April 1987, p. 7.

123. 'Eto sovsem ne kritika', *Izvestiya*, 18 April 1987, p. 7. Given the response in *Izvestiya* and the rest of the press, it seems unlikely that Mickiewicz is correct when she asserts that Bochevarov's letter represented a 'powerful expression of backlash against the provision of differing points of view'. The entire process was typical of many propaganda campaigns which occurred in the Gorbachev period. Mickiewicz, *Split Signals*, 1988, p. 55.

124. For a discussion of such campaigns see Remington, 'Socialist Pluralism', 1989, p. 282 ff.

125. See particularly, *Argumenty i Fakty*, no. 5, 7–13 February 1987, p. 8 for a round-table discussion featuring Aleksandr Bovin, Vitaly Korotich

and Vladimir Pozner. Probably the most forceful call for a new approach to international journalism was made by Fedor Burlatsky, who was well-connected and probably would not proceed with such a call without some certainty that there would not be retribution. 'Dva vzglyada', May 1987, p. 6.

126. Burlatsky said, 'Only on the basis of mutual enrichment through experience is it possible to develop our own technology and economy, and not in contradiction to the rest of civilization.' 'Dva vzglyada', 1987, p. 6.

127. Gorbachev, *CDSP*, vol. xxxix, no. 5, pp. 9–10.

128. Gorbachev, *SWB*, SU/0081/C/13, 22 February 1988.

129. Gorbachev, *SWB*, SU/0191/C13, 30 June 1988.

130. Eduard Shevardnadze, 'The 19th All-Union Conference: Foreign Policy and Diplomacy', *International Affairs* (Moscow), October 1988, pp. 3–35, especially p. 28.

131. Grigoriev (Middletown: April 1992); Volovets (Moscow: May 1990); Sukhoi (New York: September 1988).

132. Shevardnadze, *CDSP*, vol. xl, no. 13, p. 28. He said in another interview, that 'our task is to . . . shape public opinion in favor of scientifically substantiated decisions'. Shevardnadze, to *Izvestiya*'s deputy editor Golembiovskii, *CDSP*, vol. xl, no. 8, p. 19.

133. Bovin (Moscow: May 1990); A. Pumpyansky, Deputy Editor-in-Chief, *Novoe Vremya*, author interview (Moscow: June 1990). Pumpyansky illustrated the somewhat absurd extent to which the Ministry of Foreign Affairs went in order to assure 'appropriate' press coverage. He cited a case in which the Ministry went so far as to publicly condemn a comedian for his satirical representations of a friendly power, denying that his comments had anything to do with the official position of the Soviet government. In the same article he also mentioned a common scenario: 'We are told confidentially: "The man is a dictator, no question about that, but we have installed him in power at one time, so how can we criticize him today? What if he takes offence and does something rash?".' 'Tired of the Truth?', 1990, p. 32.

134. Pumpyansky, 'Tired of the Truth?', 1990, p. 33.

135. A. Lyutyi, 'Kak eto ponimat'', *Pravda*, 4 March 1989, p. 5. The original cartoon appeared in *The Times* on 27 February.

136. See Bernard C. Cohen, *The Press and Foreign Policy* (Princeton: Princeton University Press) 1963. When Lenin had spoken of *glasnost'* in the post-revolutionary period, he excluded information about many foreign policy issues, like foreign credits and Western technology transfers. See Gross, 'Glasnost', Roots and Practice', 1987, p. 70; Curry, 'Media Control in Eastern Europe', 1982, p. 110.

137. A. Denisov, 'Let's Exercise Restraint', *Moscow News*, no. 16, 22 May 1990, p. 11.

4 'OTHERNESS', ENMITY AND ENVY IN SOVIET IMAGES OF THE UNITED STATES

1. Peter Berger, 'Identity as a Problem in the Sociology of Knowledge', *European Journal of Sociology*, vol. 7, no. 1, 1966, pp. 32–40; Alexander Wendt, 'Anarchy is What States Make of It', *International Organization*, vol. 42, Spring 1992, p. 397; Prasenjit Duara, 'Historicizing National Identity or Who Imagines What and When', in Geoff Eley and Ronald Grigor Suny (eds), *Becoming National* (New York: Oxford University Press) 1996, p. 163; Etienne Balibar, 'The Nation Form: History and Ideology', in Eley and Suny, *Becoming National*, pp. 132–50; Benedict Anderson, *Imagined Communities* (London: Verso), 1992.
2. Arthur Gladstone, 'The Conception of the Enemy', in J.K. Zawodny, *Man and International Relations* (San Francisco: Chandler Publishing) 1966, p. 678; Karl E. Scheibe, *The Psychology of Self and Identity* (London: Praeger) 1995, p. 537; Samuel I. Hayakawa, *Language in Action* (New York: Harcourt, Brace and Co.) 1941; Elizabeth Spellman, *Inessential Woman: Problems of Exclusion in Feminist Thought* (Boston: Beacon Press) 1988, p. 74; Robert S. Wistrich, *The Longest Hatred* (London: Schocken Books) 1991, p. xiii; John Keene, 'Nations, Nationalism and European Citizens', in Sukumar Periwal (ed.), *Notions of Nationalism* (Budapest: CEU Press) 1995; Michale Mann, 'A Political Theory of Nationalism and Its Excesses', Sukumar Periwal (ed.), *Notions of Nationalism* (Budapest: CEU Press) 1995, pp. 50–51.
3. William A. Glaser, 'The Semantics of the Cold War', in J.K. Zawodny, *Man and International Relations* (San Francisco: Chandler Publishing) 1966, p. 678; Jerome D. Frank, *Sanity and Survival: Psychological Aspects of War and Peace* (Toronto: Vintage Books) 1967, 117 ff; John Mack, 'The Perception of US–Soviet Intentions and other Psychological Dimensions of the Nuclear Arms Race', *Journal of American Orthopsychiatry*, 1982, vol. 52, no. 4, p. 595;
4. 'It may seem melodramatic to treat the twin poles of human experience represented by the United States and the Soviet Union as the equivalent of Good and Evil, Light and Darkness, God and the Devil; yet if we allow ourselves to think of them that way, even hypothetically, it can help to clarify our perspective on the world struggle.' Richard Nixon, quoted by John Mack, 'Perception', 1982, p. 597.
5. Rogers Brubaker, 'Nationhood and the National Question in the Soviet Union and post-Soviet Eurasia: An Institutionalist Account', *Theory and Society*, vol. 23, 1994, pp. 48–50; Viktor Zaslavsky, 'Nationalism and Democratic Transition in Postcommunist Societies', *Daedalus*, vol. 121, no. 2, spring 1992, p. 105; Paul Goble, 'Ethnic Politics in the USSR', *Problems of Communism*, vol. 38, no. 4, July–August 1989, pp. 1–15. Within the multi-ethnic state, nationality was expressed as an ascriptive characteristic found on every citizen's passport and in the form of ethno-territorial sub-units (union republics, autonomous republics and autonomous regions) which often but did not always contain a plurality of the titular nationality.
6. Brubaker, 'National Question', p. 51.

7. William Bloom, *Personal Identity, National Identity and International Relations* (Cambridge: Cambridge University Press) 1990, p. 151.
8. Terry L. Heyns, *American and Soviet Relations since Detente* (Washington DC: National Defense University Press) 1987, p. 1.
9. In *What is to be Done?*, Lenin wrote, '[T]he only choice is either bourgeois or socialist ideology. There is no middle course (for mankind has not created a "third" ideology, and, moreover, in a society torn by class antagonisms there can never be a non-class above an above-class ideology).' Quoted in Kerenz, *Propaganda State*, 1985, p. 36.
10. Hyland, *The Cold War is Over*, 1990, p. 182. Georgi Arbatov, *The War of Ideas in Contemporary International Relations* (Moscow: Progress Publishers), 1973, pp. 33–6. The origins of Bolshevik foreign policy can be found in Lenin's *Imperialism, The Highest State of Capitalism*, which was first published in mid-1917.
11. Neumann's assertion that 'Europe is the main "Other" in relation to which the idea of Russia is defined', may be true looking over Russian history as a whole, but especially in the late Soviet period, the United States eclipsed Europe as the main other in Soviet thinking. Iver B. Neumann, *Russia and the Idea of Europe* (London: Routledge) 1996, p. 1.
12. Chafetz says that 'A role's main function is to provide actors with a stable sense of identity. Without them, they cannot order their environment and consequently find social behaviour intolerably difficult to understand and manage. Individuals who lack clearly defined roles may cease social function altogether.' Chafetz, 'National Identity', p. 664; Wendt, 'Anarchy', p. 400.
13. Lewin, *Making of the Soviet System*, 1991, p. 21.
14. Tucker, *Political Culture*, 1987, p. 122.
15. Rubinstein, *Soviet Foreign Policy*, 1992, p. 321.
16. Graham Gill, *The Collapse of a Single-Party System* (Cambridge: Cambridge University Press) 1994, p. 12.
17. Gellner related the following incident when Beria surprised Sakharov by asking him if he had any questions. Sakharov said 'I was absolutely unprepared ... (but) ... I asked: "Why are our new projects moving so slowly? Why do we always lag behind the USA and other countries, why are we losing the technology race?" ... I don't know what kind of answer I expected. Twenty years later, when Turchin, Medvedev and I posed the same question ... we answered that insufficient democratic institutions ... and a lack of intellectual freedom ... were to blame.' Ernest Gellner, *Encounters with Nationalism* (Oxford: Blackwell Publishers), 1994.
18. These inherent weaknesses in Soviet identity caused Soviet leaders to seek other methods of uniting the population. Too often the preferred method was unification against a common enemy, be it kulaks and other class enemies or the 'encircling' capitalist powers. This was recognized by Shevardnadze who said that 'the enemy' can instil in people 'fear, hatred and a readiness to accept the existing order of things as something natural and necessary. When you present your own people with an "enemy", you can force them to bear any privation, make any

sacrifice.' Shevardnadze, *Freedom*, 1991, p. 65. See also Robert C. Tucker, *Political Culture and Leadership in Soviet Russia* (Sussex: Wheatsheaf Books) 1987, pp. 80, 102, 110.

19. Shlapentokh, 'War Propaganda', 1984, p. 88 ff.
20. *Pravda*, 16 June 1983, p. 1.
21. Brezhnev noted that detente 'does not in the slightest way abolish nor can it abolish or alter the laws of class struggle'. *Pravda*, 12 October 1974, quoted in Gilbert, *Soviet Images*, 1977, p. 63. The irony of the situation was noted by Gorbachev's Foreign Minister Eduard Shevardnadze who asserted: 'The ideologues came out with the conclusion that in moments of warmer relations the ideological struggle must not subside. On the contrary, it must be waged more fiercely. To be honest, I cannot figure out how to make friends with a person and at the same time to carry on an implacable struggle against him.' Shevardnadze, *Freedom*, 1991, p. 5.
22. Andropov, *CDSP*, vol. xxxv, no. 25, p. 2.
23. Chernenko, *CDSP*, vol. xxxv, no. 24, p. 8.
24. Gorbachev's Report to the XXVIIth Congress of the Communist Party, *CDSP*, vol. xxxviii, no. 8, p. 6.
25. Shlapentokh, 'War Propaganda', 1984, p. 92.
26. T.V. Znamenskaya and A.V. Smyagin, 'Vneshnopoliticheskaya propaganda', *SShA*, no. 9, September 1988, p. 26.

5   US/SOVIET RELATIONS IN THE GORBACHEV PERIOD

1. Pravda, 'Linkages between Domestic and Foreign Policy', 1990, p. 2.
2. Mikhail Gorbachev quoted by Archie Brown, *Political Leadership*, 1989, p. 197.
3. Gorbachev, *CDSP*, vol. xxxix, no. 7, 18 March 1987, p. 11.
4. 'The United States' capacity to present assistance was matched only by its capacity to heighten international tension and increase the danger of war.' MccGwire, *Perestroika*, 1991, p. 268.
5. Quoted in Sylvia Woodby, *Gorbachev and the Decline of Ideology in Soviet Foreign Policy* (Boulder: Westview Press) 1989, p. 15.
6. Pravda, 'Linkages between Domestic and Foreign Policy,' 1990, p. 5; Severyn Bialer, 'The Soviet Union and the West: Security and Foreign Policy', Bialer and Michael Mandelbaum (eds), *Gorbachev's Russia and American Foreign Policy* (London: Westview Press) 1988, p. 459 ff. Woodby, *Decline of Ideology*, 1989, p. 14 ff.
7. S. Kondrashov, 'Dolgii vzglyad na Ameriku', *Moskovskie Novosti*, no. 40, 2 October 1988, p. 6.
8. S. Kondrashov, *SWB*, SU/0844/A4/2, 16 August 1990.
9. Alexander Dallin, 'New Thinking in Soviet Foreign Policy', in Archie Brown (ed.), *New Thinking in Soviet Politics* (London: Macmillan) 1992, p. 77; Malcolm, 'De-Stalinization and Soviet Foreign Policy', 1990, pp. 178–205; MccGwire, *Perestroika*, 1991, p. 124 ff.
10. See Gorbachev's speech to the United Nations, *SWB*, SU/0030/C1/3, 9 December 1988; Bialer, 'The Soviet Union and the West', 1988, p. 479; Dallin, 'New Thinking', 1992, p. 73.

11. Michael Cox, 'Hoist the White Flag: Soviet Foreign Policy in an Era of Decline', *Critique 22: Journal of Social Theory*, 1990, pp. 73–4; MccGwire, *Perestroika*, 1991, p. 319. For background on the security issue, see Stephen M. Mayer, 'The Source and Prospects of Gorbachev's New Political Thinking', *International Security*, fall 1988, vol. 13, no. 2, pp. 142–3.

12. Paraphrased by Cox, 'White Flag', 1990, p. 73; Bialer, 'New Thinking and Soviet Foreign Policy', 1988, p. 296.

13. Bialer, 'New Thinking and Soviet Foreign Policy', 1988, p. 299; MccGwire, *Perestroika*, 1991, p. 288. For Gorbachev and the need for the re-evaluation of capitalism, see his speech at the LXXth anniversary of the October Revolution, *SWB*, SU/8716/C28, 4 November 1987; Yakovlev, 'Dostizheniye kachestvenno novogo sostoyaniya sovetskogo obshchestva i obshchestvennye nauki', *Kommunist*, no. 8 (May 1987), pp. 8–10.

14. Gorbachev, *Pravda*, 3 November 1987. See also Allen Lynch, 'The Continuing Importance of Ideology in the Soviet Union', *The Harriman Institute Forum*, vol. 3, no. 7, July 1990, p. 7; Woodby, *Decline of Ideology*, 1989, p. 29.

15. Bialer, 'New Thinking and Soviet Foreign Policy', 1988, p. 299; Malcolm, 'De-Stalinization and Soviet Foreign Policy', 1991, p. 195.

16. Gorbachev, quoted in MccGwire, *Perestroika*, 1991, p. 289.

17. Dallin, 'New Thinking', 1992, p. 72; MccGwire, *Perestroika*, p. 291 ff.

18. Margot Light, 'Foreign Policy', in Martin McCauley (ed.), *The Soviet Union under Gorbachev* (London: Macmillan) 1987, p. 215 ff.

19. Shevardnadze, *Future Belongs to Freedom*, 1991, p. 5.

20. As Gorbachev said, paraphrasing (and twisting) Lenin, 'the interests of social development and pan-human values take priority over the interests of any particular class'. Quoted in MccGwire, *Perestroika*, 1991, p. 285. See *Literaturnaya Gazeta*, 5 November 1986.

21. E. Egorova-Gantman and K. Pleshakov, 'Kontseptsiya obraza stereotipa v mezhdunarodnykh otnosheniyakh', *Mirovaya Ekonomika i Mezhdunarodnye Otnoshenie*, 1988, no. 12, pp. 19–33.

22. F. Burlatsky, *SWB*, SU/8717/B/2, 5 November 1987. David Wedgwood Benn, *From Glasnost to Freedom of Speech* (London: Royal Institute for International Affairs) 1992, p. 58.

23. Sergei Churgov, deputy editor-in-chief of the journal *World Economy and International Relations*, *SWB*, SU/0273/A/7-8, 4 October 1988.

24. Vlasov, 'To Raise Quality of Information', 1988, p. 20.

25. Gorbachev seemed obsessed with psychological barriers and attributed success in international relations in part to changes in psychology. As he said in early 1988 about improving US/Soviet relations: 'All this has become possible as the result of the gradual alteration in the psychological climate in the world and as a result of changes in people's state of mind.' He then singled out 'world socialism's contribution to arousing a global impetus towards an improvement in the normalization of international relations'. Gorbachev, *SWB*, SU/0046/C/1, 12 January 1988. Shevardnadze saw 'stereotypes of the existence of the enemy' as the chief barrier to the implementation of new political thinking. Shevardnadze, *The Future Belongs to Freedom*, 1991, p. 62.

26. Gorbachev, *Time* interview, quoted in *Pravda*, 2 September 1985. For earlier expressions of Soviet concerns over the hostile international environment, see Light, *Soviet Theory of International Relations*, 1988, p. 72, n. 14.

27. Gorbachev mentioned the importance of eliminating the enemy image in his first speech calling for the 'expansion' of *glasnost* to international affairs. *SWB*, SU/0081/C/13, 22 February 1988.

28. Grigoriev, author interview (Middletown: April 1992); As then editor-in-chief of *Izvestiya* Ivan Laptev said, 'not only the Soviet people but the entire world now view the policy of glasnost' as an indicator of the progress of our restructuring'. I. Laptev, *SWB*, SU/0150/C/4, 13 May 1988. Easing of censorship and restrictions on the underground press in Poland was in part linked with the government's desire for Western credits. Ash, *Polish Revolution*, 1983, p. 19.

29. MccGwire, *Perestroika*, 1991, p. 270.

30. Morton Schwartz went so far as to state that for the Soviets, communications media were 'the most poorly understood feature of American life'. Schwartz, *Soviet Perceptions of the United States*, 1978, p. 88 ff.

31. Burlatsky, after extolling the virtues of the changes which had occurred in the Soviet media images of the West, said, 'We would like Western mass media also to take part in destroying the enemy image which remains a psychological foundation for the arms race and for difficulties in our relations. We expect objectivity, honesty and broad coverage of all aspects of our life from the Western mass media.' F. Burlatsky, *SWB*, SU/8717/B/2, 5 November 1987.

32. Georgi Arbatov, *New York Times*, 8 December 1987, p. A38.

33. Yakovlev, *SWB*, SU/0277/A1/4, 8 October 1988.

34. *Bolshaya Sovetskaya Entsiklopediya* (Moscow, 1957) vol. xx, p. 201.

35. Michael Milenkovitch, *The View from Red Square: A Critique of Cartoons from Pravda and Izvestia, 1947–1964* (New York: Hobbs, Dorman) 1966, p. 129.

36. In conducting the content analysis, every edition of *Pravda*, *Izvestiya* and *Krokodil* was examined over a five-year period separately by two individuals, one a native Russian speaker. Each international cartoon was recorded with a reference to the date and page number and evaluated as anti-American, neutral, pro-American or concerning another country. As by their nature political cartoons offer easily decipherable messages, interpretation by the two researchers was almost always consistent (following Holsti's model, the reliability measure for tested cartoons was 98.7 per cent). In the few cases where there were differences of interpretation, an evaluation was conducted by a third person.

37. S. Gribachev, interview with author (Moscow, May 1990). In the cases of Geneva (19–21 November 1985) and Reykjavik (11–12 October 1986), the changes were ephemeral. In fact, the period just after Reykjavik saw a significant increase in anti-American cartoons in all three publications, which reflected Soviet disappointment at the summit's failure and concomitant perceptions of American intransigence.

38. Gorbachev, *CDSP*, vol. xxxviii, no. 8, p. 6.

39. Gorbachev, *SWB*, SU/8389/A1/9, 14 October 1986. He was no more

sympathetic in a television broadcast in Moscow a few days later, when he said that 'The leadership of that great country is too dependent on the military-industrial complex and on monopoly groups, which have turned the race in nuclear weapons into a business, a means of making profits, the aim of their existence and the point of their activities.' *SWB*, SU/8391/A/10, 16 October 1986.
40. Gorbachev, *CDSP*, vol. xxxviii, no. 8, p. 36.
41. Gorbachev, *CDSP*, vol. xxxviii, no. 8, pp. 6–7, 27 ff.
42. Gorbachev, *CDSP*, vol. xxxviii, no. 8, p. 9 ff.
43. Gorbachev, *CDSP*, vol. xxxviii, no. 8, p. 36.
44. The period also witnessed tremendous turnover in the staff of the foreign ministry and central committee departments devoted to foreign affairs. Besides Shevardnadze, the foreign ministry also received two new first deputy heads and two deputy heads. There was major personnel turnover in the ambassadorial ranks, with new faces in over forty capitals, including Washington, Beijing, Tokyo, London, Paris and Bonn. The replacements tended to be younger, speak native languages more fluently and be better versed in the efficient conduct of public relations. Light, 'Foreign Policy', 1987, p. 213.
45. Shevardnadze quoted in Light, 'Foreign Policy', 1987, p. 216. See *Pravda*, 31 July 1985.
46. *Current Soviet Policies IX* (Columbus: The Current Digest of the Soviet Press) p. 154.
47. See Archie Brown, 'Policy and Power in a Time of Leadership Transition', in Archie Brown (ed.), *Political Leadership in the Soviet Union* (London: Macmillan) 1989, p. 187 ff; Seweryn Bialer, 'The Changing Political System', in Bialer (ed.), *Inside Gorbachev's Russia*, 1989, p. 193 ff.
48. Yakovlev, 'Dostizheniye kachestvenno novogo sostoyaniya sovetskogo obshchestva nauki', 1987, pp. 8–10.
49. Light, 'Foreign Policy', 1987, p. 215.
50. Remington, 'Gorbachev and the Strategy of Glasnost', 1989, p. 64.
51. MccGwire, *Perestroika*, 1991, p. 272; Cox, 'Hoist the White Flag', 1990, p. 76.
52. By mid-March 1987, the Soviet Union had informed the Warsaw Pact that it had adopted 'sufficiency' as its standard for determining military requirements. MccGwire, *Perestroika*, 1991, p. 319.
53. Bialer, 'New Thinking and Foreign Policy', 1988, p. 298.
54. As Grigoriev said, 'The INF was the turning-point, because it was the first thing that really worked.' Author interview (Middletown: April 1992).
55. Gorbachev quoted in *SWB*, SU/8716/C/28, 4 November 1987.
56. Malcolm, 'De-Stalinization and Soviet Foreign Policy', 1990, p. 195.
57. In his book *Perestroika*, released in November 1987, Gorbachev said that 'We certainly do not need an "enemy image" of America, neither for domestic nor for foreign-policy interests.' He also said that 'We must get rid of chauvinism in our countries (the United States and the Soviet Union), especially given the power they both possess. Chauvinism can bring into politics elements that are inadmissible.' Gorbachev,

Perestroika, 1987, pp. 216, 218. See also Gorbachev's talk with US Secretary of State George Schultz, *Pravda*, 24 October 1987, p. 1.

58. Bovin, *SWB*, SU/0316/A1/2, 23 November 1988.
59. Instead, Shevardnadze saw the defining tendency as 'the ability to build up material wealth at an accelerated rate on the basis of front-ranking science and high level techniques and technology and to distribute it fairly, and through joint efforts to restore and protect the resources necessary for mankind's survival.' Shevardnadze, *CDSP*, vol. xl, no. 30, 1988, p. 13.
60. Medvedev, *Pravda*, 5 October 1988, p. 4.
61. Yakovlev, *SWB*, SU/0277/A1/4, 8 October 1988.
62. Gorbachev, *SWB*, SU/0030/C1/3, 9 December 1988.
63. MccGwire, *Perestroika*, 1991, p. 360.
64. *Bolshaya Sovetskaya Entsiklopediya*, p. 201.
65. The absolute decline of international political cartoons, and the relative decline of anti-American cartoons is outlined below.
66. The last noted use of Nazi symbolism was in *Pravda*, 31 October 1986, p. 5.
67. *Krokodil*, no. 5, February 1989, p. 5.
68. *Pravda*, 16 April 1989, p. 5.
69. N. Entilis, interview with author (Moscow: May 1990).

6 CHANGING IMAGES OF AMERICAN MILITARY AND FOREIGN POLICY

1. 'One of the few misprints in *Pravda* during the Brezhnev era occurred in an item in July 1978 which inadvertently referred to opponents of the regime in Chile as neo-fascist instead of non-fascist. Most readers might have failed to spot the mistake were it not deemed necessary to publish a correction the following day.' Benn, *Persuasion*, 1989, p. 52.
2. The survey of terms covered four weeks per calendar year, falling in the months of March, April, September and October. The only exceptions were 1985 and 1990, in which, because of the overall periodization, only two weeks were surveyed. Also, in 1985, June and July were surveyed in order to allow some time for the transition to the Gorbachev period.

   In each week period, every article on American military and foreign policy was recorded, as were the total number of appearances of the terms 'imperialism' and 'militarism' and their adjectives. Articles referring to the terms in the domestic context, for example, 'militarization of American society', were not included. Table 6.1 only reflects the number of articles in which any of the terms were used at least once. This was preferred to citing the aggregate number of references in order to minimize the significance of certain authors who, in one article, might have used the terms as many as nine times. (See, for example, L. Klochovskii and I. Sheremet'ev, 'Latinskaya Amerika v tisakh zavisimosti', *Pravda* 14 April 1986, p. 6.)

In order to insure greater accuracy, two researchers independently analyzed the material involved. The differences were minimal. Although this type of research is inevitably prone to some degree of error, the conclusions are clear.

3. The key difference with the survey on political cartoons is that the final period here combines the June 1988 to November 1988 and the December 1988 to July 1990 periods.

4. V. Lukin, '1989: The Crossroads of History', *Moscow News*, 31 December 1989, p. 3.

5. For more on the campaign, see *Soviet Influence Activities: A Report of Active Measures and Propaganda, 1986–87* (Washington: US Dept of State) August 1987, pp. 33–49; *Soviet Active Measures in the Era of Glasnost*, Presented at the request of the United States House of Representatives on Appropriations at a hearing on 8 March 1988 by Charles Wick, Director, US Information Agency (Washington) 1988, pp. 10–12; *Soviet Influence Activities: A Report of Active Measures and Propaganda, 1987–88* (Washington: US Dept of State) August 1989, pp. 2–4.

6. *Soviet Influence Activities: 1986–1987*, August 1987, p. 44; *The Economist*, 18 April 1987, pp. 19–22.

7. There is even some debate as to whether the original letter ever appeared in the *Patriot*. The US Information Agency was never able to establish definitively if it appeared and on what date. See *Soviet Influence Activities: 1986–1987*, August 1987, p. 42, n. 6.

8. V. Zapevalov, 'Panika na Zapade, ili chto skryvaetsya za sensatsiei vokrug AIDS', *Literaturnaya Gazeta*, 30 October 1985, p. 14.

9. *Soviet Influence Activities 1986–1987*, August 1987, pp. 47–8.

10. 'Pentagonovskie spidtsialisty', *Pravda*, 31 October 1986, p. 5; 'SPID – amerikanskii 'podarok', *Izvestiya*, 25 January 1987, p. 5.

11. *Soviet Influence Activities: 1987–1988*, August 1989, p. 4. US protests and refusal of scientific cooperation in combating the disease no doubt contributed to the decision to limit the attacks.

12. A. Kuvshinnikov and A. Cherepanov, referring to an interview with R. Sagdeev and V. Gol'danskii, 'Nauka: Glavnye dostizheniya goda', *Izvestiya*, 31 October 1987, p. 6.

13. M. Ozerov, 'Fal'shivyi tryuki', *Sovetskaya Rossiya*, 30 October 1987, p. 5. See *Soviet Influence Activities 1987–1988*, August 1989, p. 2.

14. Quoted in *Soviet Influence Activities: 1987–1988*, August 1989, p. 3.

15. See *Soviet Influence Activities: 1987–1988*, August 1989, pp. 5–10.

16. Black Africa was particularly receptive to the AIDS charges because of perceptions of chauvinism and racism in Western scientists who traced the source of the virus to the continent. Latin American audiences would certainly be concerned by charges of American barbarity. See my 'Disinformation: The Soviet Union and the AIDS Virus', *Woodstock Road Editorial*, Oxford, Winter 1989.

17. *Soviet Influence Activities: 1986–1987*, August 1987, p. 1 ff.

18. TASS, 'Zhertvy genotsida', *Izvestiya*, 25 July 1985, p. 1; 'Genocide and Reforms', *Moscow News*, 23 February 1986, p. 3.

19. R. Avakov, 'Neokolonializm v mundire tsveta khaki', *Izvestiya*, 23 July 1986, p. 5.

20. M. Sturua, 'Apologiya "bolshoi dubinki"', *Izvestiya*, 12 July 1985, p. 5.
21. *Pravda* editorial, 'Kto protivitsya ozdorovlenii v mezhdunarodnykh otnoshenii', 7 January 1986, p. 4; *Izvestiya* editorial, 'K obostreniyu obstanovki v raione srednozemnomor'ya', 8 January 1986, p. 5.
22. V. Bol'shakov, 'Sindrom vmeshatel'stva', *Pravda*, 30 July 1986, p. 5; L. Medvenko, 'Martovskie klichi kholodnoi voiny', *Pravda*, 28 March, 1987, p. 4; A. Vasiliev, 'In the Heat of New-globalism', *Moscow News*, 6 April 1986, 1986, p. 6; 'Doctrine of Terrorism', editorial, *Moscow News*, 9 June 1985, p. 6.
23. There were only a few references to new-globalism at the end of 1985, then several articles in the beginning of 1986 explaining the policy and its impact. In the survey of words, the term was tracked and there was only one reference after the INF treaty was agreed to in principle. That was in *Izvestiya* in September 1987.
24. 'In other words, the fact that Libya has been pursuing an independent course not to Washington's liking has been considered grounds enough for the US to manifest naked aggression.' 'Washington Buccaneers', editorial, *Moscow News*, 21 April 1986, p. 5.
25. V. Listov, 'K 6-i godovshchine Grenadskoi revolyutsii', *Pravda*, 13 March 1985, p. 5; E. Bai, 'Grenada: Dva goda spustya', *Izvestiya*, 28 October 1985, p. 5; A. Zagorskii, 'Rastoptannaya nezavisimost'', *Pravda*, 8 February 1986, p. 5; A. Moiseev, 'Tragediya Grenady', *Pravda*, 18 August 1986, p. 5; 'The Grenada Shot of Piracy Doctrine', *Moscow News*, 2 November 1986, p. 6.
26. S. Filatov, 'Budni dzhamakhirii', *Pravda*, 3 May 1986, p. 5; V. Peresada, 'Militaristskaya voznya', *Pravda*, 13 February 1986, p. 5.
27. TASS editorial. 'Golos Sovetskikh lyudei', *Pravda* 17 April 1985, p. 5; V. Korionov, 'Obrechennaya stavka', *Pravda*, 25 January 1986, p. 5; R. Tuchnin, 'Mirolyubtsy s kasetom', *Izvestiya*, 2 January 1986, p. 5; V. Mashkin, 'Fits of Adventurism', *Moscow News*, 14 April 1985, p. 6.
28. K. Geivandov, 'Vashington protiv Arabskogo mira', *Izvestiya*, 15 January 1986, p. 5; K. Geivandov, 'Pochemu sokhranyaetsya vzryvoopasnaya obstanovka', *Izvestiya*, 7 April 1986, p. 4; V. Peresada, 'Vashington protiv Arabskykh narodov', *Pravda*, 21 January 1987, p. 5. For anti-Arab discrimination in the US, see A. Blinov, 'Neugodnykh za klyuchuyu provoloku', *Izvestiya*, 15 March 1987, p. 5; E. Ryabtsev, 'Far-Reaching Ambitions of the USA in the Middle East,' *Moscow News*, 26 May 1985, p. 6.
29. A. Moiseev, 'Tragediya Grenady', *Pravda*, 18 August 1986, p. 5; V. Korionov, 'Mnenie obozrevatelya', *Pravda*, 9 December 1986, p. 5; TASS, 'Zhertvy genotsida', *Izvestiya*, 25 July 1985, p. 1; R. Tuchnin, 'Mirolyubtsy s kasetom', *Izvestiya*, 2 January 1986, p. 5.
30. A. Bovin, 'Reik'yavik: Perelomnyi moment', *Izvestiya*, 11 October 1987, p. 4.
31. K. Geivandov, 'Obratnyi rezultat', *Izvestiya*, 2 September 1987, p. 5; V. Peresada, 'Stavka na silu', *Pravda*, 20 October 1987, p. 5; N. Ognev, 'Byli i nebylitsy', *Pravda*, 13 March 1988, p. 5.

32. On US actions in the Persian Gulf, see 'Zayavlenie Sovetskogo pravitelstva', *Pravda*, 4 July 1987, p. 3.
33. V. Kobysh, 'Pervoe desyatiletie', *Izvestiya*, 19 July 1989, p. 5; A. Cherepanov, 'Panamskii bumerang', *Izvestiya*, 6 February 1990, p. 5; E. Bai, 'Mezhdu voinoi i mirom', *Izvestiya*, 19 March 1990, p. 5.
34. A. Cherepanov and M. Kozhukov, 'Kartel prezidentov', *Izvestiya*, 16 February 1990, p. 1; A. Zagorskii, 'Sdelan pervyi shag', *Pravda*, 17 February 1990, p. 4. Both articles were in reference to US deals with Latin American countries to curb the production and use of narcotics.
35. O. Ostalskii, 'Riskovannaya strategiya', *Izvestiya*, 23 September 1987, p. 5.
36. *CDSP*, vol. xl, no. 46, p. 17; *CDSP*, vol. xli, no. 16, p. 24.
37. For those publications which appeared on a daily or near-daily basis, *Pravda*, *Izvestiya* and *Sovetskaya Rossiya*, the measurement represents the column centimetres devoted to the invasions in the seven issues following the first report of the US action. For *Argumenty i Fakty* and *Moscow News*, it represents the four issues from the first mention of the attack, inclusive. The measurements take into account only the text of the articles, not the headlines. Material has only been counted if it directly addresses the invasions. Articles which might contain a brief reference to US actions in the course of a broader discussion of, for example, the United Nations, are not included. It should be noted that the table does not even represent the full scope of change because commentary on the Libyan attack lasted far longer than it did for the invasion of Panama.
38. 'Kak eto bylo', *Argumenty i Fakty*, no. 18, 1986, p. 1; 'Izobretateli Liviiskogo sleda', *Argumenty i Fakty*, no. 20, 1986, p. 4.
39. G. Vasiliev, 'Bezrassudstvo sily', *Pravda*, 19 April 1986, p. 4; a *Pravda* editorial called America's 'act of brigandage' another addition to its 'list of bloody crimes'. 'Chuvstvitel'nyi udar po agressoru', *Pravda*, 20 April 1986, p. 5.
40. A. Mozgovoi, 'Pristup imperskogo beshenstva', *Sovetskaya Rossiya*, 16 April 1986, p. 4.
41. M. Sturua, 'Vashingtonskaya diskoteka', *Izvestiya*, 18 April 1986, p. 5.
42. 'Washington Buccaneers', *Moscow News*, 27 April 1986, p. 5. Charges of new-globalism were common throughout all of the publications. See Y. Bandura, 'Model dlya neoglobalizma', *Izvestiya*, 22 April 1986, p. 5; G. Vasiliev, 'Bezrassudstvo sily', *Pravda*, 19 April 1986, p. 4; A. Mozgovoi, 'Pristup imperskogo beshenstva', *Sovetskaya Rossiya*, 16 April 1986, p. 5.
43. M. Knyazkov, 'Kto zabyl uroki kochinos', *Sovetskaya Rossiya*, 24 April 1986, p. 3; Y. Bandura, 'Model' dlya neoglobalizma', *Izvestiya*, 22 April 1986, p. 5; M. Sturua, 'Vashingtonskaya diskoteka', *Izvestiya*, 18 April 1986, p. 5; V. Korionov, 'U pozornogo stolba', *Pravda*, 17 April 1986, p. 5; P. Demchenko, 'Mnenie obozrevatelya', *Pravda*, 16 April 1986, p. 5.
44. V. Korionov, 'U pozornogo stolba', *Pravda*, 17 April 1986, p. 5; Y. Danilychev, 'They Want to Scare Others Too', *Moscow News*, no. 18, 1986, p. 6.

45. G. Vasiliev, 'Bezrassudstvo sily', *Pravda*, 19 April 1986, p. 4; N. Bragin, 'Chuvstvitel'nyi udar po agressoru', *Pravda*, 20 April 1986, p. 5; A. Bovin, 'Prestuplenie', *Izvestiya*, 16 April 1986, p. 4; V. Mikheev, 'Zametayut sledy', *Izvestiya*, 21 April 1986, p. 4; L. Donrokhotov, 'Slepota sily', *Sovetskaya Rossiya*, 19 April 1986, p. 3; 'Where is the Evidence?', editorial, *Moscow News*, no. 18, 1986, p. 6.

46. N. Bragin, 'Chuvstvitel'nyi udar po agressoru', *Pravda*, 20 April 1986, p. 5; A. Mozgovoi, 'Pristup imperskogo beshenstva', *Sovetskaya Rossiya*, 16 April 1986, p. 5; L. Koryavin, 'Istericheskie pochesti', *Izvestiya*, 20 April 1986, p. 4; S. Kondrashov, 'Sila ne po razumu', *Izvestiya*, 17 April 1986, p. 5.

47. V. Korionov, 'U pozornogo stolba', *Pravda*, 17 April 1986, p. 5; *Pravda* editorial, 'Volyu naroda ne slomit', *Pravda*, 20 April 1986, p. 5; N. Bragin, 'Chuvstvitel'nyi udar po agressoru', *Pravda*, 20 April 1986, p. 5; A. Bovin, 'Prestuplenie', *Izvestiya*, 16 April 1986, p. 4; L. Dobrokhotov, 'Slepota sily', *Sovetskaya Rossiya*, 19 April 1986, p. 3.

48. V. Korionov, 'U pozornogo stolba', *Pravda* 16 April, 1986, p. 5.

49. Gorbachev himself wrote in a letter to Libyan leader Muammar Qaddafi of the solidarity of the Soviet people 'in the face of piracy committed by American imperialism'. He also attacked American leaders for their 'allegiance to a policy of state terrorism and the aggressive doctrine of 'new-globalism'. Finally, he supported the people of Libya and called on them to continue to 'pursue an independent anti-imperialist course in the international arena'. *CDSP*, vol. xxxvii, no. 15, p. 4.

50. *CDSP*, vol. xli, no. 51, 1989, p. 22.

51. A *Pravda* writer called the invasion a 'reversion of interventionism'. G. Vasiliev, 'Santa-Klaus s avtomatom', *Pravda*, 26 December 1989, p. 5; A *Moscow News* commentator, in one of the few comments about the invasion, referred to it as a 'relapse into imperial mentality'. V. Lukin, '1989: the Crossroads of History', *Moscow News*, 31 December 1989, p. 3. This reflected the statements of Eduard Shevardnadze, who told the UN, 'The contours of the new world order are still unclear. Relapses into imperial mentality still occur, albeit for supposedly noble and democratic reasons (recall the US intervention of Panama). However, in the main, the confrontational bipolarity is giving way to cooperation.' *Moscow News*, 7 January 1990, p. 3.

52. G. Zafesov, 'Mnenie obrazovatelya', *Pravda*, 21 December 1989, p. 5; A. Bovin, 'Litsemerie', *Izvestiya*, 9 January 1989, p. 7; V. Kobysh, 'Chto zhe dal'she', *Izvestiya*, 23 December 1989, p. 11. Kobysh wrote: 'The canal has a strategic significance for the United States and that explains everything.' N. Maslov, 'Nyeurochnyi udar kolokola', *Sovetskaya Rossiya*, 27 December 1989, p. 5.

53. There had been some references in the discussions of Libya to Reagan's fixation with Qaddafi, but they had been almost invariably subsumed under the broader arguments relating to US militarism and imperialism.

54. A. Bovin, 'Litsemerie', *Izvestiya*, 9 January 1990, p. 7; A. Bovin,

'Panamskie paradoksy', 13 January 1990, p. 5; A. Cherepanov, 'Panamskii bumerang', *Izvestiya*, 6 February 1990, p. 5. The significance of this was highlighted by Bovin who claimed that such information had been previously ignored by the Soviet press. This, however, did not suit a *Pravda* commentator who criticized those whom he claimed were accepting the US invasion, seeing the ends as justifying the means. Y. Zhukov, 'Igry s ognem i goryachie tochki', *Pravda*, 22 January 1990, p. 6.

55. I. Ivanov, 'Porochnyi krug', *Pravda*, 6 January 1990, p. 5.
56. V. Korionov, 'Bumerang', *Pravda*, 13 January 1990, p. 5; A. Shal'nev, 'Doktrina Busha', *Izvestiya*, 29 December 1989, p. 5; A. Bovin, 'Litsemerie', *Izvestiya*, 9 January 1989, p. 7; V. Kobysh, 'Chto zhe dal'she?', *Izvestiya*, 23 December 1989, p. 11.
57. G. Vasiliev, 'Santa-Klaus s avtomatom', *Pravda*, 26 December 1989, p. 5.
58. V. Lukin, '1989: The Crossroads of History', *Moscow News*, 31 December 1989, p. 3.
59. G. Petrov, 'Zachem "dzhi-ai" nuzhen general Norega?', *Sovetskaya Rossiya*, 9 January 1990, p. 3.
60. He wrote in full 'Since we have stopped being aggressive, we obligingly offer our shoulder so that our good overseas uncle, who exchanged his aggressiveness for goodwill, can pat it.' Y. Subbotin, 'Po dvoinomu standartu', *Sovetskaya Rossiya*, 3 January 1990, p. 5.
61. Y. Subbotin, 'Po dvoinomu standartu', *Sovetskaya Rossiya*, 3 January 1990, p. 5.
62. *CDSP*, vol. xlii, no. 37, p. 12; *CDSP*, vol. xlvii, pp. 8–9.
63. 'Coordination of the positions of the three centers of imperialism is most often a result of dictates or pressure by the USA, which leads not to overcoming contradictions, but to exacerbating them.' A. Menshikov, 'Triada mezhimpirialisticheskikh protivorechii', *Pravda*, 8 July 1986, p. 4. See also, R. Simonyan, 'Razglyad v klube tyazhelovesov', *Izvestiya*, 5 June 1987; S. Menshikov, 'Ekonomika zapada na perepute', *Pravda*, 16 February 1987, p. 6.
64. '(Foreign observers) believe that West Europeans are seeing with ever greater clarity that, whether discussing trade or arms control, Washington always acts on its own self-serving interest, without regard for its "junior partners".' V. Sukhoi, 'Neobkhodim trezvyi podkhod', *Pravda*, 14 June 1986, p. 5; Y. Vdovin, 'Imperskie appetity', *Pravda*, 10 June 1986, p. 5.
65. 'Washington has confirmed its reputation as a harsh partner and competitor, who in response to Tokyo's "flexibility" is demanding more and more concessions.' Y. Vdovin, *Pravda*, 20 September 1987, p. 5; I. Latyshev, 'Zhmut na partnerov', *Pravda*, 28 March 1987, p. 5; V. Matveev, 'Torgovaya voina cherez Atlantiku', *Izvestiya*, 3 January 1987, p. 4; E. Grishin, 'Torgovaya voina', *Izvestiya*, 27 December 1986, p. 1.
66. The press went so far as to accuse the US of involvement in the assassination of Swedish Prime Minister Olaf Palme. Y. Kuznetsov, 'Dotyanutsya li ruki', *Pravda*, 24 February 1987, p. 5. For other

examples, see V. Matveev, *Izvestiya*, 5 July 1985; S. Kondrashov, 'Vashingtonskii pudel ili sobstvennaya pozitsiya', *Izvestiya*, 24 April 1986, p. 6; Y. Kovalenko, 'Nedopustimoe vmeshatel'stvo', *Izvestiya*, 16 July 1986, p. 4.

67. 'Europe has paid and continues to pay today not only for the US budget deficit, but also for the continuation of its unrestrained and destructive arms race, for the Pentagon's adventures far from American shores and even from NATO's boundaries . . .'. V. Drobkov, 'Kto zaplatit za SOI', *Pravda*, 25 July 1986, p. 5. See also, V. Mikhailov, 'Zagovor protiv Evropu', *Pravda* 10 April 1986, p. 5; V. Korionov, 'Naprolom', *Pravda*, 2 August 1986; V. Chernyshev, 'Temnye zakoulki tretego etazha', *Pravda*, 14 May 1987, p. 5; V. Kukushkin, 'Bazy NATO ili bazy SShA', *Izvestiya*, 25 February 1986, p. 4; V. Matveev, 'Okhota za umami', *Izvestiya*, 19 February 1986, p. 5; I. Dorofeyev, 'What is that New Guy's Name?', *Moscow News*, 7 April 1985, p. 6.

68. Roxburgh, *Pravda*, p. 83 ff. This type of communication directed towards US allies reflected, in part, the Soviet Union's attempt to split the NATO alliance.

69. 'The allies of the US are faced with a choice – either they will, having grumbled a little, quieten down and submit to the dictate of Uncle Sam, or they will finally say that good sense and concern for fundamental interests of Europe and the whole world dictate a sharp turn away from (US) policy.' Y. Zhukov, 'Kuda tol'ko dotyanutsya ruki', *Pravda*, 25 June 1986, p. 4. See also S. Kondrashov, 'Vashingtonskii pudel ili sobstvennaya pozitsiya', *Izvestiya*, 24 April 1986, p. 6; Y. Kovalenko, 'Nedopustimoe vmeshatel'stvo', *Izvestiya*, 16 July 1986, p. 4; I. Latyshev, 'Zhmut na partnerov', *Pravda*, 28 March 1987, p. 5; V. Chernyshev, 'Temnye zakoulki tretego etazha', *Pravda*, 14 May 1987, p. 5; S. Zyubanov, 'Samouchitel' dlya Pershinga', *Pravda*, 20 March 1987, p. 5.

70. Y. Kharlanov, 'Evropeiskie perekrestki', *Pravda*, 8 April 1987, p. 4; V. Shelkov, 'Osechka v Ottave', *Pravda*, 8 April 1987, p. 5. B. Ivanov, 'Raznoglasiya ostayutsya', *Izvestiya*, 8 April 1987, p. 5; A Ignatov, 'From Europe without Love', *Moscow News*, 19 May 1985, p. 6.

71. I. Latyshev, 'V ushcherb' dobrososedstvu', *Pravda*, 27 May 1987, p. 5; V. Ovchinnikov, 'Kongressmeny s kuvaldami', *Pravda*, 12 July 1987, p. 4; Y. Yakhontov, 'Sgovor Bonn–Vashington', *Pravda*, 21 March 1986, p. 5.

72. M. Sturua, 'Dakhau i Bitburg', *Izvestiya*, 26 April 1985, p. 5; A. Maslennikov, 'Kto kogo pobedil', *Pravda*, 25 December 1986, p. 5; S. Agafonov, 'V upryazhke "zvezdnykh voin"', *Izvestiya*, 10 September 1986, p. 4; V. Korionov, 'Kto zasoryaet gorizonty?', *Pravda*, 22 May 1986, p. 4.

73. N. Portugalov, 'Reviving the Dinosaurs', *Moscow News*, 9 June 1985, p. 5.

74. V. Matveev, 'Vy uvoleny!', *Izvestiya*, 17 April 1985, p. 5.

75. E. Bovkun, 'Vokrug Bonnskoi vstrechi', *Izvestiya*, 4 May 1985, p. 4.

76. V. Matveev, 'Vy uvoleny!', *Izvestiya*, 17 April 1985, p. 5; A. Paladin, 'Za chuzhoi schet', *Izvestiya*, 1 May 1985, p. 5.

77. V. Matveev, 'Nichego sebe perspektivy', *Izvestiya*, 8 May 1986, p. 5.
78. V. Merkov, 'The Bonn–Bitburg Summit', *Moscow News*, 12 May 1985, p. 6; A. Lazarev, 'The Seven Hold a Council of War', *Moscow News*, 11 May 1986, p. 6; D. Yakushkin, 'Is Obedience Always Good', *Moscow News*, 18 May 1986, p. 6.
79. Y. Kovalenko, 'Preobladayut opaseniya', *Izvestiya*, 1 May 1985, p. 5.
80. V. Matveev, 'Vy uvoleny!', *Izvestiya*, 17 April 1985, p. 5; E. Bovkun, 'Vokrug Bonnskoi vstrechi', *Izvestiya*, 4 May 1985, p. 4; E. Bovkun, 'Spirali Bolshoi Semerki', *Izvestiya*, 28 April 1985, pp. 4–5; A. Krivolapov, 'Bez illyuzii', *Izvestiya*, 1 May 1985, p. 5; V. Matveev, 'Nichego sebe perspektivy', *Izvestiya*, 8 May 1986, p. 5.
81. V. Matveyev, 'Komu podygryvayut', *Izvestiya*, 7 May 1985, p. 4.
82. V. Matveev, 'Vy uvoleny!', *Izvestiya*, 17 April 1985, p. 5;
83. Y. Kovalenko, 'Preobladayut opaseniya', *Izvestiya*, 1 May 1985, p. 5; V. Matveyev, *Izvestiya*, 7 May 1985, p. 4; Y. Yakhontov, 'Za shirmoi pyshnykh fraz', *Pravda*, 5 May 1985, p. 5; N. Portugalov, 'Reviving the Dinosaurs', *Moscow News*, 9 June 1985, p. 5.
84. V. Ovchinnikov, 'Venetsanskoe zerkalo', *Pravda*, 13 June 1987, p. 4.
85. N. Miroshnik, 'Chto zhdet "semerky" v Venetsii?', *Pravda*, 6 June 1987, p. 5.
86. V. Ovchinnikov, 'Venetsanskoe zerkalo', *Pravda*, 13 June 1987, p. 4. N. Miroshnik, 'Chto zhdet "semerky" v Venetsii?', *Pravda*, 6 June 1987, p. 5; V. Pershin, 'Semerka: pessimizm na starte', *Izvestiya*, 10 June 1987, p. 4; V. Simonov, 'The Seven in One Gondola', *Moscow News*, 14 June 1987, p. 3.
87. V. Gan, 'Nadezhdy i prognozy', *Pravda*, 5 June 1987, p. 5. See also V. Pershin, 'Semerka: pessimizm na starte', *Izvestiya*, 10 June 1987, p. 4; V. Ovchinnikov, 'Venetsanskoe zerkalo', *Pravda* 13 June 1987, p. 4; N. Miroshnik, 'Nikakikh konkretnykh reshenii', *Pravda*, 11 June 1987, p. 5.
88. V. Pershin, 'Semerka: pessimizm na starte', *Izvestiya*, 10 June 1987, p. 4; V. Ovchinnikov, 'Venetsanskoe zerkalo', *Pravda*, 13 June 1987, p. 4.; N. Miroshnik, 'Chto zhdet "semerky" v Venetsii?', *Pravda*, 6 June 1987, p. 5.
89. N. Miroshnik, 'Chto zhdet "semerky" v Venetsii?', *Pravda*, 6 June 1987, p. 5.
90. A. Bovin, 'Eshche odin shag', *Izvestiya* 13 June 1987, p. 6.
91. V. Shelkov, 'Syurprizov ne bylo', *Pravda*, 23 June 1988, p. 5.
92. A. Bovin, 'Semerka: Stikhiinost' i soznatel'nost' ', *Izvestiya*, 24 June 1988, p. 5; A. Shal'nev, 'Toronto: Podvedna cherta', *Izvestiya*, 23 June 1988, p. 1; V. Shelkov, 'Svidanie na zakate solntsa', *Pravda*, 19 June 1988, p. 5. One writer even quoted Margaret Thatcher, who asserted that the West was enjoying the 'longest period of economic growth since the Second World War'. V. Shelkov, 'Syurprizov ne bylo', *Pravda*, 23 June 1988, p. 5.
93. A. Shal'nev, 'Toronto: Podvedna cherta', *Izvestiya*, 23 June 1988, p. 1.
94. A. Bovin, 'Semerka: stikhiinost' i soznatel'nost' ', *Izvestiya*, 24 June 1988, p. 5.
95. A. Shal'nev, 'Toronto: Podvedna cherta', *Izvestiya*, 23 June 1988,

p. 1; A. Bovin, 'Semerka: stikhiinost' i soznatel'nost'', *Izvestiya*, 24 June 1988, p. 5; V. Shelkov, 'Vstrecha "semerki" startovala', *Pravda*, 20 June 1988, p. 1.

96. A. Shal'nev, 'Semerka prinimaet deklaratsiyu', *Izvestiya*, 22 June 1988, pp. 1, 4; V. Shelkov, 'Svidanie na zakate solntsa', *Pravda*, 19 June 1988, p. 5.

97. A. Bovin, 'Semerka: stikhiinost' i soznatel'nost'', *Izvestiya*, 24 June 1988, p. 5; V. Shelkov, 'Semerka sveryaet chasy', *Pravda*, 21 June 1988, p. 6.

98. A. Shal'nev, 'Toronto: Podvedna cherta', *Izvestiya*, 23 June 1988, p. 1; V. Shelkov, 'Vstrecha "semerki" startovala', *Pravda*, 20 June 1988, p. 1.

99. P. Bogomolov, 'Lodka v bunkere', *Sovetskaya Rossiya*, 23 June 1988, p. 3.

100. V. Bol'shakov, 'Itogi vstrechi v Arke', *Pravda*, 18 July 1989, p. 5; A. Bovin, 'Semerka v Parizhe', *Izvestiya*, 12 July 1989, p. 5.

101. A. Bogomolov, 'Semerka derzhit sovet', *Sovetskaya Rossiya*, 18 July 1989, p. 3.

102. A. Bogomolov, 'Semerka derzhit sovet', *Sovetskaya Rossiya*, 18 July 1989, p. 3.

103. V. Metveev, 'Sotrudnichestvo, a ne samoizolyatsiya', *Izvestiya*, 11 August 1989, p. 5; A. Kovalenko, 'Semerka provodit itogi', *Izvestiya*, 17 July 1989, p. 4; A. Bovin, 'Semerka v Parizhe', *Izvestiya*, 12 July 1989, p. 5.

104. Y. Zhukov, 'Edinstvo v mnogoobrazii ili zhizn' po edinomu standartu', *Pravda*, 9 August 1989, p. 4; V. Bol'shakov, 'Itogi vstrechi v 'Arke', *Pravda*, 18 July 1989, p. 5. *Sovetskaya Rossiya* did not devote significant coverage to the meeting, although one might speculate that its reporters would have agreed with the *Pravda* assessment.

7 IMAGES OF DOMESTIC AMERICA

1. Walter Lippmann, *Public Opinion* (New York: The Free Press) 1965, p. 74.

2. By domestic America it is meant institutions, processes and phenomena which exist within the United States and primarily concern it and its inhabitants.

3. Two writers described the progeny of this image of America as follows, 'Until recently, the main purpose of our foreign propaganda activity was the assertion of the unconditional superiority of socialist values and their fundamental difference from the ideals and moral standards of other cultures.' T.V. Znamenskaya and A.B. Smyagin, 'Vneshnopoliticheskaya propaganda', *SShA*, no. 9, September 1988, p. 26.

4. Spechler, *Permitted Dissent*, 1982, p. 255.

5. Spechler, *Permitted Dissent*, 1982, p. 171.

6. *Izvestiya*, 20 January 1963, quoted in Buzek, *How the Communist Press Works*, 1964, pp. 56–7.

7. Shlapentokh, 'Moscow's War Propaganda', 1984, p. 91.
8. Bar-Tal, David, 'Delegitimization: The Extreme case of Stereotyping and Prejudice', in Bar-Tal, C.F. Grauman, A.W. Kruglanski and W. Strobe (eds) *Stereotyping and Prejudice – Changing Conceptions* (New York: Springer Verlag) 1989, pp. 170 ff. Much of this definition is drawn from Bar-Tal's definition of delegitimization. See also Murray Edelman, *Constructing the Political Spectacle* (Chicago: University of Chicago Press) 1988 and Edelman, *The Symbolic Uses of Politics* (Urbana: University of Illinois Press) 1985.
9. F. Tishchenko, 'SOI protiv mira', *Pravda*, 7 December 1986, p. 5.
10. V. Kapralov, 'Maks, Teks, i inoplanetyane', *Pravda*, 3 August 1986, p. 4; A. Meshcherskii, 'Stoprotsentnyi Amerikanets', *Argumenty i Fakty*, no. 32, 5–11 August 1986, p. 4; V. Zhuravsky, 'Veselye grobovshchiki', *Pravda*, 23 August 1986, p. 5; K. Solganik, 'Rok muzyka – agressivnaya ili progressivnaya', *Argumenty i Fakty*, no. 16, 15 April 1986, p. 6.
11. G. Zlobin, 'V zerkale Amerikanskogo romana', *Pravda*, 22 September 1986, p. 6.
12. V. Sukhoi, '1986 ne dolzhna povtorit'sya', *Pravda*, 6 August 1986, p. 4; V. Gan, 'Iz shkola nenavisti', *Pravda*, 23 April 1986, p. 4; V. Soldatov, 'V krivom zerkale reaktsii', *Izvestiya*, 17 February 1986, p. 5.
13. O. Startseva, 'Strelyaite i ubivaite', *Literaturnaya Rossiya*, 13 June 1986, p. 22; N. Popuridze, 'Sto sposobov zashchity ot prestupnikov', *Argumenty i Fakty*, no. 4, 21–7 January 1986, p. 7; V. Vladimirov, 'Vospitanie i nakazanie', *Argumenty i Fakty*, no. 13, 26 March 1985, p. 4.
14. L. Koryavin, 'Zloveshchie standarty', *Izvestiya*, 8 April 1985, p. 5; TASS, 'SShA', *Izvestiya*, 20 May 1986, p. 4; Y. Gribachev, 'Korichnevyi chad', *Literaturnaya Rossiya*, 17 May 1985, p. 22.
15. A. Palladin, 'Sled, ostanavlennyi kastellano', *Izvestiya*, 29 December 1985, p. 5; B. Ivanov, 'Obshchestvo totalnogo strakha', *Izvestiya*, 20 April 1985, p. 4.
16. For the impact of anti-Sovietism on school children see S. Kondrashov, 'Svidetel'stva ochevidtsa', *Izvestiya*, 17 March 1986, p. 5. On a more general level, see G. Vasiliev, 'Ryadovoi Dzho i mal'chik Piter', *Pravda*, 17 February 1986, p. 6; B. Zabirov, 'S chernogo khoda', *Literaturnaya Rossiya*, 3 October 1986, p. 22.
17. This attitude was reflected by Mikhail Gorbachev in his book *Perestroika*, when he said, 'For our part, the Soviet Union has no propaganda of hatred toward Americans or disregard for America. In our country you won't find this anywhere, either in politics or in education. We criticize a policy we do not agree with. But that's a different matter. It does not mean that we show disrespect for the American people.' M.S. Gorbachev, *Perestroika*, 1987, p. 217.
18. V. Korotich, 'Vremya otkrovennosti', *Literaturnaya Rossiya*, 19 September 1986, p. 2. Korotich would later become editor-in-chief of the leading reform journal *Ogonek*.
19. V. Mikheev, 'Dyadya Vanya v Luisville', *Izvestiya*, 16 September 1986, p. 5; For American support of Soviet initiatives see 'My vyigraem eto srazhenie', *Pravda*, 22 August 1986, p. 4; for letters from Ameri-

cans supporting Soviet initiatives see V. Sukhoi, 'Ya odin iz prostykh lyudei Ameriki . . .', *Pravda*, 7 October 1986, p. 4.

20. V. Gan, 'Podlinnoe mirolyubie', *Pravda*, 24 October 1986, p. 4; 'Press konferentsiya G. Khalla', *Pravda*, 26 October 1986, p. 4.

21. J. Meiers, 'Svezhii veter', *Pravda*, 13 January 1986, p. 6.

22. 'Zhizn' i zaboty amerikanskoi pensionerki', *Argumenty i Fakty*, no. 1, 1–6 January 1986, pp. 4–5.

23. V. Simonev, 'An August Fantasy', *Moscow News*, no. 31, 11 August 1986, p. 5; V. Kavaliavski, 'USA: Anti-Arab Racism', *Moscow News*, no. 4, 7 February 1986, p. 4; Art Blakey, 'U menya konfiskovali svobodu', *Argumenty i Fakty*, no. 2, 1986, p. 5.

24. J. Meiers, 'Svezhii veter', *Pravda*, 13 January 1986, p. 6.

25. B. Ivanov, 'Otkrovennyi rasizm', *Izvestiya*, 24 May 1985, p. 4.

26. A. Palladin, 'Obratnaya storona 'Ravnopraviya', *Izvestiya*, 22 January 1986, p. 4.

27. A. Palladin, 'Obratnaya storona 'Ravnopraviya', *Izvestiya*, 22 January 1986, p. 4; L. Koryavin, 'Tyur'ma dlya tekh, kto khochet mira', *Izvestiya*, 11 March 1986, p. 5; V. Gan, 'Zvonok iz sektora C', *Pravda*, 3 January 1986; L. Tolkunov, 'Arest stachenikov', *Pravda*, 9 February 1986, p. 5; S. Yani, 'Za tyur'emnoi stenoi', *Argumenty i Fakty*, no. 22, 27 May–2 June 1986, p. 7; Y. Abdulayeva, 'We Have Faith in Justice', *Moscow News*, no. 3, 26 January 1986, p. 1.

28. G. Vasiliev, 'Ne luchshe sebya gospoda, oborotit'sya', *Pravda*, 16 June 1986, p. 5.

29. A. Kuvshinnikov, 'Dzhozef Mori uletaet domoi', *Izvestiya*, 1 September 1986, p. 4; M. Knyazkov, 'Korsary pera vstrechayut Dz. Mori', *Izvestiya*, 2 September 1986, p. 1; N. Paskhin, 'Eto – Amerika', *Pravda*, 16 April 1986, p. 3; Joseph Mauri, 'Ya odin iz mnogikh', interview, *Argumenty i Fakty*, no. 34, 19–25 August 1986, p. 4. For a later article on Mauri, see L. Yeltsova, 'Mauri's Last Hope', *Moscow News*, no. 22, 31 May 1987, p. 4.

30. See, for example, 'Soviet People Send Petition to President Reagan', *Moscow News*, 12 April 1987, p. 5; 'Charles Hyder: I'm not Afraid to Die', *Moscow News*, 15 March 1987, p. 5; Interestingly, *Pravda*'s Viktor Linnik, who worked in the International Information Department then in the Propaganda Department, insisted that Aleksandr Yakovlev was responsible for the campaign. V. Linnik, author interview (New York: December 1989).

31. V. Linnik, author interview (New York: December 1989); V. Sukhoi, author interview (New York: September 1988).

32. See, for example, G. Stanishev, 'Vse khorosho, prekrasnaya markiza', *Argumenty i Fakty*, no. 31, 29 July–4 August 1986, p. 7; P. Lukyanchenko, 'Spasite' svobodu', *Argumenty i Fakty*, no. 40, 30 September–6 October 1986, p. 5.

33. V. Bol'shakov, 'Linchuya zdravyi smysl', *Pravda*, 11 June 1986, p. 5.

34. Sukhoi, author interview (New York: September 1988); Fedyashin, author interview (Washington: September 1989); Linnik, author interview (New York: December 1989).

35. T. Kolisnechenko, 'V pautine stereotipov', *Pravda*, 27 March 1986,

p. 4; M. Sabin, 'Kongress v SShA, Kto v nem i pochemu', *Argumenty i Fakty*, no. 6, 1987, p. 5.

36. For differing views, compare 'Iz Gazet', *Pravda*, 25 March 1985, p. 5, with G. Vasiliev, 'Udar po nadezhdam', *Pravda*, 9 September 1986, p. 4; B. Ivanov, 'Oderzhimye Besom', *Izvestiya*, 3 July 1986, p. 5. For a general view on monopoly capitalism see B. Zabirov, 'S chernogo khoda', *Literaturnaya Rossiya*, 3 October 1986, p. 22.

37. See, for example, V. Mikheev's article on political action committees, 'Kak pokupayut kongressmenov', *Izvestiya*, 5 January 1986, or B. Ivanov's on lobbies 'Chetvertaya vetv' vlasti', *Izvestiya*, 9 June 1986, p. 5.

38. For a good discussion of State Monopoly Capitalism, see Malcolm, *Soviet Political Scientists*, 1984, p. 19 ff.

39. The powerlessness of the people was a frequent subject of discourse. The attitude was summed up well by *Pravda*'s V. Peresada in 1986. After claiming that 80 per cent of Americans support a nuclear test moratorium, he stated, 'Of course, the USA has its own treatment of the concept of "democracy". But, if in general human understanding "democracy" means the "power of the people," then what kind of democracy is it when not the slightest attention is paid to the opinion of the people.' V. Peresada, 'Unikal'nyi Shansi', *Pravda*, 14 September 1986, p. 4.

40. Thomas Kolisnechenko pointed out the particularly base nature of the American ruling elite while describing the attitude of the ruling classes towards the masses: 'The ruling elite is guided not by the general interests of the nation (which characteristically guide such groups everywhere else in the world) but purely by selfish interests that benefit it alone . . .'. T. Kolisnechenko, 'V pautine stereotipov', *Pravda*, 27 March 1986, p. 4.

41. V. Korionov, 'Za kulisami Belogo Doma', *Pravda*, 17 November 1986, p. 5.

42. See M. Gorbachev, *SWB*, SU/8389/A1/9, 14 October 1986.

43. *Argumenty i Fakty*, no. 46–47, 11–17 November 1986; Y. Gribachev, 'Na puti k miru', *Literaturnaya Rossiya*, no. 10, 6 March 1987, p. 3; M. Sturua, 'Four Days in August', *Moscow News*, no. 35, 7 September 1986, p. 6. Although some of the articles appeared in 1986, they carried the same themes as those in early 1987: 'Posle Reikyavika vremya deistvii', *Pravda*, 16 October 1986, p. 1. Further, on the military-industrial complex see D. Kraminov, 'Vremya deistvovat', *Literaturnaya Rossiya*, 17 October 1986, p. 2; 'Sila i bessilie', *Pravda*, 17 November 1986, p. 6.

44. A. Buzek, *How The Communist Press Works*, 1964, p. 58.

45. Vladimir Sukhoi, 'Gorod v gorode', *Pravda*, 28 March 1987, p. 5.

46. V. Afanas'ev, 'Odinadtsat' dnei za okeanom', *Pravda*, 12 January 1987, p. 6.

47. Sukhoi was very critical of New York in the article which he wrote about his arrival as *Pravda*'s New York correspondent. V. Sukhoi, 'Ulybaites': vy – Americantsy', *Pravda*, 21 July 1986, p. 6.

48. See, for example, Sukhoi's 'Taims-skver: staroe i novoe' (*Pravda*, 3 May 1987, p. 5) about renovations in Times Square; his 'Robot

pomogaet politsii', about American police robots (*Pravda*, 24 March 1987, p. 5); V. Prokhorov's 'Nad chem smeemsya?', about American humour (*Pravda*, 13 May 1987, p. 6); A. Cooperman, 'Baseball Has Come to Moscow', *Moscow News*, no. 28, 12 July 1987, p. 15.

49. A. Luk'yanov, 'Kto eta devchonka?', *Pravda*, 7 September 1987, p. 7.
50. A. Shal'nev, 'Dusha reya Charl'za', *Izvestiya*, 4 March 1988, p. 4; A. Ivan'ko, 'Akter i prodyusor Maikl Duglas', *Izvestiya*, 29 March 1988, p. 5; I. Kovalev, 'Stallone menyaet ampula', *Izvestiya*, 29 September 1989, p. 6; A. Ivan'ko, 'Kumir Amerikantsev', *Izvestiya*, 5 January 1990, p. 4.
51. 'Greta Garbo – zhizn' v odinochestve', *Pravda*, 17 April 1990, p. 6; V. Sukhoi, 'Vudstok: tri dnya mira i muzyki', *Pravda*, 20 August 1989, p. 5; A. Ladynin, 'My vse ostavalis' pyatnadtsatiletnimi . . .', *Pravda*, 3 February 1990, p. 6; V. Sukhoi, 'Skol'ko stoit Oskar?', *Pravda*, 16 May 1988, p. 7; Sukhoi, 'Teatral'nyi kalendar' Brodveya', *Pravda*, 1 January 1988, p. 5; V. Sukhoi, 'Gorod vetrov i blyuzov', *Pravda*, 7 January 1990, p. 7; V. Sukhoi, 'Raznotsvetnye avto-mobili', *Pravda*, 1 October 1988, p. 5. For an earlier example of coverage of the Oscars, see Y. Ustimenko, *Argumenty i Fakty*, no. 23, 17–23 June 1986, p. 8.
52. D. Makarov, 'Vse na prodazhu', *Argumenty i Fakty*, no. 21, 21–27 May 1988, p. 7; V. Pozner, 'Vershki i koreshki . . . kul'tury', *Argumenty i Fakty*, no. 33, 22–28 August 1987, p. 5; G. Konavapov, 'Vzleti padenie zhurnala', *Argumenty i Fakty*, no. 20, 20–26 May 1989, p. 7; N. Soldatenkov, 'Zhizn' i smert' porno svezdy', *Argumenty i Fakty*, no. 47, 25 November–1 December 1989, p. 5.
53. *Argumenty i Fakty*, no. 7, 13–19 February 1988, p. 8.
54. V. Linnik, 'Amerikanets v voskresen'e', *Pravda*, 4 April 1988, p. 7.
55. A general article on Americans' free time was V. Sukhoi's 'Svobodnoe vremya amerikantsev', *Pravda*, 9 August 1988, p. 5. For exercise, see V. Gan, 'Kuda bezhit Amerika', *Pravda*, 9 April 1989, p. 5; bingo, V. Sukhoi, 'Igra i bingo', *Pravda* 16 February 1990, p. 7; flea markets, V. Gan, 'Chego dushe ugodno . . .', *Pravda*, 3 May 1989, p. 5.
56. Alaska, S. Dardykin, 'Blizkaya Alyaska', *Izvestiya*, 17, 18 March 1989, p. 5; New England, V. Matveev, 'Ugolok Novoi Anglii', *Izvestiya*, 23 October 1989, p. 5; the Amish, V. Sukhoi, 'Svad'by? Tol'ko po vtornikam', *Pravda*, 5 May 1990, p. 7.
57. V. Sukhoi, 'Indeika v nebesakh . . .', *Pravda*, 29 November 1986, p. 5. For a comparison with a story he did on hallowe'en, see Sukhoi, 'Chto takoe khellouin', *Pravda*, 22 October 1988, p. 5.
58. In early 1987, the author of another article on Atlanta spoke of the Ku Klux Klan and concluded that 'National politics in the USA – it is most of all politics of the violation of human rights, constitutional norms and the violation of international law.' L. Koryavin, 'Nasledniki konfederatov', *Izvestiya*, 19 February 1987, p. 5. See also L. Koryavin, 'Ne unesennie vetrom . . .', *Izvestiya*, 30 December 1985, p. 5.
59. V. Sukhoi, 'Dva dnya v Atlante', *Pravda*, 28 February 1988, p. 4.
60. On the superiority of Soviet health care, G. Balyuzhenich, 'SSSR-SShA – Statistika Zdorovya', *Argumenty i Fakty*, no. 4, 21–27 January

1986, p. 4; On athletic trainers, V. Kozakov, 'Trener v SSSR i na Zapade', *Argumenty i Fakty*, no. 14, 1–7 April 1986, p. 5; On housing, B. Bulatov, 'Kak reshaetsya zhilishchnaya problema v SSSR i SShA', *Argumenty i Fakty*, no. 17, 17–22 April 1986, pp. 4–5.

61. See 'Prodolzhitelnost' zhizni v SSSR', *Argumenty i Fakty*, no. 18, 9–15 May 1987, p. 7; *Argumenty i Fakty*, no. 23, 13–19 June 1987, p. 5. See also V. Linnik, 'Amerikanets v voskresen'e', *Pravda*, 4 April 1987; A. Telyukov, *Argumenty i Fakty*, #41–42, 17–23 October 1987, pp. 8–9.

62. They form an interesting contrast with material which Zaichenko and others had produced in earlier periods. A. Zaichenko, 'Chto takoe cherta bednosti?', *Argumenty i Fakty*, no. 16, 15 April 1986, p. 4; 'Zhizn v SShA i v SSSR glazami amerikantsa', *Argumenty i Fakty*, no. 13, 26 March–1 April 1988, p. 6 and no. 15, 9–15 April 1988, p. 5.

63. A. Zaichenko, 'On Our Daily Bread', *Moscow News*, no. 34, 21 August 1988, p. 12.

64. 'Editor's note', *Moscow News*, no. 34, 21 August 1988, p. 12.

65. A. Zaichenko, 'Imushchestvennoe neravenstvo', *Argumenty i Fakty*, no. 27, 8–14 July 1989, p. 3.

66. A. Popov, 'Bogatye i bednye', *Argumenty i Fakty*, no. 42, 21–27 October 1989, p. 5.

67. Scott Shane, 'Tipichnie Amerikantsy', *Argumenty i Fakty*, no. 45, 5–11 November 1988, p. 4; A. Telyukov, *Argumenty i Fakty*, no. 35, 27 August–2 September 1988, p. 8; *Argumenty i Fakty*, no. 33, 22–28 August 1987, p. 5. In the next period, for more information on lifespan, GNP, and pensions, see *Argumenty i Fakty*, no. 41–42, 17–23 October 1987, p. 8.

68. By major articles, it is meant articles which cover more than four column inches. Articles were considered only when they contained direct accusations of human rights violations. Common subjects considered under the broad category of human rights violations include poverty, unemployment, homelessness, discrimination and political prisoners. If anything, this resulted in an under-representation, especially early in the period, because many articles which focused on subjects like unemployment and discrimination did not contain accusations of human rights violations. Only articles on domestic issues were considered.

69. The increase of accusations in the period from January 1987 to August 1987 is probably due to Soviet disappointment with the failed Reykjavik Summit in late October 1986 and a final anti-American campaign designed to counter potential Reagan administration accusations which appeared just prior to the Moscow Summit.

70. An example of the new more analytical approach is A. Lopukhin's analysis of racism. See 'Chernaya Amerika: Vzglyad iznutri', *Pravda*, 6 October 1989, p. 6.

71. A. Shal'nev, 'Konflikt v Brukline', *Izvestiya*, 14 May 1990, p. 5.

72. Calery Chalidze, 'Socio-Economic Rights – East vs. West', *Moscow News*, no. 3, 21 January 1990, p. 6.

73. P. Moss and Dzhon Sveidi, 'Amerikantsy sami o sebe', *Pravda*, 18 July 1988, p. 1; Djek Toma and Karl Gutekanst, 'Amerikantsy pishut v Moskvu', *Pravda*, 12 September 1988, p. 6.

74. A. Lyuty, 'Uilmingtonskoe delo', *Pravda*, 5 February 1989, p. 5.
75. B. Ivanov, 'Chetvertaya vetv' vlasti', *Izvestiya*, 9 June 1986, p. 5, V. Mikheev, 'Kak pokupayut kongressmenov', *Izvestiya*, 5 January 1986, p. 5.
76. L. Koryavin, 'Tret'ya palata kongressa: Lobbi-professiya, yavlenie politicheskaya traditsiya v SShA', *Izvestiya*, 21 October 1988, p. 5.
77. Amy Elizabeth Ansell, *New Right, New Racism* (New York: New York University Press) 1997, pp. 33–48. One may refer here to Ansell's notion of 'symbolic conflict' which is concerned with 'the struggle over the set of meanings which helps to determine the mental criteria by which the distribution of (material or political) resources are perceived and judged'. *New Right*, p. 35. On the importance of symbols and the creation of meaning, see Murray Edelman, *Constructing the Political Spectacle* (Chicago: University of Chicago Press) 1988 and *The Symbolic Uses of Politics* (Urbana: University of Illinois Press) 1985; Pierre Boudrieu, *Language and Symbolic Power* (Cambridge: Harvard University Press) 1991, and Ansell, *New Right*. Those who write about language and political power, of course, rely on broader analyses of language, action and thought of theorists such as Foucault, Derrida and Habermas.
78. 'Sokhranyaet zrenie', *Izvestiya*, 17 January 1986, p. 5; D. Vasilieyev, 'Two Models', *Moscow News*, 20 October 1985, p. 12; B. Alexeyev, 'The Less Misunderstanding the Better', *Moscow News*, 10 October 1985, p. 4. Even specialty journals were slow to change. For example, *SShA*, the journal of the Institute for the Study of the United States and Canada, only showed minor changes until 1988. R. Mills, *As Moscow Sees Us*, 1990, p. 136. For a broader discussion on *SShA*, see Malcolm, *Political Scientists*, 1984, p. 160 ff.
79. V. Medvedev, 'Sovremennaya kontseptsiya sotsializma', *Pravda*, 5 October 1988, p. 4.
80. Vladimir Sukhoi, 'Izobresti ... lestnitsu', *Pravda*, 23 March 1987, p. 5.
81. G. Vasiliev, 'Esli ne zavoditsya avtomobil'', *Pravda*, 13 July 1987, p. 7.
82. S.M. Geints, 'V odin ruki ...', *Pravda*, 7 September 1987, p. 7.
83. Editor V. Afanas'ev estimated that in 1988 *Pravda* would receive 800,000 letters. *SWB*, SU/0146/B/2, 9 May 1988. On letters to the editor, see Dzirkals, Gustafson and Johnson, *Inter-Elite Communication*, 1982, p. 67.
84. See the following articles: design – V. Sukhoi, 'Luchshee–vrag khoroshego: Zametki o promyshlennom dizaine v SShA', *Pravda*, 1 September 1989, p. 6; management, A. Blinov, 'Professiya-menedzher: Kak i chemu uchat upravlyayushchykh amerikanskykh firm', *Izvestiya*, 9 September 1988, p. 5; product guarantees, V. Gan, 'Pust' nadoedayut ...', *Pravda*, 8 August 1988, p. 7; research and development, A. Shal'nev, 'Esli u tebya est' ideya ...', *Izvestiya*, 4 August 1988, p. 5; the use of modern technology – V. Sukhoi, 'U menya zazvonil telefon', *Pravda*, 9 September 1988, p. 6; overnight delivery, *Pravda*, 'V pogone za vremenem', 7 May 1987, p. 5; A. Zaichenko, 'Pensioners and Pensions', *Moscow News*, no. 2, 8 January 1989, p. 10.

85. On books, see G. Vasiliev, 'Chtoby uberech' pamyat' chelovechestva', *Pravda*, 27 July 1987, p. 7 and L. Koryavin, 'Za vitrinoi Kraun buk', *Izvestiya*, 25 December 1987, p. 5; farming chemicals – G. Vasiliev, 'Murman', fermer Rich i drugie', *Pravda*, 11 June 1987, p. 4.
86. On abortion – V. Linnik, 'Esli vybor sdelan: Kak rabotaet ginologicheskaya klinika v SShA', *Pravda*, 16 September 1989, p. 5; On restaurants – A. Shal'nev, 'Libo plati, libo soblyudai chistotu', *Izvestiya*, 19 March 1988, p. 6. The article described government inspections of New York restaurants.
87. On parks – V. Sukhoi, 'Voz'mite s soboi vospominaniya', *Pravda*, 20 June 1988, p. 7; healthcare – V. Gan, 'Polpredy dobroty', *Pravda*, 8 December 1989, p. 6; archival information – D. Raleigh and O. Teryokhin, 'The Trials and Tribulations of Professor Raleigh', *Moscow News*, 14 August 1988, p. 2; freedom of information – *Argumenty i Fakty*, no. 40, 1–7 October 1988, p. 8; theatre – V. Linnik, 'Dzhon Dzhori i ego rebyata', *Pravda*, 31 May 1990, p. 6. The latter was interesting, because the author, Viktor Linnik, explained in some detail how personal, corporate and foundation donations sustained the company. He then sent a message to Soviet troupes: 'I think that these details are not without interest for some of our statesmen of art, our leaders of theaters, groaning about the dominance of native bureaucrats, but not thinking about rejecting government donations.'
88. A. Shal'nev, 'V park, na operu', *Izvestiya*, 11 September 1988, p. 5.
89. On professionalism and ethics – Kerri Woods, 'Zhizn' v politike', *Argumenty i Fakty*, no. 25, 24–30 June 1989, p. 6; V. Savelyev, 'Soviets Appreciate US Congress' Ethics', *Moscow News*, no. 46, 12 November 1989, p. 10; V. Gan, 'Na ostrie britvy', *Pravda*, 11 December 1989, p. 7. The articles were complimentary about the standards of the US Congress and were thus different from traditional approaches. The US Congress at its core was traditionally presented as a bastion of the ruling elite which was dominated by interests of their class and constantly swayed by leading monopolies, the military-industrial complex. M. Savin, 'Kongress SShA: Kto v nem i pochemu?', *Argumenty i Fakty*, no. 6, 14–20 February 1987, p. 5; V. Soldatov, 'Tryuki vmesto debatov', *Izvestiya*, 3 December 1985, p. 5 about the absence of Senate debate and its class-oriented nature. It should be noted that there were sometimes countervailing messages concerning individual Congressmen, some of whom were singled out for their liberal attitudes and who served, in effect, as middlemen between the reactionary Reagan administration and the increasingly progressive American public. N. Kurdyumov, 'Mnenie obozrevatelya', *Pravda*, 25 April 1985, p. 5; TASS, 'Pora prezidentu otkazat'sya', *Pravda*, 15 February 1986, p. 5; on local governments – L. Koryavin, 'SShA: Vlast na mestakh, podchinena zakonu i izbiratelyam', *Izvestiya*, 26 March 1990, p. 5; on civil service – A. Shal'nev, 'Shkola Byurokratii: Kak gotovyat pravitel'stvennykh chinovnikov v SShA', *Izvestiya*, 3 April 1989, p. 5; on complaints against government – A. Shal'nev, 'Nado pozhalovatsya? Net problem!', *Izvestiya*, 11 July 1989, p. 5; on state natural disasters – L. Strzhizhovskii, 'Zemletryasenie i my', *Pravda*, 21 November 1989,

p. 5.; on the FBI – A. Shal'nev, 'Odin den' v Akademii FBR', *Izvestiya*, 23 May 1990, p. 5.

90. Remington, 'A Socialist Pluralism of Opinions,' 1989, pp. 281–2.
91. The law was published in *Pravda* on 6 March 1988 (See 'O kooperatsii v SSSR,' p. 2 ff.). The law was ultimately passed in June. For debate on the law, see A. Protsenko, 'Proekt odobren', *Izvestiya*, 24 May 1988, p. 3. See also J. Tedstrom, 'Soviet Cooperatives: A Difficult Road to Legitimacy', *Radio Liberty Research Bulletin*, 224/88, 31 May 1988.
92. V. Gan, 'Tri dnya v zhizni ADM', *Pravda*, 27 May 1988, p. 6.
93. 'Tezisy Tsentral'nogo Komiteta KPSS k XIX Vsesoyuznoi partiinoi konferentsii', *Izvestiya*, 27 May 1988 p. 1 ff.
94. V. Sukhoi, '22 milliona – c odnoi "vilki"', *Pravda*, 10 May 1988, p. 5.
95. See V. Sukhoi, 'Rybnoe chrevo N'yu-Iorka', *Pravda*, 26 September 1988, p. 7, about a cooperative which sells fish; V. Sukhoi, 'Klyukova-yagoda', *Pravda*, 3 April 1989, p. 7, about Ocean-Spray cranberry cooperative.
96. D. Shnyukas, 'Dub, dikaya roza i shchegol', *Pravda*, 5 September 1988, p. 7; V. Ryabchun, 'Kak ya byl Amerikanskim fermerom', *Izvestiya*, 28 February 1989, p. 3; V. Matusevich, 'Prizrak Fermera', *Izvestiya*, 23 March 1990, p. 6; W. Sloane and A. Bekker, 'A Socialist Farm in the State of Ohio', *Moscow News*, no. 28, 9 July 1989, p. 6. On the plenum, see *CDSP*, vol. xl, no. 9, p. 1 ff.
97. L. Lyubimov, 'V plebu stereotipa, ili o tom, kak rabotaet plyuralizm sobstvennosti pri kapitalizme', *Izvestiya*, 9 February 1990, p. 5.
98. 'Pora zadumat'sya vser'ez', *Pravda*, 3 March 1987, p. 4.
99. *CDSP*, 27 July 1988, vol. xl, no. 26, p. 11. While democratization had been spoken of often since January 1987, there were not really any major steps taken towards it until 1988.
100. Archie Brown, 'Political Change in the Soviet Union', *World Policy Journal*, vol. vi, no. 3, Summer 1989, p. 477 ff. See B. Konovalov, 'Taim' konstitutsiya SShA i poluchasnost''', *Argumenty i Fakty*, no. 30, 1–7 August 1987, pp. 4–5. There was significant criticism of the US Constitution as a whole, including an anti-American propaganda campaign on the eve of its 200th anniversary. See 'Bil o pravakh', *Argumenty i Fakty*, no. 12, 28 March–3 April 1987, p. 1; A. Meshcherskii, 'Na krylyakh demokratii', *Argumenty i Fakty*, no. 14, 11–17 April 1987, p. 1; V. Simonov, 'The Scorched Constitution', *Moscow News*, no. 20, 17 May 1987, p. 3.
101. Gorbachev stated, 'Thus, one may say, comrades that our socialist system of 'checks and balances' is taking shape in this country, designed to protect society against any violation of socialist legality at the highest state level.' Quoted in Brown, 'Political Change in the Soviet Union', 1989, p. 478.
102. The concept of checks and balances had received attention earlier in the Gorbachev period. Archie Brown traces it back to a meeting of the Soviet Association of Political Sciences in February 1987 which was presided over by Georgi Shakhnazarov, informal adviser to Mikhail Gorbachev and soon to be named *pomoshchnik*, one of four formal aides. At the same meeting, it was suggested that relevant Western

theoretical writings about the subject should be taken into consideration. Brown, 'Political Change in the Soviet Union', 1989, p. 477 ff.
103. A. Mishin, 'Dve storony filadel'fskogo chuda', *Izvestiya*, 19 September 1987. In *Argumenty i Fakty*, a Soviet jurist, while rejecting the concept of separation of powers, called for the Supreme Soviet to have a measure of constitutional oversight. This was perhaps a sign of nascent change and one of the first examples of learning from the American political system. 'Diskusii s Amerikanskami prokurorami', *Argumenty i Fakty*, no. 43, 24–30 October 1987, p. 8.
104. S. Kondrashov, 'Dolgii vzglyad na Ameriku: Menyayushchiesya obrazy v menyayushchemsya mire', *Moskovskie Novosti*, 2 October 1988, pp. 6–7.
105. Viktor Linnik, 'Koe-chto ob iskusstve sokhranit' respubliku', *Pravda*, 14 November 1988, p. 6.
106. See, for example V. Gan, 'Osen' v kapitolii: Novaya sessiya kongressa SShA', *Pravda*, 2 October 1989, p. 7, and A. Blinov, 'Prikhoditsya iskat' zamenu', *Izvestiya*, 10 March 1989, p. 5. V. Nadein, in his article 'Nichego, krome zakona', considered the separation of powers to be of lesser importance than guarantees of individual rights, but was complimentary about both and particularly about American democracy. *Izvestiya*, 24 February 1990, p. 5.
107. V. Nadein, 'Nichego, krome zakona: Predely i vozmozhnosti presidentskoi vlasti', *Izvestiya*, 24 February 1990, p. 5. See also, V. Dolganov and A. Stepovoi, 'V povestke dnya – vopros o prezidentstve', *Izvestiya*, 27 February 1990, p. 1; E. Teague, *Radio Liberty Research Bulletin*, 9 March 1990, pp. 12–13.
108. S. Kondrashov, 'Mnogopartiinost' – fundament demokratii', *Izvestiya*, 5 March 1990, p. 3.
109. L. Koryavin, 'Dvorets devyati mudretsov: Verkhovnyi sud v sisteme amerikanskoi yurisprudentsii', *Izvestiya*, 25 May 1990, p. 7. For other articles laudatory of the American legal system, see also V. Linnik, 'Sud prisyazhnykh v SShA', *Pravda*, 6 December 1989, p. 5, and an interview with American jurists, 'Razreshat' vygodnee, chem zapreshchat'', *Izvestiya*, 12 April 1989, p. 5.
110. For Lithuania see *CDSP* vol. xli, no. 7, pp. 6–7; Moldavia – E. Kondratov, 'Uslyshat' drug druga', *Izvestiya*, 31 January 1989, p. 3. There were also increasing demonstrations in the Ukraine among other republics. See Bohadan Nahaylo, 'Inaugural Conference of Ukrainian Language Society Turns into Major Political Demonstration', *Radio Liberty Research Bulletin*, vol. 1, no. 9, 3 March 1989, pp. 13–17; Don Ionescu, 'Soviet Moldavia: A Breakthrough on the Alphabet Issue', *Radio Liberty Research Bulletin*, vol. 1, no. 12, 24 March 1989, pp. 25–8.
111. A short article in *Pravda* which appeared at the same time pointed out that the states 'do not have the right to leave the federation of their own will'. 'Chto takoe amerikanskii federalizm?', *Pravda*, 26 February 1989, p. 4.
112. L. Koryavin, 'Amerikanskii federalizm : korni i vetvi', *Izvestiya*, 8 February 1989, p. 5.

113. L. Koryavin, 'Amerikanskii federalizm : korni i vetvi', *Izvestiya*, 8 February 1989, p. 5.
114. L. Koryavin, 'Zakony vlasti – zakony protivovesov', *Izvestiya*, 9 March 1990, p. 5.
115. A. Shal'nev, 'V park, na operu', *Izvestiya*, 11 September 1988, p. 5.
116. In an article on a Louisville theatre troupe, *Pravda*'s Viktor Linnik addressed not only the artistic quality of the troupe, but its entre-preneurial qualities in pursuit of personal, corporate and private donations: 'I think that these details are not without interest for some of our statesmen of art, our leaders of theaters, groaning about the dominance of native bureaucrats, but not thinking about rejecting government donations.' V. Linnik, 'Dzhon Dzhori i ego rebyata', *Pravda*, 31 May 1990, p. 6.
117. A. Lyutyi, 'Nam sverkhu vidno vse', *Pravda*, 26 May 1989, p. 7.
118. Melor Sturua, 'Ogneopasnyi stereotip', *Izvestiya*, 12 June 1988, p. 1, and A. Shal'nev, 'V kogo strelyaet Rembo', *Izvestiya*, 24 May 1988, p. 4.
119. T. Kolisnichenko, 'Neuzhto snova k bar'eru?', *Pravda*, 15 April 1990, p. 7.
120. A similar concern about the military-industrial complex was also voiced by *Pravda*'s Vitalii Korionov, 'Est o chem pogovorit?', *Pravda*, 18 September 1989, p. 6.
121. P. Bogomolov, 'Grani dukhovnoi razryadki', *Pravda*, 25 June 1990, p. 6.
122. To give an idea of the degree of change, an author, responding to a reader's question about minority representation in the American Con-gress, placed a greater stress on increasing minority representation throughout all levels of American government than on their remark-ably low levels of representation. See S. Cheremin, 'Monopoliya ne vechna', *Pravda*, 22 October 1989, p. 4.
123. Indeed, in the middle of 1988, just prior to the Moscow Summit, the liberal *Moscow News* participated in the anti-American campaign, publishing letters and articles in three consecutive issues criticizing American human rights violations. V. Simonov, 'A Subject to Discuss with the US President', *Moscow News*, no. 18, 1 May 1988, p. 3; E. Cheporov, 'Deprived of our Freedom', *Moscow News*, no. 19, 8 May 1988, p. 5.
124. Linnik, author interview (New York: December 1989).
125. Although the primary leaders seemed to have some affinity with social-democratic states, there was a distinct coolness amongst many, including Aleksandr Yakovlev and Mikhail Gorbachev, towards the United States. Moreover, it was quite clear that Gorbachev and his allies' side of the leadership was interested in restructuring social-ism, not creating an American-style system. This was evident from the General Secretary's address in opposition to Yeltsin's candidacy for the chairmanship of the Russian Supreme Soviet in May 1990, when he criticized Yeltsin for not once referring to 'socialism' in his candidacy speech, and for his attempt to 'with one stroke of the pen . . . invite us to bid farewell to the socialist choice of 1917'. *CDSP*, vol. xlii, no. 21, 27 June 1990, p. 4. Bill Keller wrote of Aleksandr Yakovlev,

'Yakovlev assuredly does not see America as a model for his country. Like many European leftists he argues that intellectual freedom and economic pluralism can be had without America's insularity, urban underclass and mass culture of rock, sex and violence.' Bill Keller, 'Moscow's Other Mastermind', *New York Times Magazine*, 19 February 1989, p. 51.

126. Y. Gribachev, author interview (Moscow: May 1990). Indeed, *Literaturnaya Rossiya*'s was consistently more critical of domestic America than any of the other four publications consulted. As early as July 1987, it warned that reform proposals, such as those by economist N. Shmelev and writer A. Strelyanii, threatened to turn the Soviet Union into a 'second America'. The author, Mikhail Antonov, made it clear that 'What we need is not a second America, but an inviolable union of free people which unite around great Russia.' M. Antonov, 'Perestroika: Ekonomika i Moral'', *Literaturnaya Rossiya*, 31 July 1987, pp. 2–3. See also O.T. Lefchenko and R.A. Galtsevoi, 'Rok-n-roll, ili naplyv muzykalnogo neistovstva', *Literaturnaya Rossiya*, 5 May 1989, pp. 16–17.

8   THE RUSSIAN PRESS AND IMAGES OF THE UNITED STATES

1. Free press systems are associated with political pluralism found in modern liberal democracies. Traditional approaches suggest that a 'free press model' is distinguished by two basic elements: access and autonomy. In terms of access, it has traditionally been posited that anyone with sufficient economic means has the right to use the media. This right of access is reinforced by the relative autonomy of the press *vis-à-vis* the government. The concept of freedom of the press was a product of the Enlightenment. For some, it was viewed as an extension of individual rights, specifically freedom of speech. For others, press freedom served more utilitarian roles, empowering a fourth estate which operates as an independent check on government or fostering a free marketplace of ideas which reveals truth and exposes error. For more on the origins, see McQuail, *Communication*, 1983, p. 87; Keane, *Media and Democracy*, 1991, p. 1 ff; Rivers and Schramm, *Responsibility in Mass Communication*, p. 25 ff; Ralph Negrine, *Media in Britain* (London: Routledge) 1989, pp. 23–5. For more on relative autonomy, see Dahl, *Dilemmas*, 1982, p. 26. For a more complete discussion of relative autonomy and socialist societies see Archie Brown, 'Political Power and the Soviet State', in Neil Harding (ed.), *The State in Socialist Society* (London: Macmillan) 1984, pp. 59–61.

2. Julia Wishnevsky, 'Media Still Far from Free', *RFE/RL Report*, vol. 2, no. 20, 14 May 1993, p. 86; David Wedgwood Benn, 'The Russian Media in Post-Soviet Conditions', *Europe-Asia Studies*, vol. 48, no. 3, 1996, pp. 471–2.

3. On limits within free press systems, see Ben Bagdikian, *The Media*

Monopoly (Boston: Beacon Press) 1990; Noam Chomsky and Edward Hermann, *Manufacturing Consent* (New York: Pantheon) 1988; Holmes, *Governing the Press*, 1986, pp. 7–8; Hedrick Smith, *The Power Game* (London: Collins) 1988, p. 121 ff; Gregory R. Nokes, 'Libya: A Government Story', in Serfaty (ed.), *The Media and Foreign Policy*, 1991, pp. 33–46; Antoine de Tarlé, 'The Press and the State in France', in Smith (ed.), *Newspapers and Democracy*, 1980, pp. 127–51; C.R. Eisendrath, 'Press Freedom in France, Private Ownership and State Controls', in Curry and Dassin (eds), *Press Control*, 1982, p. 70 ff.

4. Stephen Lovell, '*Ogonek*: The Crisis of a Genre', *Europe-Asia Studies*, vol. 48, no. 6, 1996, p. 995.

5. Lovell, '*Ogonek*', pp. 995 ff.

6. Yassen N. Zassoursky, 'Media and Politics in Transition: Three Models', *Post-Soviet Media Law and Policy Newsletter*, 23 January 1997, p. 11.

7. Mikhail Gulyaev, 'Media as Contested Power in Post-Glasnost Russia', *Post-Soviet Media Law and Policy Newsletter*, 30 April 1996, p. 13.

8. Benn, 'Russian Media', p. 474; Zassoursky, 'Three Models', p. 12; European Institute for the Media (EIM), *Media in the CIS (Media Structures)* (www.internews.ras.ru/books/media/russia.html) 1997, pp. 7–10. Although the regional press also declined in this period, there is still stong evidence which indicates that its readership is increasing *vis-à-vis* the centre. Unfortunately, the regional press is under significant constraints of local administrators and thus is less free than the national media. Gulyaev, 'Contested Power', p. 13 ff; Anne Nivat, 'The Vibrant Regional Media', *Transition*, 18 October 1996, pp. 66–9.

9. Gulyaev, 'Contested Power', p. 13. According to Chugayev, the special council reviewed the applications of around 800 newspapers and 400 magazines for subsidies. Out of these, 500 applications were approved. Sergei Chugayev, 'The Independent Press is Forced to Ask for Handouts', *CDSP*, 3 August 1994, pp. 14–15; EIM, *Media in the CIS (Media and Government)*, pp. 4–7.

10. EIM, *Media in the CIS (Media and Government)*, pp. 4–5; Lovell, 'Ogonyek', pp. 995–7.

11. Gulyaev, 'Contested Power', p. 12.

12. 'According to Ivan Laptev, the head of the State Press Committee, 92 per cent of all Russian printing equipment will have to be replaced by the year 2000. 'Ivan Laptev, New Head of Press Committee, Fires up Troops in Inaugural Remarks', *Post-Soviet Media Law and Policy Newsletter*', 27 September 1995, p. 7.

13. Zassoursky, 'Three Models', p. 13; *EIM, Media in the CIS (Media Structures)*, p. 1.

14. *EIM (Media Structures)*, p. 2.

15. Elena Vartanova, 'The Russian Financial Elite as Media Moguls', *Post-Soviet Media Law and Policy Newsletter*, 27 February 1997, pp. 18–23; Mark Whitehouse, 'Buying the Media – Who's Behind the Written Word?', *Russia Review*, 21 April 1997, pp. 26–7. The MOST banking group, headed by Vladimir Gusinsky, owns 51 per cent of NTV, the popular ECHO radio station and the publishing company

which owns the daily *Segodnya* and the news magazine *Itogi*; Boris Berzovsky, who heads LogoVAZ and Ob"yedinyonnyi Bank, owns a significant share of the ORT television station, and controls the daily *Nezavisimaya Gazeta* and the weekly *Ogonyok*; Gazprom owns 30 per cent of NTV, shares in *Trud* and *Komsomolskaya Pravda* and a series of local newspapers; LUKoil controls 19.5 per cent of *Izvestiya* through the LUKoil pension fund; Stolichny Bank provides significant credits to the *Kommersant* newspaper. See EIM, *Media in the CIS (Media Structures)*, p. 2; Vartanova, 'Media Moguls', p. 18 ff; Whitehouse, 'Buying the Media', p. 27.

16. On criticism of market influences on the press, see Ben Bagdikian, *The Media Monopoly* (Boston: Beacon Press) 1990 and Noam Chomsky and Edward Hermann, *Manufacturing Consent* (New York: Pantheon) 1988.

17. The EIM survey suggested that media ownership in Russia is about 'buying a voice, controlling a voice or the abilitilty to let others use that voice'. *EIM, Media in the CIS (Media Structures)*, p. 2; Vartanova, 'Media Moguls', p. 18 ff. According to Sergei Markov of the Carnegie Moscow Centre, 'In order to influence politics you need the media. It's perfectly rational economic behavior.' Whitehouse, 'Buying the Media', p. 27.

18. Stephen White, Richard Rose and Ian McAllister, *How Russia Votes* (London: Chatham House Publishers) 1997, p. 251; *EIM, Media in the CIS (Media and Government)*, p. 7.

19. Benn, 'The Russian Media', p. 472.

20. Paul Greenberg, 'Untruthful *Pravda* Publishes Final Edition', *Albuquerque Journal*, 7 August 1996, p. A13.

21. As Lovell said of *Ogonek*, 'The coup marked the ideological transition in . . . radical circles. It was recognised that anti-communism was not equivalent to a coherent democratic programme; in the future the political press would have to put forward constructive ideas instead of engaging in polemics.' Lovell, '*Ogonek*', p. 997.

22. Wishnevsky, 'Far from Free', p. 87; Gulyaev, 'Contested Power', p. 13. In 1994 while working for a non-profit organization, the author was offered a positive half-page feature in the publication *Poisk* for a fee of $500.

23. As Tolz said, 'By the early 1990s, such openness was no longer a novelty, and politics has moved from words to deeds. People started to expect from the media not only criticism of the past but also advice on how to build democracy. Unable to give such advice, journalists began to lose the respect they had acquired in the period of glasnost.' Vera Tolz, 'Russian Media', *RFE/RL Report*, vol. 2, no. 27, 2 July 1993, p. 3; Aleksandr Minkin and Laura Belin, 'The Press Has Lost the Trust of Readers', *Transition*, 6 September 1996, p. 40.

24. A liberal television commentator expressed what is likely to be the view of many reporters when he said of the election coverage, 'I am not sure that people in the West understand that a political fight is going on here that has no rules. If the communists win, then the media will lose their independence. There is no choice.' Quoted in

White, Rose and McAllister, *How Russia Votes*, p. 251. See also Belin, 'Private Media Come Full Circle', *Transition*, 18 October 1996, p. 62.

25. *EIM, Media in the CIS (Media Structures)*, p. 9. Vyacheslav Kuznetsov, counsellor to the chairman of the Gazprom group which owns 29 newspapers and television outlets, lends credence to such conclusions, when he claims that 'these magazines, newspapers and television stations (owned by Gazprom) will support the line which is the line of the president and the government.' David Hoffman, 'For Russian Magnates a Rush Toward Media,' *International Herald Tribune*, 1 April 1997, p. 6.

26. *EIM, Media in the CIS (Media Structures)*, p. 9.

27. I would agree with Valdez, that 'A nation's identity is neither fixed nor infinitely malleable, as primordialists or modernists would have us believe. Instead, a nation's identity is constantly subjected to a process of reinterpretation, usually by each succeeding generation. In the case of 'new' states, this process is even more easily observable, as commonly accepted aspects of the nation's identity are questioned or discarded in light of institutional and societal change.' Jonathan Valdez, 'The Near Abroad, the West and National Identity in Russian Foreign Policy', in Dawisha and Dawisha (eds), *The Making of Foreign Policy in Russia and the New States of Eurasia* (New York: Armonk) 1995, p. 84.

28. See Yitzakh Brudny, 'The Heralds of Opposition', *Soviet Economy*, vol. 5, no. 2, 1989, pp. 162–200.

29. Valdez, 'Russian Foreign Policy', p. 84. Karen Dawisha and Bruce Parrot, *Russia and the New States of Eurasia* (Cambridge: Cambridge University Press) 1994, p. 199.

30. Jeffery Checkel, 'Structures, Institutions and Process: Russia's Changing Foreign Policy', in Dawisha and Dawisha (eds), *The Making of Foreign Policy in Russia and the New States of Eurasia* (New York: Armonk) 1995, p. 55; Valdez, 'Russian Foreign Policy', pp. 94 ff. Hannes Adomeit, 'Russia as a "Great Power" in World Affairs: Images and Reality', *International Affairs* (London), vol. 71, no. 1, 1995, p. 49 ff.

31. Michael McFaul, 'Revolutionary Ideas, State Interests and Russian Foreign Policy', in Vladimir Tismaneanu (ed.), *Political Culture and Civil Society in Russia and the New States of Eurasia* (New York: M.E. Sharpe), 1995, pp. 33–4. As McFaul put it, 'To be a democrat was to be Western, was to be American, was to be wealthy.' Valdez, 'Russian Foreign Policy', p. 90.

32. Gregory Guroff and Alexander Guroff, 'The Paradox of Russian National Identity', in Roman Szpourluk (ed.), *National Identity and Ethnicity in Russia and the New States of Eurasia* (New York: M.E. Sharpe), 1994, p. 89; Valdez, 'Russian Foreign Policy', p. 87.

33. J.F. Brown, 'Everybody Needs Russia – Including Eastern Europe, *Transition*, vol. 2, no. 23, 15 November 1996, p. 6.

34. McFaul, 'Russian Foreign Policy', p. 41.

35. D. Trenin, 'Russia and the West', *International Affairs* (Moscow), vol. 42, no. 1/2, 1996, pp. 30–31; Adomeit, 'Great Power', p. 53.

36. Vladimir Shelkov, 'Priliv podnimaet tol'ko roskoshnye yakhty', *Pravda*, 15 February 1996, p. 3.
37. Dmitrii Radyshevskii, 'Nikson po Oliveru Stounu', *Moskovskie Novosti*, no. 5, 4–11 February 1996, p. 44.
38. Vasilii Safronchuk, 'Chubais priviraet, Kozyrev otdykhaet', *Sovetskaya Rossiya*, 8 February 1996, p. 7; Stanislav Menshikov, 'Rossii gotovyat uchast' Mavrikiya', *Pravda*, 13 February 1996, p. 3; Vladimir Nadein, 'Tovarishch Zyuganov obeshchaet obespechit' amerikanskim investoram luchshe usloviya, chem nyneshnie', *Izvestiya*, 3 February 1996, p. 5; A. Tsipko, ' "Bunt" El'tsina stal neozhidannostyu dlya Vashingtona', *Nezavisimaya Gazeta*, 8 February 1996, p. 5; I. Ivanov, 'Novoe napravlenie aktivnosti TsRU', *Nezavisimaya Gazeta*, 27 July 1996, p. 2.
39. Anatolii Druzenko and Vladimir Hadein, 'Rossiiskii vzglyad na Amerikanskie igry', *Izvestiya*, 6 August 1996, p. 6.
40. I. Potar', 'Priklyucheniya Amerikanskogo bezdomnogo v Rossii', *Izvestiya*, 14 February 1996, p. 7.
41. 'Za bugrom tozhe obuvayut', *Argumenty i Fakty*, 20 February 1996, p. 16; I. Epifanov, ' "Russkoi mafii" v Amerike nastupili na khvost', *Argumenty i Fakty*, 19 March 1996; I. Filimonov, 'Kak ya rabotal "pod stolom" ', *Argumenty i Fakty*, 20 February 1996, p. 7.
42. S. Modestov, 'Klyuchevoi pomoshchnik prezidenta', *Nezavisimaya Gazeta*, 8 August 1996.
43. Igor Maksimov, 'Bill Klinton soglasilsya na uzhestochenie sotsialnykh programm', *Segodnya*, 2 August 1996, p. 4.
44. Nikolai Zimin, 'Bob Doul v Aiove pervyi', *Segodnya*, 14 February 1996, p. 8; Nikolai Zimin 'Delaverskii shans Forbsa', *Segodnya*, 24 February 1996, p. 7; Vladimir Abarinov, 'V Nyu-Gempshire pobedili populizm i demogogiya', *Segodnya*, 22 February 1996, p. 7.
45. Appolon Davidson, 'Vozmozhen li "Chernyi internatsional"?', *Moskovskie Novosti*, no. 7, 18–25 February 1996, p. 14.
46. Vasilii Saphonchuk, 'Praimeriz i kokasy', *Sovetskaya Rossiya*, 22 February 1996, p. 7.
47. Aleksandr Shakhmativ and Viktor Kozhemyako, 'Neuzheli udastsya peredelat' russkikh v Amerikantsev?,' *Pravda*, 17 February 1996, p. 4; 'Vtoroe prishestvie "Volshebnika" ', Moskovskie Novosti, 4–11 February 1996, p. 43; 'Iz zhizni Gollivuda', *Moskovskie Novosti*, 4–11 February 1996, p. 45; 'Kto takoi Denzel Vashington?', *Moskovskie Novosti*, 4–11 February 1996, p. 45; 'Zvezdnyi konveier', *Argumenty i Fakty*, 26 March 1996, p. 8.
48. Elena Rykovtseva, 'Amerika Rossii podarila serial', *Moskovskie Novosti*, 4–11 February 1996, p. 39.
49. Dmitrii Radyshevskii, 'Nikson po Oliveru Stounu', *Moskovskie Novosti*, 4–11 February 1996, p. 44.
50. Maiki Praus, 'Amerikanskie spetsialisty razrabotali novuyu tekhnologiyu rascheta VVP', *Finansovye Izvestiya*, 30 January 1996, p. 6; Maikl Skapinker, Maikl Lindemann and Kerolain Sauti, 'SShA zaklyuchayut soglashenie po "otkrytomu nebu", s Germaniei', *Finansovye Izvestiya*,

8 February 1996, p. 6; Roderik Oram, 'Prokter end Gembl namerena snizhat' tseny', *Finansovye Izvestiya*, 22 February 1996, p. 6; 'SShA i EC obedinilis v borbe c piratami na muzikalnom rynke', *Finansovye Izvestiya*, 27 February 1996, p. 1.

51. 'Borba za zhenskie koshelki v Amerike', *Moskovskie Novosti*, 18–25 February 1996, p. 45. The article was a translation of a piece in *US News and World Report*.

52. D. Baluev, 'Moderation in the National Idea', *International Affairs* (Moscow), vol. 42, no 5/6, 1996, pp. 105–15.

53. For more complete discussions of Russian foreign policy and its over-lapping camps, see: Pravda, 'Politics of Foreign Policy', pp. 208–33; Checkel, 'Russia's Changing Foreign Policy', pp. 42–65; Valdez, 'Russian Foreign Policy', pp. 84–109; Glenn Chafetz, 'The Struggle for National Identity in Post-Soviet Russia', *Political Science Quarterly*, vol. 111, no. 4, 1996–97, pp. 661–88; Adomeit, 'Great Power', pp. 35–68.

54. McFaul, 'Russian Foreign Policy', p. 41.

55. Pravda, 'Politics of Foreign Policy', p. 218; Chafetz, 'National Identity', p. 673.

56. Chafetz, 'National Identity', p. 677.

57. Eduard Baltin, 'Tret'ya mirovaya? . . .', *Sovetskaya Rossiya*, 20 February 1996, p. 3.

58. Ivan Bondarev, 'Bankuyut', *Sovetskaya Rossiya*, 22 February 1996, p. 3.

59. E. Popov, '"Pincher" na novyi lad', *Sovetskaya Rossiya*, 1 February 1996, p. 7.

60. Ivan Bondarev, 'Bankuyut', *Sovetskaya Rossiya*, 22 February 1996, p. 5; Anatolii Tille, 'Lyudi i krysy na iskhode veka', *Sovetskaya Rossiya*, 3 February 1996, p. 3.

61. Boris Tvetkov, 'Risunok na "motiv" chastushki', *Sovetskaya Rossiya*, 29 February 1996, p. 3. The note appeared together with a cartoon drawn by the author which depicted Boris Yeltsin shipping Russian assets to the West, and Uncle Sam unfurling a banner listing Western income from Russia, including income derived from savings on the training of specialists for science, technology, culture and sport. This was one of only a handful of anti-American cartoons identified in 1996, most of which appeared in *Sovetskaya Rossiya*.

62. Vasilii Safronchuk, 'Chubais priviraet, Kozyrev otdykhaet', *Sovetskaya Rossiya*, 8 February 1996, p. 7.

63. Vasilii Safronchuk, 'Snova karibskii krizis?', *Sovetskaya Rossiya*, 27 February 1996, p. 1; Vasilii Safronchuk, 'Rossiya opyat' primknula', *Sovetskaya Rossiya*, 29 February 1996, p. 7.

64. Boris Poklad, 'Interesy Rossii – prevyshe vsego', *Pravda*, 22 February 1996, p. 3. See also V. Shelkov, 'Barabany "zvezdnykh voin" v yubilei Ronalda Reigana', *Pravda*, 21 February 1996, p. 3.

65. Leonid Ivashov, 'Global'nye igry: Chem budet Rossiya – velikoi derzhavoi ili rynkom syr'ya?', *Pravda*, 20 February 1996, p. 2.

66. Boris Poklad, 'Interesy Rossii – prevyshe vsego', *Pravda*, 22 February 1996, p. 3. Similar sentiments were expressed in *Sovetskaya Rossiya:* 'In politics and intergovernmental relations there is no such thing as

friends or enemies; there either is or is not a convergence of national interests.' Baltin, 'Tretya mirovaya? ...', *Sovetskaya Rossiya*, 20 February 1996, p. 3.

67. Andrei Loshakov, 'Vyzov Ameriki. A nash otvet?', *Pravda*, 1 February 1996, pp. 3–4.

68. Vasilii Arbekov, 'Dzhon Shalikashvili posetil Bukharest', *Segodnya*, 10 February 1996, p. 8; F. Lukyanov, 'Amerikanskie zakonodateli prizvali rasshirit' NATO', *Segodnya*, 25 July 1996, p. 7.

69. N. Zimin, 'Dzhessi Khelms predlagaet annulirovat' dogovor po PRO', *Segodnya*, 10 February 1996, p. 8.

70. V. Skachko, 'V SShA Leonidu Kuchme poobeshchali mnogo deneg', *Segodnya*, 23 February 1996, p. 8.

71. E. Spiridonov, 'Ex-IM Bank of the USA predostavit MTK "Sirena" kredit v summe 90 mln doll', *Segodnya*, 19 February 1996, p. 4. It also ran an article about a computer game designed by former officials of the KGB and CIA. N. Zimin, 'Oleg Kalugin nashel obshchii yazyk s Uil'yamom Kolbi', *Segodnya*, 15 February 1996, p. 8.

72. Vladimir Abarinov, 'Kitai poluchil rossiiskie istrebiteli', *Segodnya*, 14 February 1996, p. 8; V. Abarinov, 'Proiski NATO iskazhayut luchezarnuyu kartinu mira', *Segodnya*, 24 February 1996, p. 8.

73. V. Abarinov, 'Proiski NATO', *Segodnya*, 24 February 1996, p. 8.

74. I. Ivanov, 'Novoe napravlenie aktivnosti TsRU', *Nezavisimaya Gazeta*, 27 July 1996, p. 2.

75. M. Gafarly, 'SShA otmenili embargo na postavku oruzhiya', *Nezavisimaya Gazeta*, 27 July 1996.

76. Y. Lebedev and A. Podberzkin, 'Tri goda ozhidanii i sporov', *Nezavisimaya Gazeta*, 10 February 1996, p. 3.

77. A. Tsipko, '"Bunt" Yeltsina stal neozhidannostyu dlya Vashingtona', *Nezavisimaya Gazeta*, 8 February 1996, p. 5.

78. A. Tsipko, 'Neozhidannostyu dlya Vashingtona', *Nezavisimaya Gazeta*, 8 February 1996, p. 5.

79. Tsipko, 'Neozhidannostyu dlya Vashingtona', *Nezavisimaya Gazeta*, 8 February 1996, p. 5.

80. A. Konovalov and S. Oznobishchev, 'Novoe otkrytie Ameriki', *Nezavisimaya Gazeta*, 17 February 1996, p. 4.

81. B. Vinogradov, 'Oruzhie iz SShA idet v SNG', *Izvestiya*, 30 July 1996, p. 3.

82. M. Yusin, 'Amerikanskii kongress priglashaet v NATO Ukrainu, Moldaviyu i strany Baltii', *Izvestiya*, 25 July 1996, p. 3; V. Mikheev, 'Amerikantsy prishli v Vostochnuyu Evropu ne za tem, chtoby ukhodit"', *Izvestiya*, 16 February 1996, p. 3.

83. S. Kondrashov, 'Vzglyad na Rossiyu – 96 iz Vashingtona', *Izvestiya*, 3 February 1996, p. 3.

84. S. Kondrashov, 'Vzglyad', 3 February 1996, p. 3.

85. M.F. Uiliyams, 'SShA i ES v borbe s piratami na muzykal'nom rynke', *Finansovye Izvestiya*, 27 February 1996, p. 1; M. Skapinker and K. Sauti, 'SShA zaklyuchayut soglashenie po 'otkrytomu nebu' s Germaniei', *Finansovye Izvestiya*, 8 February 1996, p. 6.

86. Sergei Solodovnik, 'SNV-2: lyubov' kongressa SShA mozhet ostat'sya

bezotvetnoi', 'Kak otdelit' serna ot plevel', *Moskovskie Novosti*, 18–25 February 1996, p. 13.

87. V. Malinkovich, 'Rasshirenie NATO: chto skazhet Ukraina?', *Moskovskie Novosti*, 17–24 March 1996, p. 11.

88. Solodovnik, 'Zerna ot plevel', *Moskovskie Novosti*, 18–25 February 1996, p. 13.

89. A. Pushkov, 'Neokommunizm: ispytanie Davosom', *Moskovskie Novosti*, 11–18 February 1996, p. 12.

90. V. Malinkovich, 'Rasshirenie NATO: chto skazhet Ukraina?', *Moskovskie Novosti*, 17–24 March 1996, p. 11.

91. B. Trubetskoi, 'Uchenye v Rossii popali v seti Internet', *Moskovskie Novosti*, 17–24 March 1996, p. 28; D. Radyshevskii, 'Sud'ba Amerikantsa na Kavkaze', *Moskovskie Novosti*, 17–24 March 1996, p. 8.

92. Oleg Cherkovets, 'Bol'shaya Pyl' . . .', *Sovetskaya Rossiya*, 10 February 1996, p. 3.

93. Vasilii Safonchuk, 'Chubais priviraet, Kozyrev otdykhaet', *Sovetskaya Rossiya*, 8 February 1996, p. 7; Safonchuk, 'MVF slezam ne verit', *Sovetskaya Rossiya*, 1 February 1996, p. 7.

94. Vladimir Shelkov, 'Vot prem'er priedet', *Pravda*, 30 January 1996, p. 3.

95. S. Kashilev, 'Slabaya pozitsiya Moskvy', *Nezavisimaya Gazeta*, 31 January 1996; S. Kashilev and S. Mitrofanov, 'Moral'nyi uspekh Viktora Chernomyrdina', *Nezavisimaya Gazeta*, 2 February 1996.

96. EkoTASS, 'Iz Vashingtona – s lyubovyu k sotrudnichestvu', *Moskovskie Novosti*, 4–11 February 1996, p. 22.

97. O. Romanov and M. Leontev, 'V Vashingtone otkrylas ocherednaya sessiya komissii "Gor–Chernomyrdin"', *Segodnya*, 30 January 1996; O. Romanov, 'Komissiya Gor–Chernomyrdin uveklas' kosmicheskimi programmami,' *Segodnya*, 1 February 1996.

98. Aleksei Portanskii, 'Viktoru Chernomyrdinu predstoit podtverdit' reformatorskii obraz Rossii', *Finansovye Izvestiya*, 30 January 1996, p. 1.

99. Melor Sturua, 'Makarova v Ameriku ne pustyat. Ne cheloveka, a pistolet', *Izvestiya*, 7 February 1996, p. 3.

100. Vladimir Nadein, 'Rossiisko-Amerikanskoe partnerstvo eshche zhivo', *Izvestiya*, 31 January 1996, p. 3; Nadein, 'Amerika i vpered gotova pomogat' nam besplatnymi sovetami', *Izvestiya*, 30 January 1996, p. 3.

CONCLUSION

1. S. Volovets, author interview (Moscow: May 1990). A similar view was expressed by *Komsomol'skaya Pravda*'s Sergei Zavorotny, author interview (Oxford: November 1990).

2. E. Uotson, 'Sdelat' istinu ochevidno', *Pravda*, 15 October 1989, p. 1; TASS, 'Na put' realizma', *Pravda*, 6 April 1990, p. 6.

3. Shal'nev, author interview (New York: March 1991).

4. In analyzing the newspapers, I noted all articles referring to Canada

and West Germany as a means of comparison with the United States. I also noted affirmative-didactic articles referring to the experience of other countries. While there were many, no one country or even region could compete with references to the United States.

5. Victor Yasmann, 'Can Glasnost' Be Reversed?', *Radio Liberty Research Bulletin*, vol. 3, 1 February 1991, p. 26.

Index

226